MAINSTREAM   *SPORT*

THE PEOPLE'S GAME

THE HISTORY OF FOOTBALL REVISITED

JAMES WALVIN

MAINSTREAM
PUBLISHING

EDINBURGH AND LONDON

For Gavin and Jack again

Copyright © James Walvin, 1994
All rights reserved
The moral right of the author has been asserted

First published by Allen Lane in 1975

First published in Great Britain in 1994 by
MAINSTREAM PUBLISHING COMPANY (EDINBURGH) LTD
7 Albany Street
Edinburgh EH1 3UG

Second edition 2000

ISBN 1 84018 322 5

A catalogue record for this book is available from the British Library

Printed by WS Bookwell, Finland 2000

Contents

Introduction

The People's Game Revisited

In an early history of sports in England, Joseph Strutt made the bold claim that:

> In order to form a just estimation of the character of any particular people, it is absolutely necessary to investigate the Sports and Pastimes most generally prevalent among them.

For all its exaggeration, such a claim would receive warm support from a range of modern scholars. Time and again, sociologists have regarded sports as a lens they can hold up to particular societies and see in it a refraction of deeper social patterns. Indeed it would be hard to think of any modern society where sport does not occupy a central and influential role, not merely in the way local people seek their pleasures, but more especially how they see and define themselves. Contemporary evidence is abundant, readily available and ubiquitous; we are assailed, in print, on the radio and television, with images, discussion and analysis about modern sports. Those who do not enjoy sports are often driven to distraction by the cacophony of sporting noise and the blur of athletic imagery which permeate British life. Major sporting events, of every imaginable sort, characterise the weekly, seasonal and yearly calendar. For the house-bound sports lover, it is delight; an endless parade of games, matches, races, tournaments, Tests, and contests. Beamed from the far ends of the earth, bounced from circling satellites, the skills and strengths of the world's greatest sportsmen and women provide a display of sporting pleasures on a scale and with an intensity and coverage which was unimaginable a mere generation ago. But for those who do not like sport (and it is hard for sports lovers even to comprehend that such people exist), it is a source of irritation and annoyance. The powerful men in charge of the media seem to assume that people the world over enjoy sport; enjoy watching it, listening to it or reading about it.

It is one of the great, and largely unnoticed, curiosities of this global fascination with sports that a host – perhaps even a majority – of the world's most popular sports (athletics, the Olympics, football and cricket) have their origins deep in British history. Even those games which took local root and flourished in distinctively local form (for example, American or Australian football) had cultural roots which could be traced to Britain. But of all the world's major sports, few can rival football – soccer – for ubiquity, for the numbers who play (on dirt patches and slum streets the world over), for the armies who watch it and for the passions the game inspires. It is, quite simply, a game played by more people – mainly men – and watched by more people than any other.

It is difficult to dispute the figures. No other sporting event – not even the Olympics – attracts such colossal audiences as soccer's World Cup. The language, folk-memory, heroes and stars of this remarkable game are universal, serving to u..ite (and periodically to divide) millions of people who would otherwise have little in common. Football is a universal, powerful force. Yet it is also a very British institution; a game fashioned from particular British circumstances and spread around the world by the British. It is a game born of British circumstances, forged by British history; given its form, its nature and its purpose by the changing patterns of British life. It is, then, a game with its own rich and revealing history. But more than that, it is a game which throws light on the unfolding patterns of British life, especially in the nineteenth and twentieth centuries. The history of football is interesting in itself, but, more revealing still, it provides a unique entrée to British society in the recent past. Yet for a very long time indeed the significance of football went largely unnoticed.

When I wrote the first version of this book, twenty years ago, I was keen to stress how little serious attention and academic research had been devoted to the history of football – and to the history of sports in general. There seemed a huge gap between the obvious and undeniable importance of sports, at any point in the western world over the past century, and the failure of historians to rise to that interesting challenge. Now, twenty years on, the position has changed fundamentally. Then, the difficulty was locating the data; now it is knowing how to keep abreast of the profusion of literature, and how best to make sense of the sometimes highly specialised material. In less than two decades there has been a prodigious output of serious work, acknowledging the game's proper importance, and helping to locate the role of sport within its defining social context. Much of what I wrote in the early 1970s has simply been superseded by this long-overdue and welcome turn of events.

Curiously, it was this richness and profusion of scholarly literature which convinced me that there is still a place for the type of book I sought to write in *The People's Game*: a crisp and concise volume, which brings together current findings in a style which is accessible to a wider readership. This revised version – greatly rewritten, though maintaining the original structure – has set itself that same task. What follows is not a scholarly book, but it could not have been written, in its current form, without the efforts of a number of researchers, whose findings appear in the bibliography.

Rewriting an old book has not been an easy task. Like the historiography of the game, the author too has changed. But I have thought it best to try to stick to the original tone and form of the book; to maintain the existing structure and write to my old brief. But what follows is a very different book; it is not simply a reprint. While keeping the same overall structure, each individual chapter is different, trying to keep older relevant material, but updating it and recasting it in the light of recent findings. I have, in brief, sought to keep the best of the old book and align it with the best of the new scholarship.

Twenty years ago I could confidently preface my book with the remark that sports have failed to make much of an impact on historiography; that football in particular had 'failed to find an adequate place in written history'. Today, that claim is simply untrue. Month after month, excellent scholarly books and articles come flying off the presses – quite apart from that voluminous and important cottage industry of local, amateur, fan-based literature. The two traditions – scholarly and antiquarian – co-exist comfortably together. And this is quite apart from the amazingly profuse world of journalism and fanzines (now measured in their thousands) which feed the apparently insatiable demand for printed words about the story of football.

What follows, then, is an effort – revised and in a new format – to bridge the gap between scholarly professionals and a broader readership; to tell an important story, to tell it crisply, untrammeled by scholarship yet acknowledging the crucial work of colleagues without whom it could not have been written. This book looks at the history of football; at the game which by the early twentieth century was widely recognized throughout Britain as the people's game. By the end of that same century, its claims to the same status were even stronger. No longer primarily the game of British people, football was now the game of people the world over.

1 Pre-Industrial Football

Numerous forms of informal or regulated games in which balls were kicked around and handled by opposing teams were a common feature of pre-industrial society. From the late Middle Ages onward, in town and country, the evidence for social history is peppered with references to footballing incidents – sometimes bizarre, always colourful and frequently tragic. Until the emergence of a recognizably modern urban society in the early nineteenth century, forms of football remained a common denominator of male social behaviour and a continuing theme of popular recreation. The origins of the game (or games) are shrouded in mystery, though historians of football have spent an inordinate amount of time seeking them. Such a task is unrealistic and unrewarding (despite the scope offered by historical study of the game), for games of football were ubiquitous, spontaneous and traditional. The killing of animals, for example, provided people with bladders, unusable for most other purposes but ideal to inflate and play with.

Even before we have evidence for early games in Britain, games of football had been recorded in a host of other civilizations. A Chinese writer, Li Yu (AD 50–130), wrote eulogies to the local game, designed to be hung on the goal posts:

> A round ball and a square goal
> Suggest the shape of the Yin and the Yang.
> The ball is like the full moon,
> And the two teams stand opposed;
> Captains are appointed and take their place.
> In the game make no allowance for relationship

And let there be no partiality.
Determination and coolness are essential
And there must not be the slightest irritation for failure.
Such is the game. Let its principles apply to life.

How far a similar game existed in classical Greece and Rome is unclear. Curiously, ball games played little or no role in the development of the Olympic Games in Greece, where interest focused on wrestling, boxing and athletics. Ball games were considered the preserve of children and women and had no role in the classical conventions of male athleticism, itself shaped by military needs and the adoration of certain forms of fitness. Even some of the earliest claims for the existence of the game in Britain remain unsubstantiated, though Nennius wrote in the ninth century of a 'game of ball' in Britain. Between 1170 and 1183, however, William Fitz Stephen, biographer of Thomas à Becket and witness to his death, offered an early account of a possible game of football in a description of London.

> After dinner all the youth of the City goes out into the fields for the very popular game of ball. The scholars of each school have their own ball, and almost all the workers of each trade have theirs also in their hands. The elders, the fathers, and the men of wealth come on horseback to view the contests of their juniors, and in their fashion sport with the young men; and there seems to be aroused in these elders a stirring of natural heat by viewing so much activity and by participation in the joys of unrestrained youth.

From the first, here was a game played by younger men and watched by their seniors. Equally, many of the earliest references are concerned with the game's physical toughness and violence, and the frequent threat which it posed to the life and limb of players and spectators and to the peace and property of the neighbourhood. From the thirteenth to the nineteenth centuries, football was to appear in legal records, court cases and contemporary denunciations as a violent game; a cause and occasion of social unrest in which personal and collective scores could be settled. It was a game of indeterminate numbers, unspecified time and local conventions, in which marauding bands of young men tested their strength, enjoyed themselves and displayed their prowess in the pursuit of a ball. At its worst, it was a game which at times came perilously close to testing to the limits the social control exercised by local and national governments.

It was, above all, a tough, often violent game. Personal injury and even death characterized many of the early references to football. Had there been no such incidents, the games would, and presumably did, go unrecorded. In 1280, for example, 'Henry, son of William de Ellington, while playing at ball at Ulkham on Trinity Sunday with David le Ken and many others ran against David and received an accidental wound from David's knife of which he died on the following Friday.' A similar fatality occurred 50 years later, in 1321, which resulted in Pope John XXII granting a dispensation to William de Spalding, a canon, for his role in the accident. 'During the game at ball as he kicked the ball, a lay friend of his, also called William, ran against him and wounded himself on a sheath knife carried by the canon, so severely that he died within six days.' Violence and accidental death haunted the game for centuries; sometimes footballing quarrels spilled over into mayhem after the game. Injuries of a less serious nature were commonplace. John Hendyman remembered an incident in 1425 because 'he played with other companions at football, and so playing broke his left leg'. One of the posthumous miracles allegedly worked by Henry VI in the fifteenth century was on William Bartram of Caunton near Newark, who 'was kicked during a game, and suffered long and scarce endurable pain, but suddenly recovered the blessing of health when he had seen the glorious king Henry in a dream'. Not surprisingly, contemporaries were often appalled at a game which habitually led to such injuries. It was a game:

> in which young men, in country sport, propel a huge ball not by throwing it into the air, but by striking and rolling it along the ground, and that not with their hands but with their feet. A game, I say, abominable enough, and, in my judgement at least, more common, undignified, and worthless than any other kind of game, rarely ending but with some loss, accident or disadvantage to the players themselves.

Quite apart from the injuries to players, medieval observers were more alarmed by the wider social unrest caused by football.

The game was simply an ill-defined contest between indeterminate crowds of youths, often played in riotous fashion, often in tightly restricted city streets, producing uproar and damage to property, and attracting to the fray anyone with an inclination to violence. Understandably, regular efforts were made to control it just as, in the thirteenth century, there had been efforts to control tournaments, for similar reasons. In 1314, for instance, a proclamation of Edward II complained of 'great uproar in the City, through certain tumults arising from great footballs in the fields of the public, from which many evils may arise'. Through succeeding centuries, riotous crowds (of players rather than spectators) continued to test the precarious ability of government to maintain law and order. In 1576 a group of artisans in Ruislip 'with unknown malefactors to the number of a hundred, assembled themselves unlawfully and played a certain unlawful game, called football, by reason of which unlawful game there arose amongst them great affray, likely to result in homicides and serious accidents'. Fully three centuries after the proclamation of Edward II, football in the City of London continued to cause 'great disorders and tumults' (1615) as it did across the length and breadth of the country, from Devonshire to Manchester, from Worcester to Northumberland.

The game proved most troublesome when played in towns. In Maidstone in 1656, John Bishop, a local apothecary, played football in the High Street, 'to the disquiet and disturbance of the good people of this Commonwealth'. Similarly in Manchester, in 1608 and 1609, 'a companye of lewde and disordered persons using that unlawful exercise of playinge with the footbale in ye streets of the a said towne breakinge many men's windows and glasse . . .' Games of football were played across the face of the nation, in urban and rural settings. When played on open or common land, football was unlikely to cause the problems created when it was played in towns. Threats of damage and fears for social tranquillity lay behind the frequent protestations against the game by men in authority. And their fears were regularly reflected in attempts to ban or limit the game by monarchs or local authorities.

When played in towns and cities, few doubted what the consequences would be. If the results of football matches, then as now, were always in doubt, it was nonetheless predictable that damage, violence and chaos would ensue, as the game surged through streets, into buildings, through rivers and local ponds, until the contestants tired or reached a particular goal. A game at Hitchin in 1772 saw the ball 'drowned for a time in the Priory pond, then forced along Angel Street across the Market Place into the Artichoke beer-house, and finally goaled in the porch of St Mary's Church'.

Some of football's worst excesses took place in games which from the sixteenth century became a feature of Shrove Tuesday. On that day excessive outbursts of popular exuberance came to symbolize the last fling of human frailty before the onset of the austerities of Lent. It may well be that this 'carnival' spirit of pre-industrial Shrove Tuesdays, similar in kind to that enjoyed today in parts of Southern Europe, the Caribbean and Latin America, provided the ruling elites with a safety valve for the escape of dangerous tensions from below. In a world which lacked effective policing systems, and in which the control of men in authority was often uncertain and tenuous, public turbulence, even in the pursuit of pleasure, was a volatile and potentially threatening force. To allow the common folk to have their day, to permit them to rule the streets and public space, through their boisterous enjoyments, if only for a day, was to turn the world upside-down. But such outbursts were permitted on the strict understanding that the *status quo* returned the following day. Games played on Shrove Tuesday seemed to fit this pattern, and from the sixteenth century onward they were synonymous with a flurry of communal, turbulent pleasures; animal sports, cock-fighting – and football. The cultural habits of the people were, however, shaped by local forces; their pleasures and games tended to be specific and very parochial. Shrove Tuesday games often differed enormously from one place to another. In their turn, local games spawned their own distinctive customs. In Dorset the football was provided by the last man to have been married; in Glasgow local shoe-makers supplied the ball. In London, footballing fraternities were sufficiently well organized by the 1420s to hold football dinners. The games, predictably, often led to violence, but, so quickly did the game sink its roots as a folk-custom, that attempts to prohibit Shrove Tuesday football were likely to cause as much unrest as the game itself. Yet such local 'village' games often had complex rules and conventions. Too often they have been seen simply as incoherent, turbulent outbursts. In places, their rules were as complicated as modern games. They were part of a much broader popular culture which grew from religious, agricultural, seasonal and generational roots. Games took place between the married and the unmarried, on certain religious days, or at key moments in the local agricultural cycle.

Among the best-known Shrove Tuesday football games were those played in Ashbourne and Derby. In Ashbourne the game, played by two teams consisting of anyone who lived in the town, surged between 'goals' three miles apart. The teams tunnelled through crowded streets before fanning out into an open brawl in a nearby stream. Innumerable attempts were made to prosecute the players and to transplant the game into remoter, less vulnerable places, but order and regulation were only finally imposed in the twentieth century. The similar contest in Derby, a contest between the parishes of St Peter and All Saints, plagued generations of local law officers, and gave birth to the term a local 'derby'. This 'coarse sport' threw up its footballing heroes and more than its quota of 'black eyes, bruised arms and broken shins'. A local historian commented acidly in 1790, 'I need not say that this is the delight of the lower ranks, and is attained at an early period.' In keeping with the unrestrained traditions of popular footballing violence, the Derby game claimed its share of victims. In 1796 John Snape was killed, 'an unfortunate victim to this custom of playing at Football at Shrove Tide; a custom which . . . is disgraceful to humanity and civilisation, subversive of good order and Government and destructive of the Morals, Properties, and very Lives of our Inhabitants'. Consequently, determined attempts were made to outlaw the game but such prosecutions were, again, doomed to failure by the strength of popular resistance. Indeed prosecutions for Shrove Tuesday footballing incidents continued through the late nineteenth century and into the present century. In Derby and other parts of Britain, football was regularly denounced and proscribed, but nonetheless continued to survive because of its deep popularity among ordinary people. It had in fact become a folk-custom. Folk games littered the face of pre-modern Britain. Many of them survived to the present century; many more thrived longer than historians traditionally recognized. In Scotland, for example, the Old Handsel Monday football match, played on the Roman

Camp at Callander, was described in 1853 as a 'custom of immemorial usage'. Folk football had extensive and popular roots throughout Scotland.

Throughout the history of folk football, from its beginnings to the development of the modern game in the nineteenth century, official attitudes to it have often been marked by distrust and suspicion. Where it was seen to serve a special purpose, football could be tolerated – within strict limits. More often, however, folk football was a game seen to be in need of careful control and limitation.

From the fourteenth century onward we know of a battery of laws, proclamations, edicts and regulations against football which regularly issued from monarchs, governments and local authorities, all compounded by informal though influential denunciations of the game. But to understand such continuing hostility on the part of successive governing and propertied classes, to appreciate fully the fears of government about the mass leisure pursuits and recreational outbursts of the lower orders, we need to probe behind these laws and regulations and try to assess the strains placed upon the fabric of society by the apparently volatile forces of certain popular recreations.

The history of football before the nineteenth century could be written in terms of the attempts to suppress it. London, for example – always a sensitive complexity of social problems for English governments – witnessed regular impositions against local games from 1314 onwards. In that year, as Edward II went north to fight the Scots, football and other tumultuous games were banned in the city. The ban was repeated in 1331 and again in 1365, when football was considered to be interfering with more useful pursuits, particularly archery. This same motive inspired a similar interdict against football in 1388. In both cases the emphasis on 'useful' pastimes was ostensibly dictated by military needs. Unhappily for successive governments, the bans on football continued to be ignored and had to be reinforced, again, in 1410 by a fine of 20s and six days' imprisonment. Four years later, however, Henry V introduced a further proclamation ordering men to practise archery rather than football. Such prohibitions seemed to fail for the basic reason that they were attempting to uproot a simple and attractive pastime which had already established itself as an aspect of social life for young males in the capital.

The exigencies of defence, however, remained a prime concern of governments and dictated their response to various sports. A statute of Edward IV in 1477 noted that 'no person shall practise any unlawful games such as dice, quoits, football and such games, but that every strong and able-bodied person shall practise with bow for the reason that the national defence depends upon such bowmen'. Outlawed again by Henry VII in 1496, football nonetheless remained sufficiently popular to require repeated preventive legislation by Henry VIII. One of his statutes remained on the books until 1845.

London was not alone in seeking to ban football. A number of provincial towns enacted prohibitions against local games. In Halifax, in 1450, men were forbidden to play on pain of a fine of 12d; four years later the fine had to be increased by 4d. Leicester, taking its cue from Parliament in 1467, levied a fine of 4d on local footballers, but the order had to be revived again in 1488. The game was similarly banned in Liverpool in 1555 and, in 1608–9, in nearby Manchester. In the latter, despite the ban, so troublesome was the game that in 1618 special 'football officers' were appointed, but still in 1655, 1656 and 1657 new orders were issued against it.

Objections to the game were varied and complex. Often they were very local. There were, however, a number of objections which recurred from one place to another. Concern about damage and personal injury (and, in the earlier cases, concern about military skills) clearly help to explain a great deal of formal alarm about folk football. But the problems posed by the game were often of a more fundamental order. The game appealed primarily to young, healthy men whose vigour and collective boisterousness could not easily be contained by a society which lacked effective police forces or similar agents of social control. In London, for example, the apprentices – traditionally radical groupings, always willing to test the resilience of national and local governments – were often the chief cause of footballing incidents. By the reign of Edward III the game had gained great popularity among the apprentices, and their street games were directly responsible for a number of legal prohibitions. One (fictional) apprentice complained, in a play of 1592, that his master 'will allow me not one hour for sport, I must not strike a football in the street, But he will frown'. Then – as now – the game provided apprentices with a perfect way of happily wasting their working hours. As late as the eighteenth century, footballing apprentices frequently disrupted London life.

> I spy the Furies of the Football War:
> The Prentice quits his Shop, to join the Crew,
> Increasing Crouds the flying Game pursue.

Football clearly offered an ideal excuse for a crowd to collect – and a young, excitable, moody crowd at that. Apprentices, moreover, were no ordinary crowd. Overworked, exploited and generally harbouring a range of grievances, they formed a frequently disaffected body of young men, living close to each other in the same areas of the city and thus easily in touch with each other. They posed a regular threat of unruliness and often erupted into outbursts of radical agitation. Not surprisingly, they were readily recruited for football, especially for matches on Shrove Tuesday. On that day, apprentices' (and in other areas, rural workers') outbursts became an accepted annual institution. But as long as such spasms could be restricted to infrequent holidays, the social forces unleashed could be tolerated. But such popular pleasures were strictly on condition that matters returned to normal on the following day; the world, upside-down for a day, was expected to right itself within 24 hours. Yet the history of football suggests that nothing could be taken for granted. The fact that it was a game against which legal enactments and prohibitions continued to be implemented points to a game which was, for centuries, often uncontrolled and spontaneous, sometimes threatening, and always a matter of unease for men worried about the problems of civil order and social stability.

It would be easy to dismiss the alarm of contemporaries as an exaggerated response to popular rowdiness, but pre-industrial society was a delicately balanced order in which the maintenance of the peace fell to an informal collection of vested interests and prominent individuals. The uncertainty of social control was an ever-present factor in the minds of the governing orders, certainly until the nineteenth century when the advance of urban society recast both the nature of the population and the machinery of regulation available to the government. Social unrest in pre-industrial society was easily precipitated; food

prices, military impressing, religious passions and plain hunger
frequently sparked off public disturbances. Football, with its
robust teams and its mayhem, like many other apparently non-
political and innocent phenomena, could easily become the
spark for a wider disturbance.

With the exception of violence, perhaps the most recurrent
complaint against football was that it violated the Sabbath. To
a degree this was inevitable; for many ordinary people Sunday
was the sole day of rest. Football on Sunday (and on other
religious days) came in for frequent ecclesiastical criticism. In
1572 the Bishop of Rochester demanded its suppression. At
Chester in 1589, Hugh Case and William Shurlock were fined
2s for playing football in St Werburgh's cemetery during the
sermon. Four years later, Richard Jeffercy of Essex was charged
with having 'procured company together and plaid at foot-ball
in Hackwell, on Easter Monday, in the Evening Service time'. At
the Essex Quarter Sessions in 1599, Thomas Whistock of White
Notyle was accused 'with nyne other of his fellows the XXVth
day of February in the XLY yere of her Ma/jes/ᵗⁱˢ rayne being the
sabaothe did play at an unlawfull game called the fote bale
wheron grew bludshedd contrary to her Ma/jes/ᵗⁱˢ peace'. In
1609, twelve men were prosecuted in a similar vein, at Thirsk.
A year later men were fined in Bedford for simply watching
football on Sunday. At Guisborough in Yorkshire in 1616, a man
was prosecuted for organizing a banquet for footballers on a
Sunday. Despite such frequent prosecutions, men continued to
use their day of rest for football and a multitude of other
recreations. In 1688 ten men were prosecuted at Richmond in
Yorkshire for playing football during divine service.
Condemnation of such activities was the usual reaction, but
there were exceptions. The Revd Thomas Robinson, vicar of
Ousby in Cumberland, made use of football, 'It was his common
practice, after Sunday afternoon prayers, to accompany the
leading men of his parish to the adjoining alehouse, where each
spent a penny and only a penny; that done, he set the younger
sort to play at football (of which he was a great promoter) and
other rustical diversions.'

Such active clerical support for football was to remain
exceptional until the nineteenth century, when church ministers
came to appreciate that the game was enjoyable and offered a
useful entry to working-class life. Ironically, in 1722 at East

Looe in Cornwall footballing diversions on the Sabbath saved many lives, for 'during the usual time of Divine Service, there happened such a violent Hurricane, that a great part of the Steeple of the Church was blown down; which would have done very considerable Damage to the Parishioners had they been at Church: But they happened to be luckily at a Foot-ball Match, by which means their lives were probably saved'.

At the heart of this clash between popular recreations and defenders of the Sabbath (and other holy days) lay the complicated story of Puritanism, though in fact complaints against sports in general and football on the Sabbath in particular, predate the emergence of the forces of Puritanism in the sixteenth and seventeenth centuries. The frequency of these later Puritan-inspired attempts to curb Sunday recreations is as revealing about popular recreation as about Puritanism itself. Earlier claims that the Puritan embargoes of the late sixteenth and seventeenth centuries marked a new departure in British history by driving out the last vestiges of traditional pleasures hinge largely upon the prosecutions of Sunday sports. Such prosecutions, however, had, as we have seen, been commonplace long before, and all we can usefully deduce from the evidence is that prosecutions became more common under Puritan direction. As we might expect, the games – including football – continued as before. Because of the Puritan presence, it is claimed by Brailsford that sport came 'nearer to being a political issue than at any other period in our history'. The reason was straightforward: the breakdown of parliamentary government in the seventeenth century produced more frequent attempts by the Court to interfere directly into the details of everyone's lives, an intervention which stemmed in part from a concern for social stability. Paradoxically, the result of this royal initiative was a conjunction of interest between the far-from-Puritan early Stuarts and local Puritans, to intervene against unruly Sunday sports which many had come to regard as their ancient and rightful prerogative. But Puritan antipathy towards sports, and the unease of James I about football in the early years of the seventeenth century had firm historical precedents, for they belonged to the traditional resistance to popular recreations. Indeed the edicts against football in the fourteenth and fifteenth centuries were remarkably similar to the Puritan objections of the next two centuries. From the sixteenth century, denunciations of the game became more common (partly also because the printed word became more widespread), more bitter and riddled with the fears traditionally expressed by the privileged towards the activities of their social inferiors. In 1531, for example, Sir Thomas Eliot thoroughly denounced football, which was, he claimed, a game 'wherein is nothinge but beastly furie and exstreme violence whereof proceedeth hurte and consequently rancour and malice do remaine with them that be wounded; wherefore it is to be put into perpetual silence'. But perhaps the most withering attack on the game came in 1583 in Phillip Stubbes's *Anatomy of Abuses*, provoked in part by the continuing violations of the Sabbath. According to Stubbes, men amuse themselves 'in foot-ball playing, and such other devilish pastimes'.

> Any exercise which withdraweth us from godliness, either upon the Sabaoth or any other day, is wicked and to be forbidden . . . For as concerning football playing, I protest unto you it may be rather called a friendly kinde of fight than a play or recreation, a bloody and murthering practise than a felowly sporte or pastime. For dooth not everyone lye in waight for his adversarie, seeking to overthrowe him and picke him on his nose, though it be uppon hard stones? . . . So that by this means, sometimes their necks are broken, sometimes their backs, sometime their legs, sometime their arms; sometime one part is thrust out of joynt, sometime another; sometime the noses gush out with blood, sometimes their eyes start out and sometimes hurt in one place, sometimes in another.

Nor was Stubbes' feeling peculiar to Puritans. James I, though anxious to uphold traditional sporting rights against the intrusions of Puritans, allowed no place for football in the education of his son Henry, debarring from the Court 'all rough and violent exercise, as the football; meeter for laming, than making able the users thereof'.

The Puritan denunciations of football were part of a more broadly based drive to secure the Sabbath; to ensure that the Lord's Day was preserved for godly matters. It took its most extreme form, of course, in the Puritan settlements in New England, and under Cromwell's godly government. But even in those regions of America where the godly ruled, they could never purge the people of their desire to play traditional games. And few games were more traditional than football. Yet it would be wrong to think that only the devout took exception to popular recreations. The turbulence of football, its common indiscipline and the passions it provoked left many others uneasy. Many men of property and enterprise, anxious to promote social calm as well as economic well-being, thought that here was a game which simply got in the way. Though the formal trappings and vernacular of Puritanism had rapidly waned by the late seventeenth century, its objections to football – and other sports – survived among those keen to see society change. Traditional folk football was disliked as much by eighteenth-century social improvers (and dissenters) as it had been by seventeenth-century Puritans. To the latter, it was an offence to God's name (and a desecration of his day); to the former it was an obstacle to social and material advancement.

Until the nineteenth century, open acceptance of folk football was rare among men of property and influence. Rarer still was the enthusiastic support for the game shown by Richard Mulcaster, headmaster of Merchant Taylors' (1561–86) and later of St Paul's School (1596–1608). In retrospect, Mulcaster's support for football seems to have been well ahead of its time, closely resembling the sporting attitudes of the 'muscular Christians' in the nineteenth-century public schools. In fact his views were perfectly in accord with sixteenth-century (especially Italian) humanism. Mulcaster appreciated the social and physical benefits of organized sports, proposing a game with smaller teams, an impartial judge – and no violence. Under careful supervision, football would provide:

> much good to the body, by the chiefe use of the armes. And being so used, the Footeball strengtheneth and brawneth the whole body, and by provoking superfluities downeward it dischargeth the head, and upper parts, it is good for the bowells, and driveth downe the stone and gravell from both the bladder and kidneies.

Mulcaster conceded that the British version, for all its popularity, was 'neither civil, neither worthy of the name of any traine to healthe'. The inspiration for his belief in the healthy potential of football was drawn not from British but from Italian football, *calcio*, which had developed into a highly disciplined and controlled recreation and spectator sport by the sixteenth century. Mulcaster, like other humanists, turned for his evidence on this, as on a number of other political and social issues, to sixteenth-century Italian sources which, in concentrating on the local game, stressed the social and physical virtues of football. Mulcaster was, moreover, a prominent educationalist working within a grammar-school system which did much to create wider opportunities for a more articulate and self-confident gentry. He seems to have been in a strong position to convert other schools to his humanist views on recreation and to encourage them to attend to the physical well-being of their pupils. Unhappily, Mulcaster died in poverty and obscurity and there seems little evidence that the pupils in the grammar schools (from the social groups to which Puritanism made its strongest appeal) were much affected by his ideas.

Football seems to have been more securely based among the young men of Oxford and Cambridge in the sixteenth and seventeenth centuries. There, college and university records are littered with references to the popularity of football among undergraduates. Inevitably, and like the traditions of folk football to which it was related, football at Oxford and Cambridge created problems – for players and local officials. It was a game in need of regulation. At Cambridge, there is record of scholars playing football as early as the 1570s, and in the 1580s the Vice-Chancellor ordered students to play 'Only within the presincts of their several colleges, not permitting any stranger or scholars of other colleges or houses to play with them or in their company.' Such regulations proved as ineffective as other legislation we have encountered, and in 1595 the Vice-Chancellor ordered 'That the hurtfull and unschollerlike exercise of Footeball and meetings tending to that ende to from henceforth utterly cease (excepte within the places severall to the Colledges, and that for them only that be of the same Colledge without noyse or outcry . . .)'. The game in Cambridge was as notable for its vigour as the game traditionally played by the common people. Not surprisingly, further detailed regulations were introduced, in 1632, to control football within the university. In common with the outside world, football at seventeenth-century Cambridge was sometimes played on feast-days – with the predictable results and attempts at regulation. In 1660 a football match took place 'where several disorders were committed, and affronts offered to the officers of the University . . .' In September of that year it was alleged of an undergraduate that 'he was in a companie that did in a Riotous manner throw clotts or stones at the deputy Proctor, and M^{rs} of Arts who came to prevent scholars from playing at football, and other disorderly meetings there . . .'. Such offences led to heavy fines and, in extreme cases, to imprisonment. Nonetheless, by the early seventeenth century, football at the university seems to have established itself as an undergraduate recreation in its own right. It may have been helped by the popularity of a form of football, 'camp-ball', which was played nearby in East Anglia.

At Oxford there seems to have been no such particular local traditions. But within the university the game was nevertheless well represented during the same period. Football was explicitly forbidden at Oxford in 1555 (some twenty years before the first ban in Cambridge). By 1584, however, it had become apparent that 'diverse ministers abiding in the universities, especial nonresidents, so use open plainge at football and maintininge of quarrelles to the great discredit of this universitye' that more stringent regulations had to be introduced. But students still continued to be attracted to the game. In 1607 'the schollars of Oxford at a match of football burned the furnesses of Bullington Green contayning 3 acres or thereabouts'. In 1636 the heavy-handed rule of the Chancellor, Archbishop Laud, challenged the physical recreations of Oxford students by ordering that 'no scholars of any condition (and least of all graduates) are to play foot-ball, within the University or its presinct (and particularly not in the public streets and places of the city) whether alone by themselves, or in company with townsmen'. The Restoration of the monarchy in 1660 led to a relaxation of the more severe restrictions and atmosphere which had characterized Cromwell's government. Even so, the Oxford statute against football continued to be enforced against student footballers.

By the late seventeenth and early eighteenth centuries, football – impromptu or ritualized – had become a notable aspect of popular cultural life. Foreign visitors, those barometers of social life who often registered phenomena which went unnoticed by locals, frequently commented on this, by now distinctively British pastime. A Frenchman in 1698 noted many such games. 'En hiver, le Footbal est un exercise utile et charmant. C'est un ballon de cuir, gros comme la tête et rempli de vent; cela se belotte avec le pied dans les rues par celui qui le peur attraper; il n'y a point d'autre science.' A correspondent in the *Spectator* of 1711 noted a country game: 'I was diverted from further observations of these combatants [cudgel players] by a football match which was on the other side of the green, where Tom Short behaved himself so well that most people seemed to agree that it was impossible that he should remain a bachelor until the next wake.'

Men in authority, however, continued to worry that football might generate unrest. Certain incidents seemed to confirm their fears. There is, for example, evidence from the seventeenth and eighteenth centuries that football was deliberately used to rally a crowd for specifically political ends. In 1638, for example, in Lilleport and Ely, a football match was organized deliberately to attract a crowd and to pull down the banks designed to drain local fens (a cause of popular resentment in seventeenth-century East Anglia). An informant, meeting three of the game's organizers, reported that, 'they asked me if I came to playe a game at footbale, to which I replied and asked "What game at footbale?" and they told me Anderson would bring a bal and meete the towne of Lilleport in Burnt Fen to play at Footbale'. The result, as intended, was the destruction of the embankments. Clearly a crowd could prove an effective political tool in the hands of men who remained beyond the political pale and had little or no recourse to formal politics. It was no easy matter to assemble a crowd in a rural area. What better way was there of convening local people than by calling a football match? In 1740, 'a Mach of Futtball was Cried at Kettering of five Hundred Men of a side, but the design was to Pull Down Lady Betey Jesmaine's Mills'.

A similar incident occurred in 1764 over the question of enclosures – that great eighteenth-century development which transformed the face of rural England and displaced armies of people from lands to which they claimed a variety of traditional rights. At West Haddon, Northamptonshire, in 1764 an enclosure of 2,000 acres destroyed not only the livelihoods of a number of people on the land, but also the common land used by many others. Despite numerous formal objections, the enclosure bill passed through Parliament, leaving its victims with no alternative but action of a more informal kind. Consequently, the objectors had the imaginative idea of playing football on the enclosed land. The *Northampton Mercury* of 25 July 1765 advertised a forthcoming match, to be played on 1 and 2 August, and asked potential players to report to the public houses in West Haddon. The message was clear and the outcome predictable. Within moments of kick-off, the football match degenerated into an overtly political mob which tore up and burned the enclosure fences. Dragoons, specially drafted from Northampton, could do nothing in the face of such resistance and the damage amounted to some £1,500. Though five men were later jailed, the organizers of the 'football match' disappeared; their game had been a resounding success.

Another enclosure in Holland Fen, Lincolnshire, in 1768 triggered off no fewer than three political 'football' matches in one month.

> July 1st, the insurgents, consisting of about two hundred men, threw up a football in the fen, and played for about two hours, when a troop of dragoons, some gentlemen from Boston, and four constables, having seized four or five of the rioters, committed them to Spalding gaol. Dr Shaw, of Wyberton, set three women rioters, at liberty, and the men were admitted to bail. On the 15th another ball was thrown up, and no person opposed them . . . On the 29th, another ball was thrown up without opposition.

These are just four examples of a pre-industrial rural crowd determined (under the right circumstances) to find solutions to its own political and social problems. Such actions merely compounded authority's dislike of folk football as anti-social and possibly dangerous; a potential flash-point for social ills which could scarcely be contained.

By the late years of the eighteenth century, as the first trends towards urbanization and industrialization began to make themselves felt, some fundamental changes began to overtake the social habits and recreations of the common people. Strutt, one of the earliest historians of sport, noted of football in 1801, 'It was formerly much in vogue among the common people of England, though of late it seems to have fallen into disrepute, and is but little practised.' In fact there is a great deal of evidence to the contrary, and football continued to be played, particularly on feast-days in rural parts, and in certain public schools. But Strutt was undoubtedly right in pin-pointing a change in the social role of football (in common with many other popular pastimes). As Britain lurched into the painful early days of industrialization and urban growth, dislocation and upheaval

became a common experience in the personal and collective lives
of working people, particularly in the new urban areas. In older
cities, London above all, the new machinery of state and local
government, ineffective and cumbersome as it might seem to
modern eyes, began to provide more effective means of regular
law enforcement. Old fears about a volatile populace remained
of course, but from the 1830s a change had taken place and
government could expect and guarantee that its laws would be
enforced in the capital. For all the unknown threats of outcast
London – the city of Mayhew's surveys, of Doré's engravings
and Dickens's novels – the days had gone when authorities stood
by helplessly while their subjects took the law into their own
hands with impunity. It may seem a simple point (though it
illustrates a wider phenomenon) but henceforth, in the capital,
bands of footballers ceased to be able to create mayhem at will.
Folk-customs of street football in the old cities were one of the
victims of effective law enforcement.

In the new towns of the midlands and north, football similarly
began to fade away, but for different reasons. Dislocated and
alienated people, whether natives of the town or immigrants
from the countryside, were purged of their recreational rights
and traditions by the joint disciplines of urban and of industrial
life. New policing systems, policemen on the beat and local
Watch Committees armed with punitive local bye-laws all served
to drive traditional games from the streets of urban Britain.
Overcrowded and overworked, with little time or opportunity
to indulge in the boisterous recreations of their ancestors – or
even of their country cousins – the working class found their
leisure habits undergoing a fundamental transformation. In
those cities which, before the end of the century, were to witness
the birth of a new kind of working-class football, traditional
recreations of the lower orders began to fade away or change.
These changes, which affected practically every form of popular
recreation, were largely a result of the impersonal changes set in
train by urban growth. But there were other, more deliberate,
conscious forces at work.

The decline of the old folk recreations was only partly
accidental. In addition to new urban restrictions, there were the
restraints imposed by a new generation of employers anxious to
secure a new form of labour discipline from their labour force.
The whole process was greatly accelerated by a new middle-class

mentality which, to bolster the industrial and urban injunctions against popular recreation, sought to deny the rights of industrial people to any leisure at all, insisting instead only on economic utility. 'A spirit has lately arisen in the land [said a Liverpool man in 1831] that instigated the magistracy and other high and influential persons, to curb, restrain and almost absolutely forbid the lowly, the humble of society from indulging in any pastimes whatever.' Even *The Times* noticed this trend. Writing of Liverpool in 1842, the newspaper commented, 'The poor have been deprived of their games, their amusements and their mirth.' This was of course an exaggeration, overlooking the durability and vitality of working-class social life. But, like Strutt's earlier comments, it highlighted the problem. Football, one of the most traditional of games, was thus transformed. Even in the countryside, the game was under pressure from the changing rural economy. 'Football [noted a man in 1838] seems to have almost gone out of use with the inclosure of wastes and commons, requiring a wide space for its exercise.' This lack of space was nowhere more pressing than in the cities. In both town and country, football began to change as a game, as players were forced to adapt to new circumstances, a changing physical environment and new restrictions. Football had to adapt. Tighter rules began to evolve: the format and regulation of football began to take on a recognizably modern shape.

> When a match at foot-ball is made, two parties each containing an equal number of competitors, take the field, and stand between two goals, placed at the distance of eighty or an hundred yards the one from the other. The goal is usually made with two sticks driven into the ground, about two or three feet apart. The ball which is commonly made of a blown bladder, and cased with leather, is delivered in the midst of the ground, and the object of each is to drive it through the goal of the antagonists, which being achieved the game is won. The abilities of the performers are best displayed in attacking and defending the goals; and hence the pastime was more frequently called a goal at football than a game at football. When the exercise becomes exceeding violent, the players kick each other's shins without the least ceremony, and some of them are overthrown at the hazard of their limbs.

Whatever the changes within the internal conduct of the game, contemporaries were in no doubt that football by the

early nineteenth century was less popular, was played less
frequently and was hence less noticeable, though it continued to
be characteristically plebeian. Football remained, to use the
words of Samuel Butler, head of Shrewsbury School from 1798
to 1836, 'fit only for butcher boys . . . more fit for farm boys and
labourers than young gentlemen'. An Etonian added a similar
view in 1831: 'I cannot consider the game of football at all
gentlemanly: after all the Yorkshire common people play it.'

Paradoxically, various forms of football were played within
the public schools, educational enclaves of upper-class society
which seemed to remain immune to the encroachments of social
discipline in society at large. At Charterhouse, Eton, Harrow,
Rugby, Shrewsbury, Westminster and Winchester, variants of the
game featured in school life and, like school life in general, they
were tough, robust and dominated by the older, bigger boys. In
fact public-school football, in the years before Dr Arnold's
educational revolution, closely resembled the popular folk game
so condemned by the social class which traditionally sent its sons
to the schools. The paradox was that football was kept alive in
the public schools exactly when its traditions had begun to
disintegrate in society at large.

For those in charge of early nineteenth-century public schools
and for many who sent their sons there, the indiscipline within
the schools was disturbing, since it made any kind of 'useful'
education impossible. External pressures, notably from parents,
began to demand more control and a more effective education.
But how to begin? The irony of the reform movement which
emerged in response to these and other pressures was that one
of the agents of the new discipline was to be the sport which
itself had so characterized indiscipline in the schools. Athleticism
and physical recreation were harnessed to the task of bringing
order into the schools, and in the process a new game of football,
and a new attitude towards the game, began to emerge. In the
process the pre-industrial game was gradually transmuted into a
team game which demanded rigid discipline, selflessness,
teamwork and physical prowess, and in which the strengths and
skills of the individual were subsumed by the greater needs of the
team. Modern football thus began to evolve from the peculiar
circumstances of public-school life.

By the 1830s it was abundantly clear that Britain was
changing, rapidly and beyond recognition. As its people became

progressively more urbanized and industrialized, few aspects of their social lives remained unaffected. Even the games they played, the pleasures they pursued, were forced to adapt to the new physical and social circumstances of life around them. It was, in a way, ironic, that the game which had for centuries been rootedly plebeian, was effectively saved by the public schools. The rules, conventions and shape of the game were altered by the changing needs of those schools; by the altered requirements of a new breed of headmaster and a new generation of parents who, above all else, wanted discipline. And football, suitably altered, was to be the agency for shaping that discipline. Later in the nineteenth century, this new, highly disciplined game was to fuse with the survivals of the folk game and with the residual passion of young men for ball games, to become the game we know today.

When Arnold at Rugby and Butler at Shrewsbury looked at the turbulence within their schools, salvation seemed to lie in games, especially football, which had appeared on the surface to be part cause, part function of the problems they faced. Games were soon to be appreciated as a tool for revitalizing and controlling the schools. The game which, since the fourteenth century at least, had been frowned upon by men in authority, the game which had been consistently stigmatized as socially inferior and regularly outlawed – the people's game of football – came to the assistance of the groups which had traditionally done their best to prevent the playing of football. In the process, and for the first time, the plebeian game of football acquired an unaccustomed respectability.

7886

2 The Public Schools and Football

The public schools of the late eighteenth and early nineteenth centuries were bizarre institutions, and quite unlike their modern-day descendants. Education at Westminster, Eton, Harrow, Winchester, Charterhouse, Rugby and Shrewsbury was a curious affair generally involving a heavy emphasis on Latin and Greek administered with liberal doses of the birch. The boys were largely unsupervised and normally under the dominance of the young men at the top of the school. Inevitably life, before the reforms of the mid-nineteenth century, was coarse and brutal. 'Often enough the only virtues which the life at public school with any certainty inculcated seem to have been those of the dark ages – courage, ability to bear pain and loyalty to immediate companions.' Social and recreational behaviour reflected the general style of life in the schools and the games played consequently mirrored the hierarchical and physical, and sometimes violent nature of school society in general. Football seemed an ideal game.

Despite the pride which people took in these institutions – in their antiquity, in their famous old-boys, and in their links to British elites – it was ever clearer that the public schools were unsuited to the rapidly changing world of the early nineteenth century. Suitable perhaps for the training of indulged aristocrats in a less competitive age, the schools found their classical-based education seriously deficient in the new age of industrial change and urban growth. Too often, however, those who traditionally sent their sons to their schools did not want the 'useful' training in science or commerce demanded by the many parents from the newly emergent middle class, nor even a formal education worthy of the name. Such parental indifference had its effects within the schools; the masters interfered as little as possible in the lives of the pupils, preferring to vest control in the hands of senior pupils – the aristocracy of the school system. The overall result was that the public schools greeted the nineteenth century with the faces of eighteenth-century roués.

Not surprisingly, the public schools were infamous for disorder among their pupils. At its worst, pupil indiscipline spilled over into violence. In these years all of the major public schools underwent rebellions of varying severity. Between 1770 and 1818 six outbursts of pupil violence affected Winchester; the last was quelled by the militia with fixed bayonets. A riot at Rugby in 1797 was put down by the army (on standby for a threatened French invasion) and a reading of the Riot Act. At Harrow in 1808 the young Byron began his school career as a schoolboy mutineer in a rebellion against an unpopular headmaster.

Anarchic sports were in keeping with the disordered tone of the schools. Not surprisingly, most games (with the striking exception of cricket) were played with an aggression which lacked even the social restraints which qualified popular recreation in the world outside. Football was perhaps the most prominent of such school sports, with a history which stretched back, in some cases, to the sixteenth century. But the game of football varied from one school to another. Like folk football, it had specific local rules and conventions. Football at Eton, for instance, developed according to the capacity and limitations of the school's playing fields or playgrounds, and by the mid-nineteenth century it had become a regular institution of school life. From such simple and yet practical considerations of adapting to the physical environment, the rougher edges were gradually knocked off Etonian football and the game slowly developed a marked degree of regulation.

The same was true of other schools. The peculiarities of the local environment dictated what could be played and how games evolved. At Charterhouse, based in London before its move to Godalming in 1872, football was played within the cloisters of the old Carthusian monastery. Space was limited and a game developed which depended on 'dribbling', since the ball could not be kicked high or punted long distances, as it could at Eton. But even in the cloisters, football was rough: 'The ball very soon got into one of the buttresses, when a terrific squash would result, some fifty or sixty boys huddled together, vigorously "roughing", kicking, and shoving to extricate the ball.' Once the ball was moved out by a 'dribbler', 'fags would rush out and engage the onset of the dribbling foe, generally to be sent spinning head over heel for five yards along the stones'. Following regular scrimmages for the ball, 'shins would be kicked black and blue; jackets and other articles of clothing almost turn into shreds; and fags trampled under foot'. Care was taken not to damage the windows, but no such care was shown towards the younger boys who were considered fair game for the older 'stars' of the game.

At Westminster, like Charterhouse, playing space was restricted and dribbling came to distinguish local football. Roughness was again integral to the game. 'When running . . . the enemy tripped, shinned, charged with the shoulder, got down and sat upon you . . . in fact did anything short of murder to get the ball from you.'

Harrow, on the other hand, did not have such physical and geographical limitations, and boys there had a large playing field at their disposal. But the location of the field made drainage difficult and the field was regularly and swiftly reduced to a quagmire. Consequently, Harrovian football demanded a heavy ball, and the rules which emerged were designed to encourage movement and to avoid the static scrimmages of other schools. The result was that Harrow boys became experts in the art of dribbling on heavy surfaces. The game played at Winchester on the other hand, on a pitch of eighty by twenty-five yards, encouraged 'accurate kicking and dashing play' and skill in scrimmaging.

Rugby, too, had its own distinctive game which reflected the usual dominance of the older boys, who forced the fags to play in the more prosaic (and dangerous) defensive positions while they monopolized the more glamorous attacking roles. At Rugby, 'All fags were stopped on going out after three o-clock calling over . . . and compelled to go into the Close . . . two of the best players in the school commenced choosing in about a score each side. A somewhat rude division was made of the remaining fags, half of whom were sent out to keep goal on the other side, the other half to the opposite goal for the same purpose.' These boys faced special football boots, known locally

– and for obvious reasons – as 'navvies' and having 'a thick sole, the profile of which at the toe resembled the ram of an ironclad', and could be used to the same effect on the limbs of young boys as on the ball.

At Shrewsbury, football had failed to flourish under the headship of Samuel Butler but his successor, Benjamin Kennedy, encouraged the pursuit of sports. The brand of football which developed, known as 'douling', was strictly a dribbling game with firmly enforced rules about 'off-side' positions and it was this game which two old boys, J.C. Thring and H. de Winton, transposed to Cambridge in the mid-1840s.

Football was thus, in various shapes and guises, played – and played roughly – in all the major public schools. All the games permitted handling and holding the ball; the later division into the handling Rugby game and the non-handling Association game was as yet unknown. The widespread belief, enshrined on a plaque at Rugby School, that in 1823 a pupil named William Webb Ellis picked up the ball and ran with it, thereby inventing the art of Rugby football, is a myth fabricated in 1895 by a committee of old boys who were angered at the allegation that the game had not originated at Rugby. It is nonetheless true that between the 1820s and 1840s the practice of clutching and running with the ball, rather than kicking the ball after catching it, came to characterize the Rugby game. Most schools insisted, however, that once the ball had been caught, the player must kick it. Thus, in permitting running with the ball, Rugby School became distinctive and lent its name to the game which evolved from this practice.

Football at Rugby in the 1830s is best captured by *Tom Brown's School Days*, in which the author, Thomas Hughes, described the game he knew in the mid years of change under Dr Arnold's invigorating headmastership. On Tom's first Sunday at Rugby, he learned:

'Today's the School-house match. Our house plays the whole of the School at football. And we all wear white trousers, to show 'em we don't care for hacks. You're in luck to come today. You just will see a match; and Brooke's going to let me play in quarters. That's more than he'll do for any lower-school boy, except James, and he's fourteen.'

'Who's Brooke?'

'Why, that big fellow . . . he's cock of the School and head of
the School house side, and the best kick and charger in Rugby.'

'Oh, but do show me where they play. And tell me all about it.
I love football so, and have played it all my life. Won't Brooke let
me play?'

'Not he,' said East, with some indignation; 'why you don't
know the rules – you'll be a month learning them. And then it's
no joke playing-up in a match, I can tell you. Quite another thing
from your private school games. Why, there's been two collar-
bones broken this half, and a dozen fellows lamed. And last year
a fellow had his leg broken.'

Rugby was more fortunate than other schools. It had an
exceptionally large playing field which allowed plenty of scope
for the more traditional, free-ranging type of football, though a
number of regulations were gradually introduced to eliminate
the more violent aspects of the game. Other schools refined their
game even further and eventually Rugby remained the only
school where it was legitimate both to catch, and to run with the
ball. Crudely stated, the football game which emerged in the
third quarter of the nineteenth century as 'soccer' was in origin
the game played at Eton, Harrow, Westminster, Charterhouse
and later in other schools, where handling was allowed but
where it was forbidden to catch the ball and run with it.

Though Rugby became the isolated exception in terms of
public-school football, the school was soon to play a seminal
role in the emergence of a new attitude both to learning and to
physical recreation within the schools. Public schools were
changed by reforms initiated by a new generation of
headmasters, anxious to purge the schools of their more
unpleasant traditions and to reform education and social life
within the schools. There were of course a number of such
reforming heads – Butler and Kennedy at Shrewsbury, for
example. But the most pre-eminent – and certainly the best
remembered – was Dr Thomas Arnold at Rugby. Headmaster
between 1828 and 1842 (the setting for *Tom Brown's School
Days*), Arnold revitalized his school by a totally new emphasis
upon 'godliness and good learning', introducing a system of
education which, in contrast to what went before, was rigorous
and scholarly. Moreover, Arnold tried to open his school to
upper-middle-class boys from the professional and business
communities. The result was that sons of both aristocrats and

merchants were subjected to a new kind of education, designed to mould them into Christian gentlemen with wide cultural pretensions, a sophisticated moral code and a firm belief in social responsibility. But first Arnold had to discipline the school. He began to work with the existing power structure (which had been responsible for the earlier chaos), vesting authority in the hands of senior boys who were now made directly responsible to himself.

Central to Arnold's reforms within the school was the prefect system: once the cause of so much disorder and violence, it now became the head's instrument for social control and for improvement. Arnold's main drive for reform was through the chapel and the classroom. But he also had a place for games in his schemes for change (though personally he had little time for games, and was not the staunch advocate of athleticism which so many of his followers and admirers imagined). In introducing discipline, he sought to legitimize the existing sub-culture among the boys. He allowed existing sports to continue: they reinforced the control of the older boys over the juniors and therefore that of the head over the whole school. But Arnold's tolerance of sports was only a means to an end, and not an end in itself. He would doubtless have been appalled by the cult of athleticism and manliness which his followers introduced into the public schools from the 1850s. The irony remains, however, that Arnold's methods of reforming were later so transmuted by men who worked in his name that his ideals were totally distorted. Buttressed by new educational ideas, taken notably from Charles Kingsley, 'godliness and good learning' became 'godliness and manliness'.

In the years after Arnold's short-lived translation to Oxford, when his pupils and masters moved on to other schools, the cult of public-school sports developed, with great emphasis placed on the role of football. The game had its attractions. In the first place, a hectic game of football could keep large numbers of boys fully occupied in their spare time. Moreover, it and other games came to be viewed as a vital element in the creation of 'character', that indefinable quality of public-school men which over the past century has remained their trademark. Through carefully organized, regulated and disciplined games, the new public-school virtues (not of Arnold but certainly of his followers) of courage, selflessness, teamwork and toughness could be promoted. These qualities were not created directly by the masters, who tended not to intervene in the management of games, but indirectly through the senior boys whose preserve this had traditionally been. Football remained an extremely tough game, and to make the game more amenable to the cause of discipline, and to eliminate anomalies, written rules governing football began to appear for the first time from the mid-1840s. Through this process of codification it was increasingly possible for public-school men from different schools to recognize the common features of the game as played elsewhere.

Arnold's influence cannot be measured solely within his own beloved Rugby, for his ideals were those of a missionary. The energy he generated undoubtedly rekindled the older schools and stimulated the establishment of a new wave of schools. But the schools of the period after 1850 would have troubled Arnold. Edward Thring at Uppingham, for example, rapidly transformed the school into a team-playing institution. More spectacular still, Hely Hutchinson Almond, at Loretto school near Edinburgh for forty years from 1862, ordered an athletic regime of remarkable proportions. Boys had to play games every day, with the emphasis on rugby and running. Even the school motto and uniform reflected this sporting ethos which sought to fill the boys' every spare moment. Indeed there were *no* spare moments. Such men transmuted public-school athleticism from a disciplinary tool into an end in itself. In the process, intellectual interests and attainments were often pushed aside; relegated to the sporting imperative. In the words of Coterill of Fetes, 'Cleverness, what an aim! Good God what an aim! Cleverness neither makes or keeps man or nation.' Thus there developed the mindless attachment to athleticism above all else.

From mid-century, one school after another adopted football as part of their winter physical recreation (cricket was well established as the summer sport). The form of football adopted at a school depended largely on which school the master had attended as a boy or young teacher. The trend, however, was nationwide. Westminster school, for instance, began to keep its first football ledger in 1854. At the newly reformed Tonbridge school, football had begun to rival even cricket by 1858:

Hitherto, as has been already said, 'the ambition of the School has been monopolised by the cricket field'. But we cannot play cricket all the year round; and second to, if not equal with cricket, comes football. At the beginning of football there is a good deal of spirit in the games but after a month or so interest lags, and the games are wanting in spirit. Now this occurs to much less extent in other schools; and the reason I take it, is this; at other schools there are divisions at football corresponding to our 'elevens' at cricket and, consequently, the players feel a noble desire to be one of the 'twenty' or whatever the number may be. They have also uniforms at football as well as cricket, and far more gorgeous caps in the former.

In a wider sense the revitalization of the public schools transformed them from decayed aristocratic institutions into schools which were sought after by those who could afford the education they offered. Consequently, as the century advanced, more and more boys entered these schools, finding themselves drilled in, among other things, the arts of the newly regulated and disciplined team games. By 1864, when the Clarendon Commission reported on the public schools, sports had become an integral part of their education. 'The cricket and football fields . . . are not merely places of amusement; they help to form some of the most valuable social qualities and manly virtues, and they hold, like the classroom and the boarding house, a distinct and important place in public school education.' New generations of middle- and upper-class footballers thus emerged from these schools, moving into the varied occupations awaiting young men of their social station. Moreover, all this took place when popular football – the game traditionally played by the lower classes – could scarcely survive in the face of the economic and social changes of Victorian Britain.

The rise of the mid-century public schools was shaped of course by changing economic conditions. In this respect Rugby was exemplary, though initially untypical, for Arnold had been influenced by local pressures from the professional and middle classes. With the emergence of industrial prosperity, more and more of the bourgeoisie, many of whom could compete with the aristocracy for wealth and property, if not for station, sought places for their sons at such schools. Increasingly, the schools came to be seen as ideal training grounds for merchants as well as aristocrats. 'Look at the bottle-merchant's son and the Plantagenet being brought up side by side,' said Arnold's son Matthew to an imaginary Prussian visitor to Eton. 'None of your absurd separations and seventy-two quarterings here. Very likely young Bottles will end up being a Lord himself.' How far the reform and proliferation of the public schools were inspired by middle-class pressures is difficult to say. It is certain, however, that the rise of middle-class prosperity enabled many thousands of boys to receive public-school education. In the process a Christian athleticism evolved which, in combination with an equally pronounced public-school missionary zeal, was slowly disseminated by the swelling band of ex-pupils, into the working-class communities of Britain which had so far gained little benefit from the rise of industrial society.

The public schools became the forum for the more overt displays and development of muscular Christianity. In origin, that concept can be seen in arguments about the Anglican Church. Charles Kingsley in particular was keen to see a new generation of young clerics cast aside the emphasis on other-worldliness and, instead, confront the manifold and physical problems of society at large. What was needed was a new breed of men – muscular Christians – fit and able to tackle all the difficulties life threw at them. Team games seemed ideally suited to the task: they perfected physical fitness, encouraged co-operative effort and individual strength and commitment. More and more young clerics, steeped in public-school traditions, found the church an ideal vehicle for the pursuit of a missionary zeal which was directed towards the wretched of British society. Clerics felt equipped, by the games they had played in school, to face the physical challenges of industrial Britain. And those very same games seemed ideally suited to the task of bringing pleasure and health to their flock.

The process of transplanting ideas, customs – and games – around the country, previously so slow and complex, was made easier by the revolution in communications. From the middle of the century it was a simple matter for people, goods and social habits to be shifted rapidly around the country, thanks to the national railway system built up in the 1840s. One minor result was a change in the sporting activities of the public schools (and indeed of the whole nation within two decades). It was no longer necessary for boys to play solely against each other within their own school: teams could travel to play at other schools. Slowly but surely, public-school teams, and other sporting organizations, took to the trains. This 'nationalization' of sport in its turn generated an ever wider interest, particularly in football, and was the prototype of the social phenomenon which was to characterize the emergence of working-class football later in the century.

At the universities, but particularly at Cambridge from the mid-1840s, ex-public-school men tried to establish the games of football they had played at school. In 1846 two ex-Shrewsbury men, H. de Winton and J.C. Thring, persuaded some old Etonians to join them in forming a football club. Only four games, however, were played before the club collapsed. A more serious move was made two years later, in 1848, when according to one of the participants:

> an attempt was made to get up some football in preference to hockey then in vogue. But the result was dire confusion, as every man played the rules he had been accustomed to at his public school. I remember how the Eton man howled at the Rugby man for handling the ball. So it was agreed that two men should be chosen to represent each of the public schools, and two who were not public school men, for the 'varsity' . . . We were fourteen in all I believe. Harrow, Eton, Rugby, Winchester and Shrewsbury were represented.
>
> We met in my rooms after Hall, which in those days was at 4 pm; anticipating a long meeting, I cleared the tables and provided pens and paper . . . Every man brought a copy of his school rules, or knew them by heart, and our progress in framing new rules was slow . . . We broke up five minutes before midnight.

These rules (though no copy survives) governed the increasingly popular game at Cambridge and confirmed the drift away from Rugby-type catch-and-run football towards the dribbling game. Such matches were played regularly at Cambridge in the 1850s and, inevitably, the rules were taken to the country at large by graduates. In 1855, for example, the Sheffield club was established under the influence of Old Harrovians who persuaded local village footballers not to handle the ball, allegedly by providing the players with white gloves and florins to clutch during the game. The Blackheath club was founded in 1858 and in the following year a second Sheffield club, the Hallam, was formed. In 1859 Harrovians formed the Forest Club in Essex, playing makeshift games against ad hoc local teams. Even then their opponents were 'mostly composed of old

Public school boys, with a very limited card of matches'. But despite the initial difficulties, the game continued to permeate the country, through the good offices and enthusiasm of ex-public-school and Cambridge men.

But the games spawned across the country by returning graduates and young men fresh from their schools varied enormously. Cambridge rules were popular in a number of places. The dribbling game was introduced in Wales by the Vice-Principal of St David's Lampeter (an ex-Fellow of King's Cambridge). The Edinburgh Academicals were founded in 1857, by ex-pupils of the Edinburgh Academy; and they were later joined by young men educated at Merchiston, the Royal High School and Loretto. Football spread to Glasgow among professional men. By 1860 two more Harrow-inspired teams, Wanderers and Old Harrovians, had come into existence. But the development of the game remained sporadic and was clearly in need of more careful organization and control.

The first move to be made in this direction since the attempt of 1848 came from J.C. Thring, one of the Cambridge pioneers of football. In 1862, as an assistant master of Uppingham, he issued a set of rules known as 'Simplest Game' for the regulation of the school's football. The result was a boom in interest in the game at Uppingham but, more important, the rules were closely paralleled by regulations used in October 1862 to control a game in Cambridge between eleven Etonians and eleven Harrovians. Exactly a year later, nine Cambridge men, representing Shrewsbury, Eton, Harrow, Rugby, Marlborough and Westminster, met to draft new football rules. These 'Cambridge Rules' were to play a central role in the breach which soon followed between Rugby and Association football.

Only days after the Cambridge rules were drafted, perhaps the most significant football gathering to date was convened. On 26 October 1863 captains and representatives of several London and suburban clubs met at the Freemason's Tavern in Lincoln's Inn Fields, their purpose to codify rules 'for the regulation of the game of football'. In fact they founded the Football Association, which governs the game to this day. The teams represented were NN (no names) of Kilburn, Barnes, the War Office, Crusaders, Forest (Leytonstone), Perceval House (Blackheath), Crystal Palace, Blackheath, Kennington School, Surbiton, Blackheath School, plus one observer from

Charterhouse. With the exception of the Blackheath club, all the teams were committed to the dribbling game, best defined by the Cambridge rules of a few days earlier, and had drawn their inspiration, directly or indirectly, from public-school and Cambridge football. From these socially exclusive origins, the FA was founded. It must have been impossible at that modest founding meeting to envisage the major social revolution over which the organization was to preside within a few short years, for the sporting bureaucracy which slowly emerged from that first national footballing authority became the framework within which football established itself as the national game of the British people.

Oddly enough, the public schools themselves remained aloof from the early FA – the captain of Charterhouse even refusing to vote on anything until the views of other public schools had been canvassed. Consequently, the efforts made to draw the schools into the FA foundered. Harrow, for example, replied, 'We cling to our present rules, and should be very sorry to alter them in any respect.' Rules preoccupied the founding members. Meeting regularly in November and December 1863, they slowly began to smooth out irregularities, trying in the first place to amalgamate the best elements both of Rugby football and the dribbling game. Internal disputes, however, pointed the way to an irreconcilable gulf between the proponents of the two games. While provincial football clubs brought themselves to the attention of the FA, the main problem facing the new organization remained how best to construct the rules. The central argument pivoted on 'hacking', holding and running with the ball, and how to tackle the player in possession of the ball. Some wanted to follow the Cambridge example and to eliminate hacking, others insisted that hacking was vital to the game, alleging that without it 'you will do away with the courage and pluck of the game, and I will be bound to bring over a lot of Frenchmen who would beat you with a week's practice'.

The argument came to a head on 8 December 1863 when Blackheath withdrew from the FA in order to continue with the 'hacking' game. Around the Blackheath club and its distinctive view of football there developed the game of rugby, although the Rugby Union was not established until 1871. Soccer – and traditional forms of football – continued to survive in many of the old public schools. But it was the handling, rugby game which rapidly took hold in that proliferation of new public schools across Britain. Heads and their assistants viewed the handling game as more courageous, more useful for shaping that aggressive, physical approach to life they wanted in their boys. It was a game which, they claimed, forged a boy's physical strength, honing his physique to the arduous tasks of life outside. It was a game which obliged players to relegate self to teamwork. And – no mean factor in a boarding school – here was a game, in conjunction with others, which thoroughly exhausted growing boys. Sometimes spelled out specifically, more often only hinted at, public-school proponents of the different forms of football and sports, viewed exhausting athleticism as an antidote to the sexual impulse and habits of young males.

Whatever their motives, the public schools were rarely far from view in the early days of modern football. The first president of the FA noted in 1863: 'I took down "Fifteen" the other day to play a match and I was the only one who had not been at a public school.' Time and again this public-school presence determined the course of football in its early days. In the first place, the initiators of the game – those men who tried to devise rules in keeping with most members' experience and interests – were predominantly public-school men. Both within the central FA and in the regional FA organizations, which rapidly mushroomed across the country at county level, such men were pre-eminent, though at the grass-roots popular football continued in various guises. Many of the early teams were themselves public-school enclaves. In London, for instance, the Wanderers became a dominant force, suitably winning the FA Cup when it was introduced in 1871. 'In early days this team [was] composed mainly of old public school men resident in London.' Even when more popularly based teams began to appear (or rather when the old traditions of popular football were revived by contact with the men, the new regulations and the discipline of the FA's dribbling game) certain teams maintained their social superiority. In Walsall, for instance, one team consisted solely of 'the young men of good social position'. Army officers were particularly imbued with the public-school sporting tradition and responded eagerly to the creation of the FA. A team from the War Office was among the founders and was soon joined by one from the Royal Engineers, and by 1900 it was claimed that 'Football has been a favourite diversion with the officers of the British Army for over 40 years.' Public-school influence was equally strong in the early Civil Service team.

The second level at which public-school influence operated in the formative years of Association football was in the missionary activities of ex-public-school pupils. Wherever these men settled in their working lives, they seemed anxious to further the sporting activities in which they themselves had been drilled. Consequently, from the 1850s onward new forms of gentlemanly recreation began to appear throughout the country – a use of leisure quite distinct from the traditional recreations of the leisured class. In Liverpool, William Mather, an Old Rugbeian, invited some former school-mates, as well as some men from Cheltenham, to meet on a local cricket field to experiment with the football currently played at his old school. A Rugby man was asked to bring a team from Manchester (and a ball). From this ad hoc gathering a game emerged in Liverpool which was, predictably, a confused amalgam of the dribbling game and Rugby football. The game sprang up elsewhere in the north. An advertisement in the *Leeds Mercury* in 1864 noted, '*Football*. Wanted a number of persons to form a football club for playing on Woodhouse Moor for a few days a week from 7 to 8 o'clock a.m.' Surprisingly, 500 men turned up.

Such early, faltering steps towards the modern game were often haphazard. But there were more deliberate and organized attempts by men who had passed through the public schools to transform the games of football they found in existence around the country. Where it did not exist, they introduced it. The most striking result of this drive to establish football (and athleticism in general) throughout the country was to be seen in those urban, industrial communities which, in time, were to become the social bed-rock of the modern game. But to understand how this took place, we need to look beyond the narrow focus of the game itself.

Alongside their zeal for sports, mid-nineteenth-century public-school men were also driven by a powerful social conscience. Indeed one of the most impressive (and influential) social ideals generated within the schools was a powerful sense of social responsibility: a concern for the less-fortunate and a resolve to seek remedies. These were, after all, the years when the British well-to-do began to learn of the extent and depth of deprivation around them. A new social conscience emerged (not simply via the public schools of course) which was Christian, aggressive and self-confident. More and more people felt compelled to help their fellow citizens.

The problems were there for all to see and read. Henry Mayhew had already begun his massive and influential documentation of the hidden life of labour in London, and he was only one of an army of similarly motivated men who, spurred on by moral indignation, turned their energies to the task of exposing and relieving the conditions of the urban poor. In the year the FA was established, William Booth founded the Salvation Army and Henry Solly his Union of Working Men's Clubs and Institutes. Thomas Hughes, author of *Tom Brown's School Days*, provides a further example of a public-school man wrestling with the problems of urban life. Hughes carried 'the spirit of "fair-play" into social affairs promoting co-operation, trade unions and arbitration as well as pummelling dockers into a due appreciation of the Working Men's College'.

Those zealous young men, fresh from school or college, who were keen to help their benighted fellow citizens, needed a base within poor communities from which they could do their good works. Some knew the problems first hand. Clergymen, teachers and industrialists, for instance, had their own direct link to the world of the poor and the working class: their everyday work brought them into direct contact with many of the problems taxing the Victorian conscience. Others, however, set out to forge links with the poor, embarking on evangelical missionary work in the cities of their own country. Men from Uppingham, for example (where, under Thring, they had enjoyed unprecedented athletic facilities, including the first school swimming-pool), flocked in droves to the East End of London on missionary social work. Other ex-pupils made Liverpool and the north-west their destination for social work.

By the 1860s a distinct conjunction of forces began to draw attention to the benefits of physical fitness, for the most striking aspect of urban poverty was the physical degeneracy of the people. While public-school athleticism developed into something of a fetish, the early truths revealed about the urban poor seemed to offer proof of the need for the physical activities perfected within the schools. In the following twenty years, therefore, a concerted effort was launched by ex-public-school men to introduce the virtues of athleticism into the deprived communities, in addition to more immediately practical social work via settlements.

Social investigators, the emergence of modern medicine, the Victorian preoccupation with the healthy (and beautiful) body, all and more served to draw attention to the wretched physical condition of millions of people. To public-school men, obsessed with fitness and athleticism, it seemed clear enough that what working people needed was exposure to the benefits of the sporting culture from which they had benefited. Of course it is easy, in retrospect, to realize that British social problems were deeply rooted and could not be remedied by simple solutions. Yet athleticism had a plausible appeal.

Football fitted the bill perfectly. No other sport lent itself so easily and cheaply to the varying conditions of urban life. It was simple to play, easy to grasp and could be played on any surface under any conditions, by indeterminate numbers of men. It needed no equipment but a ball, and could last from dawn to dusk. Football could be played by anyone, regardless of size, skill and strength. Moreover, its traditions as a popular sport, though under pressure in the cities, guaranteed it an immediate appeal among working people. When ministers and school masters brought the ideals of muscular Christianity into working-class life, the game they used as a tool was consonant with the needs and traditions of working people.

But football was not a simple transplant by middle-class workers into working-class communities, for there was a powerful and spontaneous upsurge of working-class football. The first moves towards regularized football coincided with, and were in some respects related to, the embryonic framework of control which evolved from the new FA. To encourage the game of football and to tap the interest in it which was revealed at various levels of society, the FA began to organize inter-county matches (and later inter-county competitions), taking their cue from county cricket. On 2 November 1867, for instance, a football match was played between Middlesex and Kent. According to *Bell's Life*, 'A *bona fide* county match is such a complete novelty in the football world that we can hardly wonder at the numbers who thronged to Beaufort House on Saturday last . . .' Unhappily, the arrangements, and the pitch were in chaos. 'The ground was in most objectionable a state and totally unfit for football purposes and the grass, which was several inches long, and extremely thick effectually prevented all attempts at dribbling or any exhibitions of the quick play which we might have expected from the reputations of many of the players engaged in the contest.' Nonetheless, the match raised a number of important points. 'Football has lately increased to such gigantic dimension that it needs something more than ordinary club matches to bring out the rising talent. The names of the players who were engaged in this contest are a sufficient guarantee that the promoters – who we are informed, are the officers of the FA – desire impartially to perform their duties, to select the best players without regard to public schools or especial cliques . . .'

In fact the first representative game, between Sheffield and London, had been organized by the FA as early as 1866, but as the decade advanced, the need was to provide the growing number of football clubs with an organized framework for their play. The crucial step in this direction was taken by the new secretary of the FA, C.W. Alcock, an old Harrovian. On 20 July 1871 representatives from Upton Park Club, Westminster School, the Civil Service Club, Crystal Palace, Harrow, and the Royal Engineers met in London, accepting Alcock's proposal that 'It is desirable that a Challenge Cup should be established in connection with the Association, for which all clubs belonging to the Association should be invited to compete.' The FA Cup was inaugurated and the public schools were predominant at its inception. The clubs which agreed to the competition were largely ex-public-school, and Alcock borrowed the idea of the Cup from Harrow where the 'Cock-House' competition was based on a similar knockout principle. Such house competitions were also common to the other schools attended by the FA's founding fathers. In retrospect, it seems strange that a competition which came to represent such fierce loyalties and rivalries among working people in urban areas began life as an extension of public-school experience.

When the first games for the FA Cup were played, in 1872, fifty clubs were eligible to compete, but only fifteen did so. Of these, only two (Queen's Park, Glasgow, and Donington Grammar School) came from north of Hertfordshire. Interest in the Cup developed slowly (by 1876 there were still only thirty-seven teams involved) but nonetheless the principle of competition in football spread rapidly, chiefly, as with cricket, at county level. County FAs and their local competitions swiftly changed the face of the game, for they provided the growing number of teams in the midlands and north with the regulation, direction and competition which the FA had provided for the London clubs in 1863.

The Scottish Cup, inaugurated in 1873, had the same effect, providing a framework for local footballers and a focus for the activities of growing numbers of teams. Throughout that decade, the game, on both sides of the border, retained many features of its old, traditional, slightly ramshackle format. As urban growth accelerated, land for sporting activity became scarcer. In Scotland, it was claimed that cricket declined because so much suitable land succumbed to the builders. Football, on the other hand, did not require such neatly manicured surfaces. 'What,' asked a Scottish writer, 'did they care about ridges or furrows or that it was difficult to see the lower goal posts when you were at the other end.' One game, played at East Kilbride in 1873, took place on a narrow strip of land, divided by 'fifteen foot furrows, which, by introducing alternate hill and dale, no doubt lent a charm to the landscape, but while giving the place a poetic beauty, rather spoilt it for the stern prose of football'. Another game (in 1882) between Rangers and Jordanhill was delayed until a horse and plough could be used to mark the boundary of the pitch. Yet such problems – by no means uncommon – did little to staunch the game's rising popularity. Within a decade of its foundation, for instance, the Scottish Football Association counted 133 member clubs (nineteen of which are still in the Scottish League).

The growth of football in England and Scotland was striking in the 1870s. Yet it grew within a framework which, in organisational and ideological terms, remained overwhelmingly public school. Despite the early stirrings of provincial football, the 'old-boy teams' from the south maintained their primacy until the early 1880s. The FA Cup was won for its first 11 years by the Wanderers, Old Etonians, Oxford University, Royal Engineers, Old Carthusians and Clapton Rovers. This was, after all, the 'Golden Age of the Amateur', when gentlemen of leisure dominated the game and when the great technical and athletic skills and feats of football were the preserve of ex-public-school men. A.F. (later Lord) Kinnaird was perhaps the most exceptional. This aristocrat with an estate in Perthshire, later to be High Commissioner of the Church of Scotland, played for the Wanderers and Old Etonians, wearing long white trousers and quartered cap and sporting a superb flowing red beard. Kinnaird appeared in no fewer than nine Cup finals, taking home five winners' medals. Always the hero of the crowd (who, on one occasion, took the horses from his coach and hauled him, in true eighteenth-century style, to the players' entrance), at the 1882 Cup final Kinnaird stood on his head in front of the stands. Exuberance and unusual outbursts among the players were a feature of football from its early days.

The Cup final of 1882, though won by Kinnaird's Old Etonians, was a turning point in the history of football in England. For the first time, the supremacy of the southern gentlemen's teams had been challenged by the north in the shape of Blackburn Rovers. That year proved to be the last time an amateur team won the Cup. The Blackburn team represented a major change in the nature of the game, for they had cracked the dominance of the public schools.

The changes in football in the space of two generations had been remarkable. Looking back from, say the early 1880s, it was hard to imagine that this increasingly popular game was descended directly from the ancient folk game and from the turbulent games in the public schools. The transformation of school football, from uncontrollable hurly-burly to the game which is recognizably modern soccer, was the result of a complex intermeshing of internal school factors (notably the post-Arnoldian emphasis on athleticism) and the external factors which encouraged ex-pupils to move into various middle and high positions in Church and State, and to meet together in social and recreational pursuits. Moreover, the revelations about levels of contemporary destitution had provided these same men with the perfect opportunity and reason for exporting their interests and ideology into working-class communities. But the rise of working-class football was only in part an imitation of its social superior, for forces were at work in society which made possible the transformation of the social and leisure lives of working people. To grasp the context out of which the Blackburn team of 1882 emerged to challenge the Old Etonians – to appreciate how new forces came to challenge the old order – we need to adjust our historical focus and concentrate instead on the changes in industrial society. While the gentlemen of football's organizations were striving to build up a footballing organization in the 1880s, the social class which within thirty years would claim football as its own was struggling to shake off the crude limitations of early industrial life and seize the first opportunities of organized leisure. The story of the game for the rest of the century was the remarkable tale of the rise of working-class football.

3 The Rise of
   Working-class Football

'The great and widespread interest in football is a manifest fact. So much so that nowadays it is frequently urged that cricket can no longer be regarded as our "national game" in the true sense of the word. Football it is claimed, has now the first place in the popular heart.' This comment, by the great all-round athlete, cricketer and footballer, C.B. Fry in 1895, illustrates a social revolution. A mere thirty years before he wrote, football had been the virtual monopoly of a relatively small handful of gentlemen. By late in the century, football – transformed by public-school men from an undisciplined folk-game into a disciplined recreation – had been re-adopted by thousands of working people throughout the country. Long before the turn of the century, football had become the sport of the industrial working class; a social change of major proportions.

At first glance it seems unusual that the ancient folk traditions of football scarcely existed among industrial workers in the first half of the century. The reasons, however, are not hard to find. Formal holidays and time off work were unusual, as foreign visitors frequently noted. Even Sunday recreation – the traditional English day of leisure – was opposed, in almost seventeenth-century fashion, by many men of substance. 'A Sunday's holiday is looked upon as a heinous sin by so many worthy and respectable people that it cannot be indulged in with impunity.' Indeed, between 1830 and 1870 the only guaranteed national holidays were at Christmas and Easter. For industrial workers the situation in some respects was even worse, since the rigours of industrialization were bolstered by a utilitarian attitude to work among their betters which demanded total commitment to the march of progress. 'The pronounced tendency of this age to utilitarianism and the worship of wealth acting on the energies and earnestness natural to the English character,' said the Revd Martin in 1863, 'have resulted in the establishment of a highly artificial system of over-working which excludes recreation.'

It would, however, be inaccurate to suggest that the experiences of the working class were uniform and to lump together all the industrial cities of Victorian Britain. Beneath the common experience of industrialization there lay a multitude of local, regional and trade differences, each of which could determine a different style of life for local people. Nineteenth-century cities were distinct from one another. The lives of Manchester textile operatives, for example, differed markedly from those of the metal workers of Birmingham, the dock workers of Liverpool or Glasgow, or the potters of the Five Towns. Naturally enough, in each area the strength of old traditions (both political and recreational) depended on the direction of local industrial and urban change. The new industrial cities, those urban wens which seemed to owe little to eighteenth-century roots, were predictably weaker in local traditions than those industrial towns which emerged from existing social and economic structures. The Lancashire textile towns, for example, nestling in the nooks and folds of the East Lancashire hills, were smaller, and tended to be closer in distance and spirit to the fibre of pre-industrial life. Many pre-industrial traditions were thus within the reach of certain groups of industrial workers. Lancastrian Wakes provide us with a good illustration of this, for they offered a taste of the crudities of pre-industrial recreations, with their 'bull baiting, badger baiting, dog fighting, footracing in almost a state of nudity . . . eating a dishful of scalding porridge with bare hands and often the most disgusting exhibition of eating a pound of tallow and stripping the wicks through the teeth for wages'.

Among ancient spectator sports, boxing continued to hold sway, drawing vast and diverse crowds, ranging from aristocrats to the fringes of the underworld. Moreover, all these spectator sports – animal-baiting, boxing and the turf – were marked by the presence of a criminal fraternity, then as now, attracted by the free flow of money which always accompanied such sports. Even in mid-Victorian Britain there was a pronounced association between certain recreations, violence and illegality. It was of course to this sphere of sport that the older tradition of football belonged and it continued to be a truism that spectator sports and violence went hand in hand. Indeed public executions, arguably one of the most popular of spectator sports, were only finally outlawed in 1868.

In the major cities, however, the old cruel sports tended to die out in the face of all new urban regulation and the advance of industrialization. Yet the drive to curb and to end the old popular cultures was not always linked to new industry.

The drive towards a new form of labour discipline had surfaced in the eighteenth century. Men who were keen to modernise their industrial (and even agricultural) systems were unhappy with workers' traditional attitudes to work and free time. Working people enjoyed a range of saints' days, local holidays – or simply took time off work when they were able to. Josiah Wedgwood in the Potteries was only the most famous of a host of new employers who sought to inculcate a new labour discipline among their workforce. The whole point was that working people should regulate their lives by the dictates of the clock, the machine and the factory hooter – not by the whims of inclination or the patterns of local folk-customs.

This determination lay behind the campaigns against a host of local games and pastimes, none more disruptive (at least in the eyes of employers) than folk football. Time and again, in the early decades of the nineteenth century, employers joined forces with other propertied groups to ban football matches (and other such activities) which had been enjoyed since time immemorial. This pattern was, however, less striking in Scotland, but the difference may be due to the nature and pace of local industrial change. Football in Scotland seems to have survived longer as a casual rural game. But everywhere, across the face of Britain, there was a perceptible decline in folk football over the course of the nineteenth century. What is undoubtedly clear, however, is that when football began to spread in the last twenty years of the nineteenth century, it swept many other sports aside. This was especially the case in Scotland. It was a game which drew its rising strength from the amazing support it was able to marshal from one working-class community to another.

Yet that transformation was in the future. But before sports could emerge from the new industrial areas fundamental changes were needed in the economic life of the nation and one above all others: the prerequisite for a better personal and social life was a shorter working week. Campaigns aimed at reducing the hours worked in industry were as old as industrialization itself, but they first began to yield results in the 1840s. A firm provision of free time for industrial workers was finally established by a Factory Act of 1850 which introduced the sixty-hour week for women. The most important change was the coming of the free Saturday afternoon; what historians called '*la semaine anglaise*' (though *britannique* might have been better). Its major impact was, initially, in the textile industry before spreading to many other trades by the 1860s. For large numbers of people it meant that 'St Monday' (the traditional day which pre-industrial workers took for their free time) was swapped for Saturday. And in many cases, this exchange actually meant an increase in the number of hours worked. But the change from mid-century was very noticeable. Workers in one industry after another demanded a free Saturday afternoon. Writing in 1881, a Manchester industrialist looked back to life in the city in the 1830s with the comment, 'As for Saturday afternoon holiday, it was not even dreamt of. Hence people had fewer opportunities of indulging their inclinations in this direction.'

The campaigns for Saturdays partly free from work began in the textile industry and were greatly helped by a coincidental change of attitude on the part of the employers, who slowly turned to 'intensive' rather than 'extensive' methods of employment. After the first Factory Acts, designed to control working hours in the textile industry, similar regulations began to permeate industrial life (often without legislation). Industrial workers in London were granted free Saturday afternoons in the 1850s; in the Birmingham engineering trades in 1852–6; and in other cities by the late 1850s. Liverpool was exceptional: there, free Saturday afternoons did not become effective until the early 1870s.

This overall movement towards greater leisure for industrial workers involved more than industrial concessions. In the words of the Hammonds, it 'signified the success of a contention that . . . the workmen had a right to share in the culture and leisure enjoyed by others'. More and more employers realised the benefits to be had from granting free time to their workforce. They too benefited. Not only was the workforce refreshed, but, in the words of Wray Vamplew, employers were now able 'to have boilers scraped and furnaces overhauled'. Unfortunately, this concession was not evenly distributed for, on the whole, it was granted mainly to industrial workers and did not apply to the armies of clerks, shopkeepers – the very jobs which expanded quite dramatically as the service and retail industries grew – and agricultural workers, whose working hours continued to be almost as oppressive as ever. The most obvious consequence of this partial granting of Saturday afternoon off work was that *la semaine anglaise* was primarily an industrial phenomenon, allowing the industrial labour force to fill the free afternoons with organized recreation. Thus those sports, notably football, which came to dominate the Saturday afternoons of working men, tended to be watched and played by workers in the heavier industries – textiles, metals, engineering, mining, shipping and port industries. Football emerged as an industrial game, not as a palliative to the grimness of industrial life, but largely because industrial workers, unlike others, had free time. In addition, even more men (but rarely their womenfolk) had money to spend. In the historical debates about the impact of the industrial revolution on workers' lives, few would now deny that, from 1850, real wages rose. It varied enormously; there were years of decline, patches of misery caused by unemployment, ill-health and – above all – old age. Yet it is clear enough that more and more working men had spare money to spend as they wanted. The history of football and other organised sports shows that armies of them chose to spend some of that money on leisure.

Large communities of working men found themselves with leisure time and a little spare cash (for the first time in industrial society) in the years when the FA had begun to encourage the expansion of football. Contemporaries were immediately struck by the far-reaching potential of this new-found leisure time. 'The possession of the Saturday afternoon for themselves,' said a factory inspector, 'is an immense boon conferred upon the people in relation to their social state: for now the wages can be carried home in ample time for the market, and the husband and wife can spend that money together. And a still greater boon is the distinction at last made clear between the worker's own time and his masters'.' In Bradford it was claimed that a Saturday half-day had become 'as it were, a part of our religion'.

Throughout the industrial regions, Saturday rapidly established itself as the industrial equivalent of the pre-industrial St Monday, a day devoted to leisure, one to be anticipated and savoured. Writing in 1867, a working-class engineer noted, 'it is now a stock saying with many working men that *Saturday* is the best day of the week, as it is a short working day, and Sunday had to come'. In some areas the change brought about by free Saturday afternoons was easily visible. 'The working half of Saturday is up at one o'clock . . . When the bell rings the men leave the works in a leisurely way that contrasts rather sharply with the eagerness with which they leave at other times; but once outside the workshop gates, the younger apprentices and other boys immediately devote themselves to the business of pleasure. They will be seen gathering together in a manner that plainly indicates that there is "something in the wind".'

Those who enjoyed this new freedom universally praised it as 'one of the most practically beneficial that has ever been inaugurated with a view to the social improvement of "the masses" . . . It had made Saturday a day to be looked forward to by the working men with feelings of pleasurable anticipation, to be regarded as the day on which he can enjoy many things, which but for it he would not have had the opportunity of enjoying.' Within twenty years this free time was to be dominated for millions by football in the winter months, with the consequent further transformation of working-class social experience.

In the first years of *la semaine anglaise* the full potential for leisure of the emancipated labour force was not fully realized. Gradually, however, leisure became a national concern. *The Times* complained in 1871 of 'an increasing tendency of late years among all classes to find excuse for Holydays'. Many pious commentators in the 1860s expressed concern about the economic and industrial consequences of further holiday concessions. According to the *Illustrated London News* of 1863, 'There is, perhaps, no social problem more difficult of solution than that which involves the affording of more holidays to the working classes without at the same time diminishing their means of subsistence.'

In 1871 the national determination to enjoy formal holidays was revealed on the first ever Bank Holiday. The Bank Holiday Act of that year, extended in 1875 to cover other occupations, pushed through the Commons by Sir John Lubbock, was a landmark in the emergence of modern leisure patterns, for it transformed old religious holidays into secular days of recreation sanctioned by the state. *The Times* characteristically persisted in calling such days 'holydays' (and ironically the Bank Holiday became known as 'St Lubbock's Day'). On that first Bank Holiday the nation witnessed amazing and unprecedented scenes, as people collectively turned to organized leisure. Railway stations were packed – Cannon Street, Charing Cross and Fenchurch Street were a shambles. Similar chaos prevailed at steamboat piers. The boats ran out of food within ten minutes and public houses were similarly drained. By the following year, the Bank Holiday was even more widely observed, signalling the phenomenon of working-class holidays which, in the 1890s, were to become concentrated in the new seaside towns. Before the turn of the century, as social investigators were surprised to discover, working-class holidays had become commonplace among all but the very poor.

All this is not to claim that plebeian leisure and recreation were new. But the forms of leisure which emerged from the 1860s onwards were qualitatively different both from the leisure pursuits of the lower orders in earlier generations and increasingly from those of their social superiors. The years after the 1860s bore witness to the rise of a mature industrial labour force with the time, money (particularly after the 1870s) and inclination for organized leisure.

The contrast with pre-industrial leisure was stark. The new forms of leisure were as disciplined, regulated and even as timetabled as the industrial society which spawned them. The irregular, undisciplined and robust recreations of an older society (which was itself marked by these same qualities) gave way to the stringency of modern recreations. Yet for all this undeniable trend, patches of the old world remained. Sometimes traditional customs were transformed – and tamed – to suit the new society. In some places, older habits survived to give people a taste of the rowdiness of a previous generation. Even industrial workers clung to old habits; St Monday was observed in some industries well into the century. All this and more offers reminders of how rich a social mosaic British society really was. Any generalisations offered by historians can easily be punctured by examples of contrary behaviour. Despite, for instance, the rise of football, some areas remained immune. And what are we to do about the failure of the game (and most other games) to impress women? Yet it remains beyond dispute that, of all the recreational pursuits of the liberated working-class communities, none was more noticeable in its impact, more dramatic in its attractions (for both players and spectators) and more far-reaching in its consequences than the game of football.

Those who wished to encourage sporting activity among working people, the ex-public-school men keen to tackle the problems of industrial Britain, needed a point of entry to a social world which was often distant and generally alien. One of the most useful means of approaching working-class life was via the Church, of all denominations. Of course among many of the clergy belief in athleticism was almost as striking as their belief in God (one prominent headmaster had said, 'the Laws of physical well-being are the laws of God'). Few doubted the needs for large-scale recreation as part of the Churches' solution to the nation's ills. Clergymen seized on football as an ideal way of combating urban degeneracy. Robust games could, they believed, bring strength, health and a host of qualities badly needed by deprived working people – especially the young. As a result, working-class churches began to spawn football teams in the years immediately following the concession of free Saturday afternoons in local industries. Liverpool, which before the turn of the century was to establish itself as *the* footballing centre of England, was later than other cities in turning to the game, but when, in 1878, local teams began to form, they sprang most notably from churches, headed by St Domingo's, St Peter's, Everton United Church and St Mary's, Kirkdale. As late as 1885, twenty-five of the 112 football clubs in Liverpool had religious connections. Similar patterns emerged in other cities. In Birmingham in 1880, eighty-three of the 344 clubs (some twenty-four per cent) were connected to churches. Indeed many of today's famous clubs began life as church teams. Aston Villa originated in 1874 from members of the Villa Cross Wesleyan Chapel who already played cricket but wanted a winter sport. Birmingham City began life as Small Heath Alliance, organized by members of Trinity Church in 1875. Some years before, pupils and teachers of Christ Church, Bolton, formed a football club. In 1887 they took the name Bolton Wanderers. Blackpool FC emerged from an older team based on the local St John's

Church. Similarly, Everton started life in 1878 as St Domingo's Church Sunday School (and later produced an offshoot which became Liverpool FC). In 1880 men at St Andrew's Sunday School, West Kensington, organized a football team which later became Fulham FC. Members of the young men's association at St Mary's Church, Southampton, formed a team in 1885, changing the name to that of the present professional club in 1897. In Swindon, the local football team owed its origins to the work of the Revd W. Pitt in 1881. A year later members of the Burnley YMCA turned to football. Boys at St Luke's Church, Blakenhall, formed a football team in 1877, later taking the name Wolverhampton Wanderers. These surviving professional teams constitute only a small minority of the thousands of teams founded in the 1870s and 1880s from church organisations (often with the local vicar or curate as a player).

It might seem a contradictory point to note that one of the other main institutions which spawned football teams in these years was the local pub. This, after all, had been the traditional centre for a host of plebeian pleasures for centuries past. Pubs offered a place to meet, somewhere to change, a venue for news and information; a place where teams, management and supporters convened (much in fact as they still do throughout Britain).

Church teams, therefore, formed only one element in the rise of working-class football. Schools, particularly after the 1870 Education Act, similarly came to provide working-class communities with a new focus for educational and social activity. The new state education system provided ex-public-school men with an opportunity to put their widely based educational ideas into operation. Within the new state schools and particularly in educational administration, such men were able to generate wide enthusiasm for physical education. In the early years of state education this tended to take the form of drill and various forms of PT. But within ten years, schools had begun to marshal their male pupils into the various grades of football teams which to this day characterize British schools.

The process was slow, however, depending to a large extent on local initiative. As late as 1880, Matthew Arnold complained, 'Bodily exercise, also, and recreation, deserve far more care in our schools than they receive. We take too little thought for the bodies of our school children.' By 1890 this deficiency had been made good by a new elementary school code, with its recognition, 'for the first time of the duties of the State to care for the physical welfare of the children, and to make physical culture an integral part of their school life. Physical education, sports and games, out-of-door teaching in fresh air were therefore encouraged'.

Outside the public schools the move to football was initiated by pupils from the old grammar schools, who simply copied their educational superiors. In 1874, for example, old boys from Blackburn Grammar School formed a local club which became Blackburn Rovers. Ten years later old boys of Wyggeston School, Leicester, established a club, Leicester Fosse (renamed Leicester City in 1919). The origin of the professional club in Chester traces its roots to 1884, in part to the local King's School. State-school teams soon followed. One such team, among boys of Droop St School, London (1885), became Queen's Park Rangers two years later. School teachers seemed equally enthusiastic for the game and, as we might expect, some of their teams have survived in professional form. Sunderland FC was formed in 1879 as the Sunderland and District Teachers' Association AFC. In 1897 teachers in the Elementary Schools Athletic Association in Northampton formed a team which laid the foundations for the present professional club. These school-based teams, like those which emerged from churches, are merely the surviving, well-known fragment of a much wider social phenomenon.

One factor which encouraged the growth of school-based teams was the role of training colleges, and the teachers they educated. There was, quite simply, a massive growth in the number of college-educated teachers; they graduated and went out into their professional lives fired by the commitment to football inculcated in their college. Though many local education authorities remained sceptical or hesitant about football (and other sports), teachers in the schools often by-passed the system. If their schools made no provision for football, they ran teams after school hours and at weekends. Good teachers realised that such out-of-school activities also served to forge boys' loyalty to their school.

In the last twenty-five years of the nineteenth century, Britain developed an education system which, despite its local and regional differences, served to draw all children into its educational net. It was often difficult to attract pupils. More difficult still to keep them in school. But time and again teachers accepted that football proved to be the attraction which drew many boys to school and to school activities. Among the boys, the school football teams – and later the inter-school and even inter-regional school football competitions (themselves modelled on public schools) – became of crucial importance in generating and maintaining the youthful commitment to football, particularly among working-class boys whose recreational opportunities were limited. By the last years of the century, thousands of spectators paid to see the finals of local schoolboy competitions, played for trophies, medals and caps similar to those of their professional peers and their public-school betters, at the splendid new stadiums recently built on the edges of British cities.

Some bemoaned the new emphasis on sport in schools. 'Our school competitions in football and other sports have now become a severe tax on the strength of any boy and particularly of the poorly clad and ill-fed . . . In many cases a team from a poor district has to compete with a school in a better neighbourhood, where the boys are better fed, and much evil must result.' How far physical debility among the poorest boys prevented them from enjoying football to the full is difficult to say, but in general the game's popularity rapidly became a feature of schoolboy life. Indeed the new emphasis upon football in state schools by the turn of the century was perhaps *the* most important factor in guaranteeing the future of football as a mass game and was undoubtedly a determining factor in making football the national game. Critics had a point, however. It was not easy to see how the very poor, and especially the sick – of whom there were many thousands – could benefit by being pitched into vigorous physical team games. On balance, however, the game thrived on the simple test of consumer popularity. Boys and young men turned to it in their millions, as players and spectators.

Schools had a much wider importance in the emergence of working-class football than in the obvious respect of creating schoolboy teams. They helped to establish, for instance, a more sophisticated form of literacy among working men which, in its turn, laid the basis for the mass readership of the new-style national and local popular newspaper. These gave great coverage to football and in many respects helped to generate interest in and knowledge of the professional game. Supplements, cheap weekly editions, local newspapers, all gave increasing prominence to sports; all gave prompt information, about timetables, fixtures and results, helping to satisfy and encourage still further the popular demand for news about sport (and helped promote the ancillary industry of gambling). Millions took part in sport, at a distance, through the printed word. Until the rise of TV, newspapers, for the best part of a century, proved a key player in the history of modern football.

Sports teams emerged from a host of institutions. In addition to schools and churches, the work-place itself proved influential. Factory football teams became a feature of working-class recreation in the winter months and, like schoolboy football, have remained a feature of working-class life to the present day. As we shall see later, the early professional footballers were generally part-timers, continuing to work in local industries where their footballing talents had first come to prominence. Industrial football teams, like church and school teams, mushroomed rapidly throughout the industrial regions. Moreover, many of today's professional teams owe their origins to them. One of the earliest was founded in 1863 by workmen on the North Staffordshire Railway, possibly with the help of ex-public-school men teaching in a local school. This team later became Stoke City. Other railway workers, in Crewe, who had formed a cricket club in 1866, decided to form a football team in 1877 and, since they met at the Alexandra Hotel, they took the name Crewe Alexandra. In a northern suburb of Manchester, workmen of the Lancashire and Yorkshire Railway Company formed the Newton Heath team in 1880; in 1902 they took the name Manchester United. Ninety years later the professional club reverted to the original Newton Heath playing strip for their alternative colours. Workmen employed at Singer's cycle factory in Coventry formed Singers FC in 1883; by 1898 the team had become Coventry City. Workers at Morton's factory in Millwall formed a team in 1885, later to become the present-day professional club. One of the most famous of London clubs began life in this way. Workers at the munitions factory at Woolwich began to play football in 1886. Known successively as the Royal Arsenal FC, then Woolwich Arsenal, the present name, Arsenal, was adopted in 1914. In the East End of London, employees at the Thames Iron works formed a team in 1895,

partly financed by the company. Later the company
discontinued the contribution and consequently in 1900 the
West Ham United Football Company was formed. But the
origins were revealing. The company was owned by Arnold F.
Hills, a graduate of Harrow and Oxford, a talented sportsman
in his younger days and, throughout, committed to athleticism,
social progress and profitable business. The football club was
founded in 1895 as part of Hills's belief in 'the importance of co-
operation between workers and management'. The game would,
he believed, be useful (and enjoyable) for the workers and
beneficial for the company.

It was natural enough that new forms of social activities in
working-class communities should emerge, where possible,
from existing institutions and traditions. By the late
nineteenth century a number of inter-related institutions
dominated and formed the geographical and social limits of
working-class life; the home and immediate neighbourhood,
the work-place, the church, the union and, later, the local
school. In most working-class areas these institutions were
usually close to each other, dotting the tightly packed streets
and forming the reference points for local movement. Soon
they were to be joined by impressive monuments to the rise of
local leisure – the new football stadiums which at once
symbolized the confident emergence of football and expanded
the horizons of working-class fans who travelled to new parts
of the city (and even to distant parts of the country) in support
of their local teams.

Many new football teams, however, did not emerge from
existing institutions, springing instead from local, accidental or
idiosyncratic forces. Some sprang from an accident of
geography; a neighbourhood group of men who simply wanted
to play football together. Many teams were a winter by-product
of cricket, which, like football, proved difficult to transplant
into industrial cities. Cricket was, moreover, more time-
consuming and expensive than many other popular sports.
Nonetheless, cricket, a traditional rural game, and a folk-custom
especially in Kent and Yorkshire, remained the summer game of
working men throughout the nineteenth century. In addition,
those men who turned to cricket in the late years of the century
often wanted a complementary game for the winter months. The
result was that groups of footballers sometimes sprang from

cricketing organizations. Derby County FC (1884) owed its origins to the local county cricket club, while three years earlier, men from the Preston Cricket Club organized a football team which became Preston North End. One of the oldest of English clubs, Sheffield Wednesday, was founded in 1867 by members of the Sheffield Wednesday Cricket Club, anxious to keep together in the winter months. Their neighbours, Sheffield United, were formed in 1889 by members of the Yorkshire CCC. Tottenham Hotspur FC emerged in 1882 from an even older Hotspur Cricket Club.

Some groups became football teams simply by adaptation. In Nottingham, football emerged from a traditional local game known as 'shinney'. Elsewhere, purely fortuitous events led to the establishment of local football. In Doncaster, the main local football team was established in 1879 simply to play a game against the Yorkshire Institute for the Deaf. Middlesbrough's team came into being in 1876 following an exploratory tripe supper at the Corporation Hotel.

Football's most attractive charms were cheapness and simplicity but, before the turn of the century, as the organization and tactics of the game gained in sophistication – as it approached more nearly the game we know today – watching and playing football began to cost money. In the early days, free-for-all football could be played in the new municipal parks, which local authorities (led by Birkenhead and Manchester) gradually introduced as part of the wider effort to bring health and beauty into the squalid industrial cities. Oddly enough, many cities made determined efforts to prevent the playing of football and other sports in these parks (as many indeed still do). Young working men nonetheless seized the opportunities offered to play Saturday football on municipal property. But as teams, leagues and competitions became established in the 1880s, on a local trade, school or regional basis, the increasing sophistication of the game brought expense. Specially made equipment began to replace the old everyday clothing worn by players. Eye-catching kit with colourful jerseys, shorts, stockings and even caps had long been the mark of the public-school sportsman. Now it was the turn of working-class players. In 1880 Lewis's of Manchester offered for sale knickerbockers at 6s 9d, jerseys for 3s 11d – and hand-sewn footballs for 10s 6d. Custom-made footballs could be bought in most major towns by the 1880s. Football boots began to replace normal boots and shoes – that shoe manufacturers considered it worthwhile to diversify into such specialized areas indicates the growing economic importance of the game. Of course most footballers played without resort to the latest fashion, simply turning out in whatever spare clothing seemed appropriate.

Firms which had previously specialized in cricket equipment turned to the production of footballs. Manufacturers of herbal and patent medicines directed their attention to the thousands of players whose knocks, bruises and strains required swift, cheap and uncomplicated treatment; Elliman's Embrocation became the lubricant of football success. Tonics found in the footballing fraternity a new and greedy market. Grant's Morell Cherry Brandy, 'the best Tonic for Football Players', was also useful for the hardy winter spectator, being 'most comforting in chilly weather'. Even seed merchants supplied the new demand for durable turf. Football shirts in varied styles, colours, materials and qualities and football shorts, ranging from basic navy serge to exotic lambskin, appealed to the sartorial sense and team identity of the new footballers. Department stores offered the whole range of football goods, from nets to balls. In fact the economic spin-off from the game had, within thirty years of the establishment of the FA, become a sizeable industry itself, and around football there developed a cocoon of ancillary trades and services all of which were made possible (like the modern game itself) only by the increasing amount of money available for leisure.

Commercial involvement in football is, then, as old as the game; the degree of modern involvement ought not to persuade us that it is a new phenomenon. Even the present-day spate of newspapers and magazines devoted wholly or in part to football was paralleled by a late nineteenth-century wave of popular footballing journalism. Cheap magazines appealed directly to the newly awakened sporting interest among working men. Of course the format, style and tone were different. Yet in essence they were very close; using the printed word to excite interest in the game, to foster loyalties to chosen teams, to lavish adoration on particular players, and, of course, to make money from the sale of printed copy.

ARE YOU A FOOTBALLER?
We presume so, or you wouldn't
be at this Match.
Perhaps you also run a bike?
WELL
SPORTS
IS THE PAPER YOU WANT
(Illustrated 32 pages)

People Swear by it.
Rivals Swear at it.
Agents Pant for it
The Public Fight for it,
And you can Buy it EVERYWHERE.
Nothing succeeds like –
SPORTS!

From the 1880s local newspapers began to give serious coverage to organized sport in general and football in particular. Like the popular national newspapers, these ventures, and the sports magazines, depended on widespread working-class literacy for their success. We now know that literacy was widespread in a host of plebeian British communities for centuries past. But after 1870 the informal and personal drive towards working-class literacy was subsumed within the new school system. In the case of football, knowledge about the game's increasingly complex organization – its fixtures, venues, times, transport arrangements, personnel and results – was actively promoted through the medium of the press. Newspapers (led by the locals) rapidly established themselves as football's information service. Results from around the country, for instance, could be seen on the evening of the game, pasted in the windows of local press offices, thanks to the newly efficient telegraph services (a service which was the forerunner of Football Evening Specials). Equally, the establishment of football as an efficient national concern directed by the English and Scottish FAs in the last quarter of the century was made possible only by the sophistication and reliability of the postal and telegraph services. Indeed the efficiency of business and commerce in general (of which football was a part) was related directly to the evolution of reliable modern communications. Fixtures could be arranged, teams forewarned and fans informed by telegraph (and through newspapers with their own telegraph terminals) while national and municipal transport services could be relied upon to deposit mail, football teams and armies of fans at the required destination on schedule. When professional footballers threatened to strike (in 1909) they warned 'of empty trams and deserted trains . . . and withdrawal of football editions'. By then, everyone appreciated the importance of modern communications to the game's well-being.

Transport was vital in the rise of popular football. In the cities, newly introduced trams were designed specifically for a working-class clientele, providing local people with a means of reaching previously inaccessible quarters of their own cities at fares they could afford. In 1871 the system was embryonic but within thirty years it employed 18,000 men. By the 1880s the average fare was less than 1½d. The new tram systems (horse-drawn initially, later electric), criss-crossed the cities, snaking their way to the very edges of the countryside, to the new parks and playing fields, to distant schools, churches or factories and, later, right to the turnstiles of the stadiums. The electric trams were cheaper than ever – perhaps forty per cent cheaper than the old horses – and the system began to penetrate the new suburbs and even the edges of the countryside. By 1901 sixty-one local authorities ran their own tram systems; in Leeds, by then, the horses had been withdrawn.

Trains were equally vital in the rapid growth of football in the last quarter of the nineteenth century. While the debate about cheap fares and special provision for working-class passengers had originated in the 1840s, the railway companies fully appreciated the economic importance of this market only in the 1870s. Regular train travel still remained too expensive for many working people, but the provision of cheap return tickets on special occasions opened up a new market. Train-borne footballers and fans were whisked to distant parts of the country which they would otherwise not have seen. In 1879 Queen's Park left Glasgow on Friday night and played in Manchester the following day before returning to Glasgow that same evening. Perhaps more striking still was the movement of fans. Railways brought thousands of fans into the cities from working-class communities in their hinterland. The same railway companies whisked the fans away to watch games in distant towns and cities. This was particularly noticeable after the institution of the Cup finals as annual events in London and Glasgow when thousands of working men converged on the cities. These waves of men who, from the 1880s onwards regularly descended on London from the midlands and the north, were effectively the first working-class visitors *en masse* since those unusual thousands transported to the Great Exhibition of 1851 by Thomas Cook. After a new Crystal Palace site became the permanent venue for the Cup final in 1895, many thousands more were drawn to London at the end of the football season:

> All the long night overcrowded trains have been hurrying southward along the great trunk lines, and discharging cargoes of Lancashire and Yorkshire artisans in the grey hours of early morning. They sweep through the streets of the Metropolis, boisterous, triumphant. They blink round the historic monuments, Westminster Abbey, St Paul's Cathedral. They all wear grey cloth caps, they are all decorated with coloured favours; they are all small men, with good-natured undistinguished faces.

One of them, in 1909, was the author's grandfather who had paid 10s 6d to travel from Oldham Mumps station to London to watch Manchester United beat Bristol City 1–0.

These were also the years when the adult male working class came of political age. Thanks to the vote, rudimentary social reform (particularly at the municipal level), and the consequent rise of working-class and industrial agitation, the British working class became an 'estate of the realm', though clearly not an equal one. Just as the working-class presence made itself felt in political and industrial terms, their new forms of leisure and recreation equally changed the nation's social life. By 1895 an observer commented, 'The nation, we are told, is a democracy, and the game of the people must be accepted as the game of the nation . . .'

Modern football reflected then a deep-rooted social revolution within industrial society, involving the freeing of the lower strata to enjoy the first meagre benefits of a technically advanced and relatively sophisticated society. Leisure time, more money, the improvements in education, transport and communications cumulatively produced the need, desire and possibility for leisure and recreation. But this process was not unique to Britain. It could also be seen throughout the western world, notably in the USA and Australia where mass recreations became a feature of late nineteenth-century life. When we look at Australia and the USA we can appreciate that the changes discussed here were universal in the western world. In other countries and regions they resulted in the establishment of games other than Association football as the national game. Indeed even within Britain there were (and are) very obvious regional exceptions to the overall rise of football as a working-class sport. In parts of Lancashire and Yorkshire, Rugby League was to become the local working-class sport; in South Wales, Rugby Union played the same role; and in Ireland other forms of football prevailed. Yet wherever we look, the local passion – in winter at least – was for games called 'football'; games which, however dissimilar, were derived from traditional customs, and had been transformed by local usage into a modern team game with enormous local appeal. This was true for Gaelic football, Aussie Rules, soccer, Rugby League and Rugby Union.

In general, football ideally fitted the nature and needs of urban industrial life. It was rapidly adapted to the opportunities and limitations of urban life. Ironically, football in industrial cities became, at one level, what it had been for centuries past – a street game played by the young. Its skills could be mastered and enjoyed by a single boy playing alone in a cobbled street, or by teams of twenty roaming through the new parks. Once rugby established its separate identity in the 1870s, with much of its emphasis given to dragging players roughly to the ground, it could no longer compete with football as a street game. With its new rules and careful regulation, football became a relatively safe and acceptable street game, as it has remained ever since. Unlike the ancient game, football in the late nineteenth century could be permitted in streets and alleys without fear of social disruption, serious damage to property (save for the odd broken window) or physical injury. The players (though not the spectators) no longer posed a threat to law and order and football soon came to be seen as a perfect way of distracting idle youngsters from more harmful pursuits. Crudely stated, football had been rendered safe by the wider disciplines of industrial society.

By the 1880s football had begun to undermine the following and strength of other sports, and some men began to utter profane thoughts about converting football into a summer game, arguing that 'there is no logical reason why football should remain exclusively a winter sport'. Accordingly, the administrators of the game, true to their social roots and anxious to guarantee the survival of their summer game, ordered that football should be played only between 1 September and 30 April. Among the young, however, football inevitably continued to be played all the year round. Inside the formal framework of football, however – the expanding bureaucracy of FA administrations which reached into virtually every regional cranny – football became established as the winter game, no longer to compete with cricket. But arguments about the respective status of the two games continued.

> Certainly football is a more democratic game than cricket . . . a man who owns some boots, some shorts, and a shirt has all that is necessary for a football match . . . The result of all this is that football is within the reach of everybody . . . football is certainly the more feasible game of the two, from the working man's point of view . . .

Of course time was an important factor. Football required relatively little time to play or watch. Cricket, on the other hand, required days rather than hours.

The devotion of working men to their teams soon brought snorts of disapproval from their social superiors and employers. An almost utilitarian view of working-class support for football reasserted itself in the face of industrial absenteeism and partisan passions which now characterized the game. 'Nothing is more annoying to the principals of a firm than to incessantly find an unexpected absentee on Monday morning.' This same Liverpool gentleman continued, bemoaning that 'those young gentlemen, who are no use to anyone during the week, who are absent-minded at their work, careless in their duties, irregular in their habits, come out on Saturday afternoon with terrific force. It is simply monstrous to what a pitch this football-playing has arisen.' Whatever their objections to the game, however, most men were united on one point. Football had indisputably become 'the game of the busy classes and consequently of the people'.

4 Football to 1914

The pioneer gentlemen's football clubs established in the 1860s and 1870s bore little resemblance to their modern descendants. Even the game they played seemed quite unlike the football we would recognize today. The early deliberations among football's founding fathers were to a large extent concerned with fashioning a standard form of football which would be acceptable to all who played the game. The problem was that footballers played different games, depending on which school or college they had attended. From the first, there was a tension between those who preferred the dribbling game and those who supported the handling game. At their early meetings the FA members strove to incorporate the best aspects of both games. But late in 1863 a decisive argument about the two games developed within the small caucus of members and the outcome was to establish a distinctive dribbling game. The original rules had agreed that:

> (Rule IX) A player shall be entitled to run with the ball towards his adversaries' goal if he makes a fair catch, or catches the ball on the first bounce; but in the case of a fair catch, if he makes his mark, he shall not run.
> (Rule X) If any player shall run with the ball towards his adversaries' goal, any player on the opposite side shall be at liberty to charge, hold or hack him, or wrest the ball from him; but no player shall be held and hacked at the same time.

In December 1863 both these provisions were deleted from the FA rules, effectively leaving the members free to develop the

Association game in which the emphasis was on controlling the ball with the feet. The change of rules, however, persuaded others to quit the FA and, eventually, to form their own handling organization. Uniformity was still a long way off, but gradually the FA came to be accepted as the arbiter of the rules and techniques of football, and as ever more clubs came within its jurisdiction, standardization of rules, interpretation and play slowly emerged. As local FA organisations were established through the provinces and in Scotland, each local organisation served to ensure the standardization and local acceptance of football's rules and conventions.

Uniformity in football was speeded up after the introduction of the knockout competitions, the English and Scottish Cups, for all competitors were obliged to play within the same nationally supervised rules. Overall, the Cups made an incalculable impact on the nature of football in the 1870s for, in addition to uniformity, it introduced the competitiveness which was itself a spur to the formation of more and more clubs. We need to remember, however, that these were the years of a massive proliferation of sporting clubs of all sorts and conditions. But of all of them, football accounted for the greatest expansion and absorbed the activities of many more people than any other sport. In central Scotland, footballers became so numerous that they often had trouble finding somewhere suitable to play. The consequent rise of professional and semi-professional football was so profuse that clubs tended to fight for the same low-income spectators. Many thought, by the 1890s, that there were, quite simply, too many Scottish clubs and teams for the overall health of the game. Not able to charge more than 3d for their average spectator, the Scottish clubs were sensitive to local economic ups-and-downs, and to regional hardship. When boys' football teams proliferated in the 1890s, some of the older clubs simply could not compete for spectators. But in England until the early 1880s the game which evolved through the FA and which found a focus in the annual competitions for the Cup, was dominated by the gentlemen amateurs of the south. They too controlled the administration of the game. Indeed the administration of the FA was to continue in such hands long after the social composition of football had changed beyond recognition. As proof of this dominance, in the first ten English Cup finals all twenty competitors were drawn from that exclusive band of southern, middle-class amateurs which had grown directly out of the public schools and the universities. Playing in long trousers and caps (the origin of modern international 'caps') and forced to play in public parks or, for the final, on Surrey's cricket ground at Kennington Oval, these footballers gave the game its orthodoxy and skills. But it would still have remained unusual to modern eyes. Teams changed ends when a goal was scored, the original cross-bar was a tape and the pitch had no markings for the centre-circle, half-way line, goal or penalty areas.

The whole point of the game in the early years was to attack. Teams were built around the star attackers, and indeed the great majority of the team consisted of attackers – dribblers who personified the skills and attractions of the game. 'To see players guide and steer a ball through a circle of opposing legs, turning and twisting as occasion requires, is a sight not to be forgotten.' Eight men out of the eleven formed the attack; by 1874 they had been reduced to seven, three of whom were centre-forwards. In the late 1870s this was reduced still further, to six attackers and finally, in 1883, Cambridge University resorted to five, pulling back one of the centre-forwards to fill the newly created position of centre-half. This new formation rapidly established itself as the norm throughout the British game and was to last, with variations, until a changing sense of tactics induced a defensive mentality in the 1930s and again in the 1960s. Until the early 1880s dribblers dominated football, and dribbling was the basis of the game; it had been perfected many years before on the public-school playing fields. Football stars of the 1860s and 1870s would have been denounced by many modern spectators for their greed with the ball (a vice, today, allowed only to the greatest of players):

> A good dribbler stuck to the ball as long as he could, especially if he saw a good chance of outrunning the three backs, who formed the only obstacle he had to overcome. Long runs were frequent, and as a consequence, individual skill was in a great measure the source of a football reputation.

For the amateur, such a casual, individualistic approach was both ideal and unquestioned, but as players of a different social class and, more important, new spectators came to seek in the game not just skill but positive results, the emphasis within the game began to change. Spectators and players came to expect their team to win; winning rather than fancy footwork was the aim.

This, like so many aspects of the new game, drew its immediate inspiration from Scotland. There, the game had its own distinctive history which paralleled and reinforced developments south of the border. In the summer of 1867, the Queen's Park Club of Glasgow was formed, paving the way for the development of the Scottish Association game. From the first, the men of Queen's Park had close ties with the FA in London and in 1870 a representative match was arranged to be played in London between English players and some Scots. To boost the game C.W. Alcock, secretary to the FA, wrote to the *Glasgow Herald* inviting nominations for the Scottish team. 'In Scotland, once essentially the land of football, there should still be a spark left of the old fire, and I confidently appeal to Scotsmen to aid to their utmost the efforts of the committee to confer success on what London hopes to found, an annual trial of skill between the champions of England and Scotland.' From this first Scottish team of 1870, only one man played for Queen's Park; the other ten were 'Anglos' from the English public schools. But in the following year the Glasgow club was among the first competitors for the original FA Cup. A year later, in 1872, the first formal 'international' between England and Scotland, took place in Glasgow before a crowd of 4,000. The Scotland team consisted entirely of players from Queen's Park, and although the match ended in a draw, English observers were enormously impressed by the teamwork of the Scots. 'The strong point with the home club was that they played excellently well together.' Two English clubs, Sheffield and Royal Engineers, had also begun to develop a new approach to teamwork. Significantly, when Sheffield played the Queen's Park club, the match drew no fewer than 10,000 spectators. Like so many innovations inspired by the Scots, coherent teamwork spread rapidly throughout the English game and by the late 1870s teamwork, based on passing rather than dribbling, had come to dominate English football. Writing in 1888, a contemporary historian of the game noted: 'The one change, however, the introduction of a combination of passing tactics from forward to forward to the discouragement of brilliant dribbling by individual players, so far revolutionized the game that we may fairly say that there have been two ages of the Association play, the dribbling and the passing.'

In response to this change in tactics, football teams were obliged to reorganize their formation; defences became highly structured, absorbing six of the eleven players and requiring careful tactical preparation to cope with the thrusts of the opposition's teamwork and passing. What appears on the surface to have been merely a change in tactics actually involved a sudden and dramatic shift in the nature of football itself. In March 1874, for example, the winning goal in the Oxford–Cambridge game was scored by an Oxonian who had dribbled the whole length of the pitch. Within two years, however, most clubs had begun to follow the Scottish passing pattern which required forwards to keep strictly to their own half of the field and effectively ruled out such feats of individual enterprise. By 1876 the passing game had replaced the dribbling game. Moreover, this tactical innovation coincided with the rise of working-class football. These new footballers predicted a new kind of game, for the dribbling skills which had so far characterized the game were perfected in the public schools. It was felt that working-class footballers required tactics more in keeping with their own experiences. 'This special art of steering a ball up and down through opponents (and very pretty play it made) was once learnt in early youth at school, and few of the modern players have either the opportunity or the need for acquiring it.'

It is not too fanciful to claim that these tactical changes announced even more fundamental changes within the game. Tactical changes within the game represented and, in some respects, paved the way for the transformation of football from a middle to a working-class game. 'The feature of modern Association play,' said our commentator of 1888, 'is essentially the combination shown by a team. While each player has his own place to keep, the field at each kick changes like a kaleidoscope, each player shifting his place to help a friend or check an adversary in the new position of the game.'

This 'combination' did more than symbolize the emergence of working-class football; its basic skills were easily and swiftly learnt and applied by men whose education had not provided them with the talents of public-school footballers. More fundamentally, the resulting teamwork, with its strict allocation of positions and division of labour among the players, suited the style, attitudes and practices of working-class life. Working men were accustomed to a crude division of labour, to fulfil specific roles and functions; they were not expected to take upon themselves the individualist responsibilities of their social superiors. The game which working men proceeded to colonize fitted this order of social relations; by the late 1870s the game had begun to reflect the qualities of their experience.

The progress of the FA Cup mirrored the changing social progress of football. The decade of dominance by the public-school teams was ended at the 1881 final between Old Carthusians and Old Etonians. In the following year the Old Etonians were back again, this time to face Blackburn Rovers. In 1883 another Blackburn team, Olympic, travelled to the London final, taking the trophy north for the first time. Blackburn Olympic, under the control of Jack Hunter, their player–manager, had trained for the final at the booming seaside town of Blackpool and when they stepped out to meet Lord Kinnaird's Old Etonians, the social contrast could not have been greater. Among the Blackburn players were three weavers, a spinner, a dental assistant, a plumber, a cotton operative and an iron-foundry worker. Having won 1–0 in extra time, the Blackburn team was welcomed home by huge crowds headed by yet another manifestation of the new working-class social life – a brass band. Blackburn Olympic had approached the game in a most professional manner. Financed by a local iron-foundry owner, they had trained carefully for a week and had stuck to a suitable diet:

6 a.m.	Glass of port wine and two raw eggs followed by a walk along the sands.
Breakfast	Porridge and haddock.
Dinner	Two legs of mutton (one for each end of the table).
Tea	More porridge and a pint of milk each.
Supper	Half a dozen oysters each.

There was something new and unusual about the tone of these proceedings. This was not the style traditionally adopted by the gentlemen players. It was, in effect, a professional approach by a team from different social circumstances.

Like the team, the Blackburn fans who descended on London were northern working men, dismissed by observers as a 'northern horde of uncouth garb and strong oaths'. Thereafter until 1915 provincial teams won the FA Cup in every year save one. The Cup went south only in 1901 when Tottenham Hotspur won the competition; for the rest it travelled no further south than Birmingham and Nottingham. Even before the 1880s had ended, commentators considered it natural that teams from the north and midlands would dominate the Cup. 'Indeed, today the balance of power is distinctly with the provincial teams, and clubs like these . . . can as a rule be depended upon to beat the teams of either University or the old school clubs.'

Between 1883 and 1915 northern clubs won the Cup on twenty-one occasions and midland clubs on eleven. But just as important as this shift in balance within football in the course of the 1880s was the dominance which the Cup came to exert over the game. 'So great is the interest shown in the progress of the Cup-tie competitions that it may almost be said that every other match is dwarfed in comparison . . . For better or worse Cups and Cup-ties are the life and soul of the Association game.'

The new football fanatics give the FA Cup the approval of their growing numbers, and by the end of the 1880s the crowds had begun to outstrip the capacity of existing facilities. The first Cup final of 1872 had attracted 2,000 people; at the 1888 West Bromwich Albion–Preston North End final, the Oval gates closed behind 17,000 spectators. Three years earlier some 27,000 had crowded in to watch a Cup-tie between Aston Villa and Preston. After the 1892 final Surrey Cricket Club, realizing that football would soon put an end to their hallowed turf, refused further permission for the Cup final to be played at the Oval. In 1893, therefore, the match was transferred north, to the Fallowfield athletic stadium in Manchester, where 45,000 people paid to see Wolves beat Everton. In the following year Everton were hosts to the final, at their splendid new stadium at Goodison Park, Liverpool. Finally, in 1895, the Cup final was moved south to the Crystal Palace ground in London where, until 1915, it became the highlight of the football calendar. The first Crystal Palace final attracted 45,000 spectators and the figure went progressively higher: 66,000 (1897), 69,000 (1900), 110,000 (1901), and finally 120,000 in 1913. Thus even by the turn of the century the attendance at the top game of the new national sport was limited solely by the capacity of the stadiums and the interests of safety. The FA Cup provides the most spectacular examples of football's popularity. It was similarly registered, on a more modest scale, in expanding crowds across the face of Britain. In 1875 only two games attracted crowds of more than 10,000. Ten years later 13 games drew such numbers. As more people turned up, the clubs took more money, in turn investing it in grandstands (which segregated social groups) and improvements to the playing facilities. In retrospect, those facilities look crude; mounds of ash and rubble for embankments, holes-in-the-wall for entrances, carts and waggons perched round the ground to provide vantage points, tickets sold from neighbouring shops, players changing across the road in the pub. But the development of football also depended on other specialised industries: engineering companies which made turnstiles, printers making entrance tickets, pubs with their own telegraphic terminal (for results), and builders who specialised in pavilions, sheds and banking for stadiums.

However crude the facilities, fans were rarely deterred. In the 1890s especially they poured into British football grounds. Each improvement in a local ground was followed by still bigger crowds. Commentators simply stopped recording their astonishment at the communal passion for football in the major urban areas in the years 1890–1915. In the first years of the English league, in 1888–9, some 602,000 spectators watched the games. Seven years later the figures had grown to almost two million. Ten years later, with the League expanded to twenty teams, five million spectators turned up. It was a sign of the game's remarkable popularity that thousands of men simply quit the work-place – and ran the risk of dismissal – to watch important local games.

It was cheap to get in. In places, notably in Scotland, the cult of football was so powerful that money for football was set aside even in the midst of unemployment. Though it is notoriously difficult to unearth entrance fees, the evidence suggests that most clubs charged mere pennies for the cheapest places. When clubs raised the price to 1s for important games, local newspapers complained; but the ground still filled up. And it seems equally clear that the great majority of spectators were working men. There were more prosperous sections of the crowd – notably in the expensive stands (where women also tended to gather). Of course in those towns, dominated by a particular industry, the crowds were filled with, for example, miners, shipbuilders, textile workers, steel workers or whatever. Apart from such obvious evidence, and despite the imperfections in the data, the typical football spectator is clear enough. In the words of Tony Mason, 'We know that most of them were working class because contempories said so.'

Despite the game's growing sophistication, despite the disciplined nature of the players – and the millions of fans – it remained a tough game, involving punishing play and often vulgar and coarse support. Writing in 1892, Arthur Budd noted: 'To this day, despite the fact that the evidence of science has removed the coarseness of the primeval game and reduced to a minimum the risks that attend it, the horrors of football still remain a favourite theme with journalists and correspondents.' The behaviour of the crowds was often less refined than the play itself. Writing of a game at Shrewsbury in 1899, an observer noted: 'There were many thousands at Shrewsbury on Easter Monday, and the concomitants of betting, drinking and bad language were fearful to contemplate, while the shouting and horseplay on the highways were a terror to peaceful residents passing homewards.'

But was it as bad as many critics claimed? There were, inevitably, problems with the crowds. There was the simple problem of large boisterous crowds of, mainly, young men keen to enjoy themselves; vociferous – sometimes crude – in their footballing passions. Crowds were partisan, noisy (of course) and often irreverent. To the outside, unsympathetic eye such noisy, crowded support could seem threatening and unbecoming. There were not surprisingly incidents of crowd misbehaviour; against unpopular decisions, because of overcrowding (not really their fault) and sometimes irritation against unpopular club decisions, or poor performance. Objects were thrown at players and officials, on the pitch and outside. As likely as not, problems were made worse by inadequate facilities; thousands simply could not see in those crowded, primitive stadiums. It was to take some prominent disasters (not unlike the story of the music halls) before the questions of safety and comfort were addressed.

The crowds and packed stadiums taxed the local police. In time, they managed to control most situations. Sometimes, however, circumstances overwhelmed them; accidents, injuries, fighting and crowd turbulence occasionally plunged the game into disrepute. Such incidents – unusual as they were – have often reminded students of the game of the traditional, older history of football's turbulent past. In truth, the troubles of the late nineteenth and early twentieth century bore little resemblance to pre-modern upheavals. The simple fact remained that a small number of well-trained policemen could marshall and contain a crowd of tens of thousands. In retrospect, perhaps the most remarkable feature of football crowds before 1914 was their overall tranquillity. Yet, this was all of a piece with society at large. At play, at work and in everyday social life, Britain had, in the phrase of Brian Harrison, become a peaceable kingdom.

The crowds had other, less dangerous consequences. Football's popularity among working men led directly to the introduction of professionalism in football. As the crowds expanded, the potential (and real) income from football could no longer be ignored. While the gentlemen of the controlling bodies felt embarrassed about the sums of money which came their way (in the early days they solved the problem by giving the proceeds to charity), the more hard-headed among them felt no such qualms about treating football as a lucrative business. They pumped the game's growing income back into football; into stadiums, equipment and, illegally at first, into players' wages and transfer fees. As the game expanded and commitments became more far-flung and more expensive, clubs came to depend on a reliable income. Players, too, required financial guarantees, particularly for their travelling and living expenses and the time spent away from home. Their expenses soon became an issue within the FA and as early as April 1883 an FA committee decided, 'That in the semi-final and final ties of the FA Challenge Cup railway fares should be allowed to the players.'

This concession was a testimony to the presence of non-leisured footballers who, unlike the founders, quite simply could not play the game unless paid expenses. Only four years earlier, in 1879, when Darwen had played the Old Etonians, the financial problem had been resolved by the raising of a local subscription for the Lancastrian side, but such ad hoc gestures were quite inadequate for the game's expanding requirements.

The clubs were in a powerful position to provide for their players' financial needs thanks to their growing income from gate money. Aston Villa, for instance, first took money in 1874, collecting 5s 2d. Thirty years later they took £14,329 at a single match. Such a dramatic change was due entirely to the emergence of football as a spectator sport in the cities; a game watched weekly by hundreds of thousands of working men who had become deeply committed to their local teams. 'No words of ours,' said Montague Shearman in 1888, 'can adequately describe the present popularity of football with the public – a popularity which, though great in the metropolis, is infinitely greater in the large provincial towns . . . it is no rare thing in the north and midlands for 10,000 people to pay money to watch an ordinary club match, or for half as many again to assemble for a "Cup Tie".'

The drift towards professional football, towards rewarding footballers for their unique and increasingly profitable skills, was first apparent in Lancashire, the area which was the effective centre of English working-class football. But initially professionalism was made possible by the availability of Scots anxious for work and able to offer an attractive combination of industrial labour and footballing skills. By the late 1870s the number of Scots playing in the new teams of the manufacturing areas had become obvious. Like the Irish, the Scots had traditionally been drawn to the greater economic opportunities of England, and in the late 1870s and early 1880s as Scotland rapidly established herself as a natural producer of footballers, she offered a new kind of recruiting ground for English economic needs. From that period to the present day, the flow of footballers southward has enhanced the English game and debilitated Scottish football. Scots had been prominent among the early pioneering, gentlemen footballers. But the game, north and south, was transformed by the working-class Scottish footballer. In many respects he became a caricature of himself; small, hardy, from deprived circumstances, tough on opponents and blessed with skill and courage. From one generation to another there was a succession of such footballers gracing the football fields of Scotland and England. Why Scotland should produce an endless flow of footballers is difficult to say. Almost as difficult to pin-point is the origin of the migration south. Certain trends are clear, however. Visits by Scottish clubs to

Lancashire and Yorkshire exposed visiting players to greater economic opportunities. Moreover, the quality of the football they played, particularly against the Lancastrian teams, persuaded English clubs to seek new talent over the border. The search for Scottish talent escalated in direct proportion to the growing popularity and sophistication of football in the industrial cities. And the Scots came south for their own improvement, expecting work in local industries and payment for their football. As early as 1881 the secretary of the FA was forced to remark: 'There is no use to disguise the speedy approach of a time when the subject of professional players will require the earnest attention of those on whom devolves the management of Association football . . . it will be well for those who have the interests of the game at heart to recognize the existence of a problem that will in all likelihood have to be mastered before long.'

The question of payment to players exposed a number of basic problems within the footballing fraternity, more especially the regional tensions among those (in Birmingham and Sheffield) who feared that professionalism would simply enhance the success of the Lancastrian clubs. More powerful still was the social antipathy of men who considered professional sport ethically unacceptable. Whatever the doubts, there could be no denying the existence of professionalism by the mid-1880s; indeed Scottish newspapers regularly carried advertisements from the Lancashire clubs for footballers.

Attempts were made by the FA and their regional branches to prevent encroaching professionalism, but illegality merely drove payments and inducements underground. Individuals and clubs were fined and suspended, by both the English and the Scottish FAs, the latter particularly alarmed about the drain on the game at home. The issue finally came to a head in January 1884 following a Cup-tie between Preston and Upton Park (watched by 12,000). Complaints that the Preston team employed professionals were answered by a perplexing nod of agreement from Major D. Sudell, the Preston manager. Faced with official disapproval and threats, Sudell took the offensive, convening a meeting of the Lancashire clubs in October 1884 with an eye to forming a breakaway organization – 'The British Football Association'. Any such move would have broken the back of the FA monopoly and, accordingly, in the following month the FA took the first tentative steps to incorporate professionalism. The final legalisation of professional football was delayed until July 1885 when the FA launched stringent regulations, along the lines of professional cricket, thereby bestowing legality on hundreds of players. Many of the players were quite happy to play, as they worked, for twelve months in the year. To prevent this 'abuse', the FA followed up the acceptance of professionalism by limiting the season to between 1 September and 30 April (a prospect that would doubtless please present-day footballers – and cricketers).

The number of professional footballers grew rapidly. In 1891 the Football League had 448 registered players, the majority almost certainly part-time or full-time professionals. By 1914 the Players Union had 4,470 professionals on their books. What evidence we have suggests that most of them were skilled and not unskilled working men. They had in effect a combination of skills, on and off the pitch, which were sought by the businessmen who, increasingly, were in charge of professional clubs. From 1901–2, players' wages were pegged at a maximum £4 a week. Not everyone earned that much; the stars earned more – by a series of illicit and open stratagems. Thereafter the clubs and the players were locked in an often unseemly dispute about wages, a persistent struggle not ended until the abolition of the maximum wage in 1963. Overall, the wages of working-class footballers compared favourably with their peers in other plebeian occupations.

By the summer of 1885 the contours of the modern game had been clearly established. Within a mere five years, teams of working men from industrial Britain had superseded the gentlemen players, in the process bringing in professionalism and forcing the introduction of a regular winter season. Professionalism was ultimately to ensure more than the emergence of a technically superior game; it was soon to alienate the founding groups. As early as November 1884 the *Manchester Guardian* predicted that football, which between 1880 and 1884 had promised to become a social leveller – a sport in which social distinctions had no place – would, because of professionalism, come to be monopolized by working men and ignored by their social superiors. Whether professional football was the cause or occasion for the former masters of the game to turn to other more socially acceptable sports is difficult to assess. But it is clear that many middle-class institutions turned away from football in direct proportion to the rise of working-class football, with its professional elite, boisterous crowds and its blatant commercialism. Even within the FA the social bias against professionalism was prominent; some members felt no hesitation in claiming that it was 'degrading for respectable men to play with professionals'. Other more realistic and less socially conscious members, led by the secretary C.A. Alcock, trenchantly put the other view. 'Professionals are a necessity to the growth of the game and I object to the idea that they are the utter outcasts some people represent them to be. Furthermore, I object to the argument that it is immoral to work for a living, and I cannot see why a man should not, with that object, labour at football as at cricket.'

Professionalism did, however, have unpleasant side-effects. Henceforth footballers became marketable commodities, to be bought, sold, haggled over and inspected like eighteenth-century slaves. They were even offered for sale. In 1891 an advert appeared, offering:

> No 163. Right or left fullback. This is one of the most likely youngsters I have ever booked. He gives reference to a well-known pressman, who has repeatedly seen him play and knows what he can do, and has a high opinion of his abilities and future prospects. Just note – height 5 feet 11 inches; weight 12 stone; age 20. There's a young giant for you. This is a colt worth training.

Whatever the results of professionalism, and they were clearly mixed, contemporaries were convinced that it had resulted from the emergence of football as a mass, and more especially as a working-class, sport. 'As soon as there was money to be made out of football playing, it became not only natural but inevitable that the mechanic and artisan class of players should desire to share in it.'

Professionalism had profound effects on the game; the new clubs, with their professional players and increasing expenses, with an apparently insatiable local and national demand for their services, needed more than Cup-ties and impromptu games. Finance alone dictated a more coherent and ordered framework for the football season, as most leaders of the game realized. To this end, in March 1888 William McGregor of

Aston Villa, a powerful figure in the Birmingham FA (predictably a Scot), circulated a letter to all the major clubs about the need to rationalize the game. 'Every year it is becoming more and more difficult for football clubs of any standing to meet their friendly engagements, and even arrange friendly matches . . . I beg to tender the following suggestion as a means of getting over the difficulty. That ten or twelve of the most prominent clubs in England combine to arrange home-and-away fixtures each season.' Following meetings in London and Manchester, and notwithstanding the opposition shown to the league principal and the points system involved, the Football League was launched in September 1888 with twelve founding clubs: Aston Villa, Accrington Stanley, Blackburn Rovers, Bolton Wanderers, Burnley, Derby County, Everton, Notts County, Preston North End, Stoke City, West Bromwich Albion and Wolverhampton Wanderers. The original intention had been to form a national league, but the outcome was quite different; six teams came from Lancashire, three from Staffordshire and one each from Derbyshire, Nottinghamshire and Warwickshire. A second division followed in 1892, and the notion of league football spread rapidly throughout the British Isles. The Irish League was formed in 1890, the Scottish in 1891 and the Southern League in 1894. In the same decade schoolboy football was put on a league basis.

The Football League remained the pacemaker, and a great number of clubs, anxious to share in the tangible rewards of league football, unsuccessfully applied to join. But the direction was clear and it was only a matter of time and practical experience, particularly of the disputed process of promotion and relegation, before the league organization embraced more and more clubs on a genuinely national basis. Progress in this direction was slow, and even on the eve of World War I, when forty clubs were divided equally between Divisions One and Two, only six clubs were drawn from outside the north and midlands. Arsenal, admitted in 1893, Luton (1897), Bristol City (1901), Chelsea and Leyton (1905) and Spurs (1908), were the sole competitors against their fellows further north. Moreover, the pattern within league football paralleled that within the FA Cup competitions, for the game itself, and consequently its top honours, became a virtual provincial monopoly. Between the formation of the League in 1888 and the interruption of war in

1915, the championship of Divisions One and Two only once went outside the north and midlands when Bristol City topped Division Two in 1905–6.

Throughout the 1890s, as the sheer volume of play increased, professional football became a major commercial enterprise both in itself and through its ancillary services. It generated money on all hands, from the businesses providing for the millions of footballers to the humble food caterer providing hot pies to the crowds on match days. Football spawned a massive industry on the back of the game itself. Underhand bribes which had formerly seduced players to join a particular club gave way to open and ever-soaring 'transfer fees' (reaching £1,000 in 1905). The wages paid to top players were generally better than those of skilled artisans, perhaps amounting to 30–40s a week in the 1890s. Then, as now, for every well-paid star there were ranks of poorly paid footballers whose few weekly shillings generally supplemented wages earned in local industries. Naturally enough, the more successful clubs, with large followings, could afford to pay higher wages and offer bonuses for success. Players were often equally attracted to offers of payment in kind or, better still, to offers of employment with future security. But whatever the wages, and no matter how much of an improvement they constituted for the working-man-cum-footballer, there was no disguising the fact that a footballer could not make a fortune from the game. Nor was football a means to social mobility as it so often is today. To the skilled player, the game offered a slight, though invariably temporary, improvement in earnings and living standards. But the impermanence and insecurity of earnings from football could be measured by the thousands of men who fell back from footballing fame to the anonymity of their origins.

Football thus became another dimension of late nineteenth-century urban life, generating great commercial activity, but one in which the creators of the wealth, in this case the footballers, gained relatively little from their skills. The experiences of working-class footballers were in keeping with their wider social and industrial lives; substantial profits were being made from their work, but little of it accrued to them. Ironically, little seems to have gone into the pockets of the men who controlled and owned the clubs; the businessmen who sat on the boards of what were limited companies. There were no directors' fees and dividends were limited to five per cent. Big clubs made profits regularly (though some made spectacular losses too). But that money was, in general, sunk back into the game. There were, of course, examples of managing directors and club owners who seemed to do very well from football. But in almost all cases they were already wealthy men.

Why did such men – businessmen, politicians, men from the liberal professions – involve themselves in a game which sometimes cost a great deal and invariably seemed to devour their time and occasionally bring unwelcome public abuse? These men were of course from local elites, often bound together by important social and economic links; proud of their home town and keen to advance its interests and name. Then, as now, there were plenty of men of substance keen to take their seats on the board of a football club in return for whatever prominence and indirect benefits might accrue from association with the football club. For others, even a less formal attachment might bring benefits.

For politicians the years after the 1884 Reform Act posed a challenge in the form of a new mass (male) electorate which had to be wooed rather than led. What better way was there of establishing a reputation, of ensuring that one's name was before the eyes of the male electorate and for posing as a man of the people, than by belonging to the people's game; to the local football club? Similar motivations drew local businessmen. Booming clubs attracted businessmen for cash (for shares) and as guarantors of bank loans and enhanced in numerous and indefinable ways their commercial and public status in the town. Manufacturers and entrepreneurs, newspaper proprietors and merchants, established themselves as patrons, benefactors (and, less obviously, as beneficiaries) of local teams, giving employment in their businesses and providing enjoyment for the crowds, many of whom were their workmen, voters and clients. John Houlding of Liverpool was one such man; a local businessman (brewer) and alderman who had an influential hand in creating the Everton club. His money and enterprise were largely responsible for the rise of Everton as one of the country's premier teams, from a city which by the 1890s had become the football centre of England. But Houlding's brash methods alienated his colleagues within the club, leading to a major split on the question of whether or not to become a limited company. Houlding was able to have Everton removed from their playing pitch at Anfield Road (they subsequently bought new land at Goodison). This left Houlding with a pitch and no team to play on it. So he turned to Scotland for a totally new team, forming, in 1892, Liverpool FC (known for obvious reasons as the 'team of the Macs'). Houlding was only an extreme form of a type common throughout the professional clubs in these formative years, like William McGregor, founder of the League. Manchester United, for instance, was re-formed, from the initial railway team, and made into a footballing power in the land, equipped with a splendid new stadium at Old Trafford, by the control and investments of another wealthy local businessman, J.H. Davis. H.A. Mears, a London builder, developed Chelsea's stadium at Stamford Bridge. These were exceptional – and exceptionally successful – examples of a phenomenon to be found around most British football clubs.

In the early years of the present century Manchester United was as famous for the activities of its players as the achievements of its directors. The first stirrings of unionism developed among United's footballers. Once again, the national context is vital, for the last quarter of the nineteenth century, particularly the 1890s, witnessed an upsurge in union membership, power and militancy. Footballers were one – and a generally neglected one at that – of a number of new trades and occupations in need of collective protection. While footballers' wages were attractive supplements to a more traditional wage – pin-money in effect – few players received an adequate return for their efforts. With the marked tendency of the clubs to become more 'capitalistic', by becoming limited companies, players increasingly felt the need to follow the example of their fellow workers and to establish a union. As a result, in 1898 a founding meeting of a players' union was held in Manchester, but it was to take a further ten years of effort, in the teeth of dogged resistance by the League and the FA before the industrial rights of footballers were recognized. In 1907–8 the union once more became a prominent force, led by the Manchester United players and their centre-half, Charlie Roberts. In March 1908 the FA gave its consent to the formation of such a union and to a match to be played between Manchester United and Newcastle United to raise union funds. In the following year the union threatened to join the Federation of Trades Unions, in response to which the

FA and the League ordered all players to resign from the union under penalty of suspension. The players responded with a strike threat and the authorities prepared makeshift teams to take over the threatened fixtures. Weakened by internal disagreements, the union was forced to break down, finally agreeing to recognize the ultimate authority of the FA in return for its own existence. Throughout, the players' union had been characterized by militant leadership, but that militancy was a direct function of footballers' terms of employment. It was imperative that footballers should take a firm stand for, as the secretary of the union noted, the footballing authorities were demanding 'that they relinquish the rights of every worker to associate himself with his fellows so as to be better able to succour an unfortunate colleague [but] they have refused to surrender their legal rights at the bidding of a body of men who do not contribute a penny piece to the upkeep of the game'.

Both the union's militancy and the authorities' resistance may well have been influenced by the wider militancy of the period. Certainly the decade of struggle by the players provided ample evidence of the social and industrial cleavages within football. To interpret the players' efforts solely in class terms would, however, be an exaggeration, but nonetheless the basic clash was between working-class footballers anxious to defend their economic interests and the management and ownership of the clubs, the FA and the League who were equally anxious to defend their arbitrary and paternal control. From the compromise of 1909–10, in which a non-TUC players' union was accepted, to the present day, it has proved immensely difficult to apply industrial solutions to the game's problems. Even today, footballers persist in calling their manager 'boss', employing terms which have long ceased to exist in other industries. Players continue to maintain a deference towards the directors of clubs and consequently towards the disciplinary and decision-making bodies of the League and the FA. The players' union has, despite everything, been a source of strength to them and the body above all others responsible for the introduction of greater justice into the professional game. But the uneasy relations finally established between players and management, between master and man, just before World War I, were essentially an acceptance of the social and economic divisions which had characterized football since the rise of professionalism in the 1880s.

While professional football had transformed the national game, at the turn of the century the game's administration was still marked by an amateur mentality which was a hangover from the early days of organized football. In addition, the administration rightly saw itself working for more than the professional game. There were after all many more amateurs than professionals; in 1910 some 300,000 players in 12,000 clubs registered with the FA alone, not counting the myriad teams from schools and factories who played on a more informal basis. After the first decade of professional dominance of the FA Cup, it had been appreciated that a new incentive was needed to maintain the commitment and zeal of the amateurs. Consequently, in 1892 the FA Amateur Cup was instituted and a clear line was drawn between the two footballing fraternities.

In practice the distinction between amateur and professional dissolved at certain points; all professionals, for instance, began life as amateurs – if only as schoolboys. Moreover, both groups were under the common jurisdiction of the FA. Within the upper reaches of football's administration, however, there were men who resented the rise of mercenaries. Given the differing centres of footballing gravity in England (amateur in the south, professional in the north), the amateur voice was most strident in the Southern organizations and clubs, leading in the early years of the century to protracted threats of withdrawal from the FA. Indeed between 1907 and 1914 a breakaway Amateur FA set up shop for the non-professionals. Ultimately, however, the episode simply reinforced the status of the FA. Yet the changing social context of football made itself felt even within the ranks of amateurs. In the early years of the Amateur Cup the 'Old Boys' teams won the trophy three times, but they too were pushed aside by working-class teams. Public-school and university teams, finding the social ambience of the amateur competition as plebeian as the professional game, retreated into their own socially exclusive sporting world. They formalized this with the establishment of the Arthur Dunn Cup. Dislike of professionalism among the men whose schools and universities had created modern football was clearly a widespread and genuine feeling, but it also marked a deeper unease about the changing social roots and composition of the game. Unable to exert their traditional control within a changing world, the younger gentlemen players withdrew into a contracting world of their own – or quit football entirely. This pattern of events – which had its counterpart in sports played in parts of the Empire – tells us more about the nature of social and class feeling in late Victorian and Edwardian Britain than it does about football. Once again we are faced with an important element in the history of the game which can only be fully understood in its wider social setting.

The only real amateur challenge to the overall footballing superiority of the professional teams came from the Corinthians, formed in 1883 by N.L. Jackson and composed of public-school and university players. Drawing largely upon the university teams, Corinthians regularly inherited skilful players, attuned to each other's game, who had the leisure and money to devote considerable time to their Wednesday games. A string of excellent teams emerged, able to offer an equal challenge to professionals, and yet remaining rooted in an utterly amateur approach. Their performances speak for themselves; in 1904 they defeated Bury (who that year won the Cup by a record 6–0) by 10–3. Led by athletes of considerable all-round ability, G.O. Smith for example, claimed by some to have been one of England's greatest-ever centre-forwards, the gentlemen of the Corinthians were the last representatives of the dying breed who had seen their superiority slip away as society changed around them. Indeed the Corinthians exuded a distinctly imperial air – but at a time when their empire was crumbling. They were finally disbanded in 1939. For all their undoubted skills, the Corinthians were social dinosaurs, doomed to extinction by changes they could not control. They (literally) arrived at a game sporting top hats and canes, while their opponents wore cloth caps. The story of the Corinthians can be taken as an emblem of the history of the game. In the 1880s, the Corinthians were typical of the game's founding fathers; by 1914 they were utterly exceptional – toffs in a world taken over by the plebs. No greater indication exists of the changes within English football than the fact that by the early twentieth century the Corinthians were utterly exceptional; in 1880, they would have been typical.

World War I marks an obvious break in the history of football, and most other forms of social recreation. The game continued to be played for the first eight months of the war and, despite the mounting criticism directed against football in the press, football put its organization behind the war effort. It gave away its money indiscriminately to various war charities, its offices provided storage room for army supplies and, most important of all, the bureaucracy was set the task of recruiting soldiers for the war. When, in the early months of the war, the government set out to build a volunteer army, it found that it lacked the effective machinery to reach into all walks of private life to tap the manpower of the nation. To overcome this problem, all private institutions and organizations were persuaded to encourage their younger men to rally to the war effort. *The Times* appealed to its own readership: 'All Varsity men, Old Public School Boys – men who are hardened to the soldiers' life by strenuous pursuit of sport should enlist at once.'

Men of humbler station were equally in demand, and by September 1914 football clubs throughout Britain had begun to appeal to their players and thousands of fans to take the King's shilling. The FA agreed with the War Office that clubs should 'be requested to place their grounds at the disposal of the War Office on days, other than match days, for use as Drill Grounds . . . Where football matches are played arrangements [are] to be made for well-known public men to address the players and spectators, urging men who are physically fit, and otherwise able, to enlist at once.' Footballers often set the example for their followers by joining the forces in front of the assembled crowd. One poster asked, with an unconscious touch of irony:

> Do you want to be a
> Chelsea Die-Hard:
> If so
> Join the 17th Battalion
> Middlesex Regiment
> 'The Old Die-Hards'
> And follow the lead given
> by your Favourite Football
> Players

The results of these suggestions and of the FA's efforts were staggering. By November *The Times* claimed that 100,000 men had volunteered via footballing organisations. Of 5,000 professional footballers, 2,000 had joined the forces. It has even been claimed that by the end of 1914 half of the nation's volunteers had stepped forward through their local footballing recruiting system. There was, nonetheless, a vituperative correspondence in the press directed against football because it tried to continue business as usual in the early months of the war (rugby had suspended activities at the start of hostilities). Yet such feelings, understandable in a way (it seemed unacceptable that fit young men should still play for pleasure – and profit – while their countrymen were at war), ignored the enormous contribution to the war effort, quite apart from the therapeutic value of recreation. So successful was the recruiting campaign among football's followers that attendances fell by half; most of the best players were in uniform – and more and more of the fans themselves were drifting into the services. It was only a matter of time before the game was frozen for the duration, particularly since it became clearer by the month that, far from being over by Christmas, the war would be protracted and bloody. The final official game, played at Old Trafford on 24 April 1915 was the replayed Cup final between Sheffield United and Chelsea – the Khaki Final. Lord Derby presented the trophy with the words, 'You have played with one another and against one another for the Cup; play with one another for England now.' The Football League expressed much the same hope to its players: 'that every eligible young man will find in the service of the nation a higher call than in playing football'.

Despite the critics, football's response to the call-to-arms in 1914–15 was remarkable. It was an imaginative stroke to appeal to working men through the nation's footballing networks. Football was, after all, the most popular, nationwide and comprehensive forum for male recreation. In a society which lacked the highly intrusive state bureaucracy familiar today, football's administration offered the state a swift and acceptable entry to working-class communities which might otherwise have proved difficult to penetrate. Here was yet another testimony to the importance of football in British working-class life by 1914.

The war effort served to highlight the pre-eminence of football within British working-class communities (with some notable regional exceptions). In the generation before the war, employers had frequently complained that working men's attachment to football often interfered with work. Curiously, these appear almost like a reprise of the complaints which had surfaced a century earlier. 'Working men are too anxious to leave their work for the sake of seeing their favourite teams play football. Sport is very good in its way, but it must always hold a subordinate position.' Unhappily for such captains of industry, football was, for armies of men, more important than work itself. Here was the beginning of a modern phenomenon in certain cities; a sign of the emergence of new attitudes to life, work and leisure among working men.

In 1914 those men within the game able to look back at its development over the previous thirty years must have been amazed at what they saw. In the years up to 1914 an enormous pyramid of footballing activity had evolved, with an informal base of millions of boys and men, tapering away to the tip of the professional game with its annual carnivals at the Cup finals. The two FAs ruled supreme over all these players and had, between them, effectively imposed uniformity on the game throughout Britain. Yet only a generation before, football had been a mosaic of a game; fissured by conflicting rules, conventions and styles. Now, in the early years of the twentieth century, football had a uniformity and coherence; an agreed code of conduct which linked players of all sorts and conditions, from young boys playing in the streets and school playgrounds, through to the elite professionals playing in major internationals and Cup finals. Most footballers played – and even more watched – from a sheer love and passion for the game itself. Yet all this had been made possible by a fundamental revolution in the social and economic lives of the British people. Of course there was an array of other recreations which, equally, reflect those same changes. A similar story could be told of seaside holidays, popular music, the music hall and others. But football was, without question, the most spectacular. And football's rise to pre-eminence seemed to bring the process full-circle. It was almost like a return to the folk-culture of pre-industrial life.

5 Britain's Most Durable Export

In the space of a generation, the modern game of Association football spread around the world. In the quarter of a century before World War I, a host of football games sprang up, taking on local form (Aussie Rules, American football) from a basic common root. But even more spectacular was the rapid, global diffusion of soccer. Of course football was not the only sport to develop a world-wide following among players and spectators. These were the years when most of the world's modern games, from cricket to athletics, spread rapidly into all corners of the habited world. But few could match soccer for the speed and ubiquity of its spread, or for the following it quickly mustered.

There were, as we have seen, a number of pre-industrial games which locals called football. It was a ball game common to a number of societies long before the emergence of the modern game. But despite the widespread existence of footballing folk customs around the world, the Association game erupted as a global phenomenon not from existing local traditions, but as a direct export by Britons.

The speed with which football established itself as the British national game was remarkable, involving, as we have seen, crucial changes in the nature of social life. But even more remarkable was the establishment of football around the world in much the same period. The contributor to the *Encyclopaedia Britannica* of 1911 noted: 'Association football has become one of the most popular of all national sports in the United Kingdom. It is slowly but surely taking a similar position on the continent of Europe.' In fact the phenomenon was more significant than the *Encyclopaedia* claimed, for football had by that time sunk its roots deep into urban society, not only in Britain and Europe, but also throughout South America and in a host of other (sometimes unlikely) spots where the British lived, settled, governed or traded. At first sight, however, the British export of football appears to have been unusually distributed, for the game did not always thrive where the British had direct political and social control, that is in the vast areas of the Empire, but in parts of the world where they simply worked or traded. These were the years of British global industrial and imperial pre-eminence. In the period 1880–1914 large tracts of the world's map turned an imperial red while, on a more informal basis, British capital and goods and manpower poured into practically every corner of the world. Britons travelled, traded and lived right around the world. They penetrated most parts of the world, from the polar ice-caps, to the most inaccessible regions of Africa and Asia. So often, the strange, adventurous men in the van of the most daring of ventures regarded their exploratory and usually dangerous work as part of 'the great game'. More often than not, those who put down local roots, for business, governance or settlement, transplanted into their new homes many of the social institutions familiar to their own class at home. Sports and recreations inevitably followed in the train of British settlers and workers, although the spread of sports was uneven and unpredictable. It is, for instance, difficult to explain why certain sports were readily adopted in certain parts of the world and not in others where conditions looked similar. But in the case of football, it seems clear that the game percolated into differing societies throughout Europe and South America because of the missionary zeal of travelling Britons anxious to play their national game and equally anxious to encourage locals to play with them. The modern international game of football developed from these small, accidental and often peculiarly personal beginnings.

Football first took root in Europe, spreading rapidly through Holland, Germany, Scandinavia, Italy, France and central Europe. There was a familiar pattern in Europe, for the game seemed to emerge from educated, propertied players, similar to the gentlemen pioneers in Britain, before spilling out and generating a more broadly based social following. The first Danish club, for example, was formed in 1876 by British residents and encouraged by a visiting footballer. In the later

1870s the game spread to Holland, thanks to the efforts of pupils who had studied at British public schools. At the same time, the first German football association was established in Hanover, spreading rapidly through different *Länder*. Hamburg, Germany's oldest club, was formed in 1887, though it grew out of the Anglo–American club established in 1881. Football in German high schools, however, could trace its history to 1874. Again the British were influential. Germans returning from British schools, visiting British teams and British residents – especially in Hamburg and Berlin – all served to encourage footballing enthusiasm, especially in local schools. The first interest in Sweden stemmed from games played in Stockholm's public parks by members of the British Embassy staff, but more important still was the subsequent influx of British workers keen to play the games they played at home. There, and in other parts of the world, the initial pioneering play of gentlemen was secured and popularised by the arrival of British plebeian footballers. The game subsequently spread into the neighbouring dependency of Norway via interested students. Even Finland turned to the game, thanks, again, to men who had studied in Britain. In Switzerland, where the game began as early as the 1860s, football was imported by British boys studying in local schools. Later it was promoted by sporting British teachers. Significantly, when the main club was founded in Lausanne it was named the Lausanne Football and Cricket Club. In a number of European cities, the two games went together in their early days; a sure enough sign of the British influence. By the 1890s teams had begun to proliferate throughout Switzerland. In France, where pre-industrial football had been as widespread as in Britain, the first modern club was formed in 1872, in Le Havre, after a game with visiting British sailors. There and in other Channel ports, the British commercial and shipping presence was crucial in the creation of local football teams. When the game spread to Paris in the 1880s, it travelled on the enthusiasm of students and, once more, of Britons working in the capital. The first Parisian club, established in 1887, was formed by Englishmen.

In Italy, *calcio* had been a celebrated annual game, notably in Florence, since the sixteenth century at least. But Association football owed its origins, yet again, to British rather than traditional local roots. Italians working and studying in Britain and Britons working in Italy, came together in the 1880s and 1890s to play the Association game. Older games continued to be played, but the enthusiasm for the British variety rapidly put all other forms of football into eclipse and local teams were formed in direct imitation of the new British clubs. Businessmen returning to the northern industrial towns of Italy were keen to replicate the industrial-based sports teams they had seen in Britain. From Turin the game spread to Milan, thence to other major cities. Though the passions were local and deeply divided, the initial inspiration was, once more, British. In Italy, as in other European countries, football took off in the 1890s. The first Czech, Belgian, Austrian and even Icelandic teams were founded in the decade. One of the first Italians to take football home had been a commercial representative in England, returning to Turin equipped with a football and glowing accounts of the British game. In 1887 clerks in his firm were sufficiently enthusiastic to organize their own team. Five years later, in Vercelli in Piedmont, another team developed as an off-shoot from the local fencing and gymnastic club. At much the same time, football began to take root in Turin and Milan – those twin centres of Italian industrial progress. In 1897 Juventus was formed from a group of Turin students and local British residents. A year later in the rival city of Milan, the Milan Cricket and Football Club was formed by interested locals and resident Britons; shortly afterwards the football branch changed its name to AC Milan. In Turin the traditional footballing rival to Juventus is Torino, founded in 1906, but actually able to trace its roots to 1894. Torino was galvanized by Vittorio Pozzo, who emerged as the dominant influence on the formation of Italian football. Pozzo had studied English in Manchester and Bradford, becoming a keen football follower and striking up a formative and life-long friendship with Charlie Roberts, Manchester United's centre-half and leader of the players' union in the pre-war struggles. Through Roberts, Pozzo developed a passion for the game and an unrivalled knowledge of tactical concepts which bore fruit after the war, when he led Italian national teams to Olympic and later World Cup victories.

By the inter-war years Italian football had become enormously popular and Pozzo had ample local talent to draw on. Before 1914, however, the Italian game was embryonic, drawing its inspiration directly from local British encouragement or indirectly from the influence of the British game on Italians living in Britain. In Genoa, for example, in September 1892, a group of Britons formed the Genoa Cricket and Football Club. At first, Italians were not eligible to join the club, but in 1897, under the influence of Dr Spensley, the new football captain, Italians were invited to join. Thereafter football became the club's main concern and Genoa soon established itself as the premier Italian team before 1914. Games were arranged with Torino FC and Alessandria, and the first meetings were later convened, from which developed the Italian football federation and the Italian championship.

A similar pattern unfolded to the south, in Palermo, where in 1897–8 Britons, keen to play their own games, organized themselves into the Palermo Football and Cricket Club. In these early days, football and cricket went hand-in-hand among local expatriate Britons, but within a few years, in practically every case, once the Italian element in the club became more dominant, cricket gave way to a new local emphasis on football. In this way a number of Italian football clubs emerged from Anglo–Italian roots. In Bologna, for instance, the local football team was established in 1909 by the mutual interests of the British and local students. In other cases the foundation of an Italian football club was uniquely and distinctively English. Fiorentina, though founded in 1926, traces its origins to a chance meeting in 1907 of three Englishmen, Wood Jarvis, Holdgate and Rochford, in a local tea shop; they decided to form a local football team, ordering their football from Gamages.

Throughout the rest of Europe football similarly spread through direct British influence or through local contact with the British game. In Spain football was first introduced in 1893 by British engineers working in Bilbao. Local miners immediately adopted the game, evolving a highly successful team. But the oldest of Spain's teams, Atletico Bilbao, was founded in 1898 by students from northern Spain who, again, had learned their football in Britain. In that same year students in Madrid organized the team which was later to become Real Madrid. In 1899 a team was founded in Barcelona by a naturalized Swiss, Don Juan Gamper, playing its first game against a team of visiting British sailors. By 1902 the Spanish championship had been established and was won in different years by Atletico Bilbao, Madrid, San Sebastian, Barcelona, and Racing Club de

Irun. This importation of football from Britain to Spain was part of a wider British influence on Spain in the last quarter of the century, notably among sections of liberal and left-wing opinion. In such circles, British institutions, from *The Times* to the new game of football, were seen as civilizing forces within a reactionary Spain.

Barcelona's first game against naval visitors was typical of many such football matches. In these years the Royal Navy was regularly called on to form scratch sides to play against newly formed local teams around the world. The British had already become famous as natural footballers and it was assumed that British sailors, along with any other Briton on the spot, would automatically play the game. In 1906 in Rio, for instance, a team from HMS *Amethyst* played a friendly game against the local team Fluminense, which prompted the formation of the first football league in Rio. Six years later, the Santos club (later to be world famous as the home club of Pele), was established after another demonstration of football by visiting British sailors.

In widely scattered parts of the world where the British were given the task of initiating local industries, it was axiomatic that football would spring up in the neighbourhood. Perhaps the most unusual and yet most revealing example of this occurred in Tsarist Russia, the most 'backward' of European countries but anxious to modernize and industrialize with the help of European money and expertise. One such enterprise, the Vicoul Morozov textile factory at Orekhovo-Zuevo near Moscow, was under the management and direction of two Lancashire textile men, Clement and Harry Charnock. In 1887 Clement founded a football team among his workers, but the management of the team fell to his brother Harry, who advertised in the London *Times* for 'engineers, mechanics, and clerks capable of playing football well'. After the arrival of a player from Bolton, the team was renamed OKS, and again, Morozovsty, winning the new Moscow championship five times in succession. During the Revolution the team – along with the factory – was absorbed by the Soviet Electrical Trade Union, and renamed Moscow Dynamo. This Lancashire export was the genesis of the modern Russian game of football which, with the establishment of large-scale industry after the Revolution, swiftly became more popular than ancient peasant sports. But as early as the 1890s football had become hugely popular and was able to attract crowds of over 30,000. In the process of rewriting Russian history, however, the Russian Communist Party took great pains to eliminate the British influence, preferring instead to view the growth of national football as yet another aspect of the class struggle which culminated in the workers' triumph of 1917.

In the early days of the Moscow textile team Britons played alongside Russians. Two of the players were later to distinguish themselves in quite different fields; Bruce Lockhart, the secret agent, and Captain (late Field Marshall) Wavell. Lockhart's account of his Russian footballing experiences provides a colourful glimpse into the confused and fortuitous expatriate circumstances which spawned football around the world.

> Almost the first Englishmen I met were two brothers called Charnock. Both were Lancashiremen and both were connected with the cotton industry. At the time, Harry, the younger brother, was managing director of a large cotton mill at Orekhovo-Zuevo in the Province of Vladimir.
>
> Now Orekhovo-Zuevo was one of the storm centres of industrial unrest, and as an antidote to vodka drinking and political agitation among his factory hands Charnock had instituted 'soccer' football. His factory team was then champion of the Moscow League.
>
> Through some confusion with my Cambridge brother the rumour had already gone around the British colony that I was a brilliant footballer. Without waiting to inquire whether 'rugger' or 'soccer' was my game, the Charnocks invited me to join the 'Morozovsti', which was the name of their factory team in Moscow for which I was expected to play . . . Later, when I came to know these North-countrymen better, I realised what splendid fellows they were . . . I have always counted my football experiences with the Russian proletariat as a most valuable part of my Russian education . . . these league matches were great fun and excited immense enthusiasm. At Orekhovo we played before crowds of ten to fifteen thousand. Except by foreign teams we were rarely defeated. If it had been adopted in other mills, the effect on the character of the Russian working-men might have been far-reaching.

The enthusiasm for football and the potential for future development around the world was clearly enormous. But in many countries there were good political reasons for curbing this enthusiasm and limiting football's potential. Indeed in many of the more autocratic European countries before 1914, the government's response to the emergence of football among ordinary men, but more especially among subject peoples, was similar to the attitude which had characterized authority's attitudes towards the pre-industrial game. Football drew huge crowds and, in politically insecure regions where imperial authorities were unsure about their hold over local people, could easily provide the occasion and even the cause of social or political unrest. Time and again, imperial powers sought to limit or ban the convening of large (and possibly uncontrollable) sports crowds. And none were bigger or more boisterous than those for football. In the Russian, Austro–Hungarian and Turkish empires, a similar story was repeated, from one distant corner of the empire to another. Imperial power disliked large crowds. Russia, for example, tried to curb football in those areas of Poland under Tsarist rule. The same fear inspired Prussia's policy towards the rise of football in its own corner of Poland. Consequently, when football did emerge there (organized yet again by the British, working in local factories at Lodz), it did so in the teeth of official opposition, though the arrival of a new football-loving governor from St Petersburg loosened restrictions on the game. After World War I the Poles were free, for a short time, to organize their own political and social lives. One minor result of this greater freedom was the flowering of football teams throughout the country.

The Russians were equally reluctant to sanction mass spectator sports, particularly football, in their Baltic provinces, despite the enthusiasm there, rapidly fostered by British workmen. Once again, the liberation inaugurated by the 1919 Versailles Peace Treaty had the minor and unexpected consequence of encouraging the blossoming of football in the Baltic states. When the first Latvian football league was established, its first president was British. Similarly, in Romania the first effective teams were organized in the early years of the century by British workers in the Colentina textile factories and in the Ploesti works of Standard Oil. Long before 1914 a number of Romanian teams were regularly playing each other (though the Romanians had the added advantage that Prince Carol, Queen Victoria's great-grandson, had become a keen football fan).

It was no accident that in Russia, Poland and Romania, many of the British workers behind the establishment of local teams were engaged in the textile industry. These were, after all, the peak years of an expansive Lancashire textile trade, buoyant and confident enough to sponsor the development of what appear to have been rival industries throughout the world. Moreover, Lancashire was the centre of English football. But, as we have seen, the Lancashire game itself had turned to Scotland to a remarkable degree, for its players, its coaches and its administrators. So many footballing roads led back, from the far corners of the world, directly or indirectly, to Scotland. More obvious, however, were the links between world soccer and Lancashire. Football had come to dominate the social lives of Lancastrian working men and it was natural that they should export 'their' game to the rest of the world, enthusing their foreign workmates with the sporting as well as the industrial skills of their home towns.

The autocratic mentality towards popular gatherings in general and football crowds in particular was equally pronounced in the Austro-Hungarian Empire. In the far-flung marches of the Empire, particularly in Serbia, long prone to spasms of independence, the Hapsburg authorities feared mass spectator sports, for fear that they might lose social control. In the Serbian fringes, effective measures prevented the emergence of widespread football support until the end of World War I. But in Bohemia and Moravia (later to become Czechoslovakia) football flourished, led by SK Slavia and AC Sparta in the 1880s and 1890s. In Austria itself football had taken root in 1889; in 1894 FK Austria was formed, though originally known as the Vienna Cricket and Football Club. Willy Meisl, later to be the guiding spirit of Austrian football, wrote of these formative years:

In the old Austrian Monarchy, soccer started almost simultaneously in Prague, Vienna and Graz, the capital of Styria. Vienna possesses a sizable British colony. A number of British firms had branches or representatives in Austria's Metropolis. An English firm had the license to light the capital; English artists appeared on the stage; English typewriters, caps, clothes, shoes, anything and everything English was in demand. Gandon of the said Gasworks; Lowe, manager of the hat manufacturer's; Blyth of the haberdasher's and gentlemen's fashion house, Stone and Blyth; John Gramlock owner of a firm for electrical complements; Shires, who represented Underwood; Blackley, manager of the engineering firm, Clayton and Shuttleworth; the Rev. Hechter of Vienna's Anglican Church; these were some of the men who founded the first two football teams in Vienna.

Shifting our attention eastwards, to the Ottoman Empire, the pattern of football's growth and of resistance to it by arbitrary imperial authority can be seen repeating itself. The people turned enthusiastically to the game, and the authorities were equally enthusiastic to prevent it. Originally played by British residents in Turkey, football was soon adopted, particularly by Greeks and Armenians, and was consequently subjected to suspicious official scrutiny. In the politically neurotic climate which typified the pre-revolutionary Caliphate, minor incidents took on major significance. Bizarre occurrences unfolded from innocent matches and attempts to organize football, as the nervous authorities prepared to curb any gathering. Games were patrolled by troops and police and police raids were launched against meetings of footballers. One such gathering of Young Turks, assembled to translate the FA rules into Turkish, was broken up. The resulting report described the gear found in the room as 'military equipment', and the football rules as political manifestos. The 1908 Young Turk revolution had a liberating effect on social and recreational life in the Empire, and football teams sprang up throughout Turkey and her neighbouring possessions. But the Balkan Wars, followed by World War I, put an end to the evolution of mass spectator sports, and football was not revived until peacetime – and only then after encouragement by British military teams. In Portugal, the British had played football on a ground near Lisbon since the 1870s. Equally important (and repeating the pattern in Italy and Spain) were the Portuguese schoolboys returning from a British education and enthused by the game they had learnt. One man in particular, Guilherme Terreira Pinto Basto, was the architect of Portuguese football, helping to establish it as the national game by the mid-1890s. Portugal's premier team, Benfica, was founded in 1904 by Cosmé Damiao who had – inevitably – learned his football from the British. The continuing success which he helped to secure for Benfica owed a great deal to his unusual policy of recruiting his players from the Portuguese colonies. The result was the tapping, for the first time, of the enormous athletic potential of black Africa, talent which largely went unnoticed in the rest of Africa until the years of political independence after 1945. Moreover, this Portuguese policy, sponsored by Benfica, involved the transplanting of the British-inspired game into black Africa. The Portuguese were exceptional in this and in their encouragement of spectator sports among colonial peoples. Russians, Austrians, Germans and Turks feared the political consequences of popular mass sports. Much the same was true of the British, who discouraged certain mass sporting gatherings among the native peoples of the Empire.

Football had made inroads into most European countries long before 1914, from the Arctic to Malta, and the foundations had been laid upon which the inter-war game was to be built. Once the game developed local roots, it invariably followed the lines of the British game, with a rapid nationwide proliferation of clubs, the evolution of Cup competitions modelled on the FA Cup, local leagues and the emergence of professionalism, thanks to the game's increasingly profitable spectator appeal. Thus, within a few years of football becoming the British national game, and following British missionary work abroad, football's simplicity and basic attractions enabled the game to become widely popular in a number of European societies. By the turn of the century, British clubs, both amateur and professional, had begun to visit their counterparts in Europe, visits which, in their turn, helped to stimulate further the European interest in the game and formed the first tentative steps towards the modern international game. But in these early formative years British teams, led by the gentlemen of the Corinthians, travelled as unrivalled pioneers and masters of the game. It was, after all, their game and the rest of Europe were mere students. Unhappily for the later well-being of the British game, the belief that British primacy in football would automatically maintain superiority was soon to be proved false, as the pupils throughout Europe began to surpass their teachers.

In recent years, some of the finest teams and the most fanatical support for football are to be found in South America, as an American journalist found to his alarm on a whistle-stop visit to Uruguay. 'In a restaurant one evening I saw middle-aged citizens rise suddenly and smash glasses and plates and hurl beefsteaks at each other in sheer frenzied delight when they heard over the radio that Uruguay had scored a point . . .' South American football, and the local support for it, was quite different from that in Europe and yet, just as we need to know more about the history of football in specific European countries, we must resist the temptation to think of South America as a unified, undifferentiated continent. Each country has its own distinctive history, economic experience and social structure and, as in any sphere of social activity, football occupies a significantly different role from one country to another.

Until the ascendancy of Brazilian football (from the 1950s to the early 1970s) Uruguay was the undisputed pacemaker. John Gunther patronizingly noted that 'The Montevidians love two things above all – fútbol (soccer) and meat. Almost all South Americans are football-mad, but none are madder than the stout citizens of Uruguay.' The first Uruguayan team was founded by an English professor at Montevideo University but the real growth in local football came from the efforts of a group of British workmen in the 1890s. In 1891 four British workmen, Arthur Davenport, Frank Henderson, Frank Hudson and Roland Moor, all employed by the Uruguayan Central Railways, formed a sporting club in the capital. Known originally as the Central Uruguayan Railway Cricket Club (along the lines of so many European clubs), the footballing element within the club became ever more pronounced as local membership came to the fore. In 1913 the club took its present name, Penarol, from the district where the railway yards were located, and has subsequently remained one of Uruguay's top clubs. One of the original British members, a Mr Carter, also helped to form the Uruguayan FA in 1900, while John Hurley, a Scot who went to Montevideo in 1909, became the most influential figure in both Penarol and Uruguayan football at large, introducing the fast, short-passing game which had come to characterize the British game. Hurley laid the tactical foundations for the development of local football and the star players he coached became the backbone of Uruguay's rising international success. When, in 1902, a trophy was introduced for an international competition between Uruguay and neighbouring Argentina, the trophy was, fittingly, donated by the tea millionaire Sir Thomas Lipton.

British influence in South America was most notable in

Argentina. Over the years the country had attracted an abundance of British investment and industry, and became home to a large and active British colony, particularly in Buenos Aires. Predictably, football took root early in Argentina, growing out of a British sporting club organized in Buenos Aires as early as 1865 (which makes it one of the oldest clubs in the world). British clubs, British players and administrators, teams with British names and players, British schools with footballing traditions – all and more were characteristic of Argentinian football in its first twenty years. Gradually, however, this powerful British influence was eroded both by waves of immigration from other parts of Europe and by the development of indigenous Argentinian loyalties to the game. Yet both served to strengthen the local game. The new immigrants, especially the Italians, arrived familiar with, and keen on, the new game. The Racing Club of Buenos Aires, founded in 1905, for instance, was organized by Frenchmen who had played in Paris. The famous River Plate Club, however, was founded in 1901 by English residents and for a time played in the Uruguayan league under the direction of Penarol's Scottish coach, John Hurley. As late as 1911, one Argentinian team consisted entirely of Englishmen.

Brazil apparently first tasted modern football in 1884 during a Royal Navy visit, but the oldest Brazilian club, Flamengo, was not established until 1895 – another suggestion that in South America, as in Europe, the 1890s formed the take-off period for the game. One of the most influential men in its establishment in Brazil was Charles Miller, son of an English father, who played for Hampshire and the Corinthians while studying in England. On his return to Brazil, Miller was energetic in spreading the game in São Paulo. In Rio a local team, Fluminense, was formed in 1902, but it was only in 1906, following yet another friendly match against British sailors 'showing the flag', that a local football league was formed around Fluminense. Six years later, British sailors playing in Santos stimulated the formation of a local team but for the first few years the local game was kept alive by the enthusiasm of British businessmen living in São Paulo.

Across South America, the broad outlines of the history of the development of football were the same. British influence was paramount, directly or indirectly. Gentlemen pioneers, in business and schooling, British working men and military personnel, all helped to lay football's foundations, in the form of clubs, teams, leagues and competitions. Local, indigenous support came later. New European immigrations, urban change, the growth of local industry, the diffusion of schools and schooling, all provided the social base for the broadening appeal of the game among local people. As in Britain, employers realised the benefits to be gained from supporting a local team. Gradually the game was wrested from the hands of local elites and taken over by working men. New competitions, rooted in local rivalries – between districts, works, regions, and, later, countries, confirmed the pattern first shaped in Britain.

This early development of football in Europe and South America, the two areas which have remained the key centres of footballing interest, soon needed a formal institutional framework. In one country after another, following the initiative of the pioneering clubs, local football associations were formed on the British model. But the development of football around the world demanded something more than the proliferation of national organizations; the movement of men and teams from one country (and continent) to another to play and teach the game of football required some kind of international controlling body. In what was to prove symbolic of the British game, the founding English FA was, initially, reluctant to involve themselves in the efforts to create an international footballing organisation. Indeed they played no part at all, the initiative being taken by the French and the Dutch. Thus, FIFA was founded in Paris in 1904 without British involvement. The English Association joined a year later, but at first FIFA could not accept the need for separate representation from Scotland, Ireland and Wales. By 1911, however, all three had been accepted as members. It was a minor but revealing episode; vision, imagination and an ambitious view of the game's future were to be found not in the offices of the founding fathers, but among the men they had enthused with the game in Europe. The outcome, FIFA, for all its subsequent difficulties, was to be the body which managed the international development of the game from that day to this.

Before 1914 two direct British exports helped to sustain football abroad: tours by teams, and the work of former professional footballers, as coaches, trainers and managers. Teams from Oxford and amateur teams from the south of

England made periodic – and usually victorious – visits to cities in Europe. Gradually, British teams went further afield; in 1897, for example, Corinthians played twenty-three matches in South Africa. In 1899–1900 the FA sent a touring team to Germany. In 1898 Scotland's Queen's Park played in Scandinavia. Surrey Wanderers went to Germany and Austria in 1901, a tour repeated in that same year by Southampton. Three years later Southampton travelled even further afield, to South America, becoming the first English team to play there. (The first European team to play in England came from Brussels in 1900.) Understandably, many of these early tours were made not by the new working-class teams but by the older breed of leisured amateurs. Many of the professionals were part-timers, unable to afford weeks off work for foreign tours unless subsidized by their clubs. Consequently, travelling footballers were more likely to be university graduates than mill hands. In 1904, for example, the Oxbridge Corinthians played the first games by a visiting English team in Hungary (winning all their games handsomely). Ten years later a team from London University played a series of matches in Russia. The ethos which pervaded the Corinthians' approach to football and towards their opponents was rooted in the style and philosophy of the early days of football. At a farewell banquet in Budapest, the Corinthians' captain praised their opponents who, he claimed, 'were prepared to take a beating in a thoroughly sportsmanlike manner; they were also ready to take a few hints from a team with a far greater experience of the game'. Exactly fifty years later a different Hungarian team returned the compliment by thrashing the England team at Wembley.

European and South American football was anxious to learn from the unique experience of British players and, as a result, footballers from Britain began to coach around the world. The career of Jimmy Hogan offers an excellent illustration. Hogan, a native of Nelson, first played for Nelson as a professional earning 5s a week, later turning out for Rochdale, Burnley, Fulham, Swindon and Bolton. On retirement he went to Holland as a coach and later to Vienna where he helped to transform the local game. During World War I he was interned, but was later sent to Budapest to coach another team. He returned to Vienna in 1932, but in the meantime he had worked as a coach in Germany, France, Switzerland and even North Africa. After

1932 Hogan played a key role in creating the Austrian national and Olympic teams, and while his travels were unusually extensive, he was only an extreme example of many such peripatetic footballers who spread their skills.

William Garbutt of Blackburn Rovers and Arsenal was equally nomadic. Before 1914 he went to Genoa as a coach, returning again in 1919. In 1927 he moved to Rome; between 1929 and 1935 he taught football in Naples before moving to Bilbao in 1935–6. In the following year he returned to Milan, moving back to Genoa in 1938. During the war he was forced to live underground but on the resumption of peace he returned to his first post in Genoa.

Similarly long service was given in Europe by John Madden, a Glaswegian who managed the Czech side Slavia from 1905 to 1938 and who was recognized as the finest coach in the country. Another Scott, John Hurley, as we have seen, had much the same effect on football in Uruguay, through a career at Penarol which lasted more than fifty years.

This process, of British footballers encouraging interest and helping to perfect the skills of players abroad, continued during World War I, as British sailors and soldiers took the game to every theatre of the war. In the Mediterranean and the Near East, the British military presence encouraged the development of the local game; a pattern of events which was to be even more pronounced in World War II.

In the years before 1914 it appeared at times that football might take root in practically every continent for, while Europe and South America witnessed the greatest upsurge in the game, football was tentatively introduced wherever Europeans, and particularly the British, settled. Football matches were even played in Japan; in 1913 the first Asian international match was played, between China and the Philippines. The game in Australia took an unusual turn. Forms of football were popular among immigrants as early as the 1850s; by 1865 distinctive local rules were in place. Before the newly organised game of soccer could make inroads, this local game – the forebear of Aussie Rules – took root, especially in Victoria. From there it spread to other parts of Australia. Despite the subsequent emergence of the two rugby codes, and the importance of soccer, Australian football established a popular, sporting beachhead which, for all its regional variations, helped to establish it as *the*

Australian game. In a society with a fierce sense of its emergent national identity, soccer was too closely linked to Britain (later still, to other ethnic minorities) to be really Australian.

In the 1880s, as pioneering soccer players tried to secure a grip in Australia, Scottish enthusiasts embarked on a similar venture in Canada. Football put down tentative roots across Canada, thanks in the main to the Scots, aided by the development of the railway and the growth of key cities between Toronto and Vancouver. Wherever Scots settled, they transplanted a passion for the game played in their homeland. When possible they organised teams to return home to play in Britain. In 1888, for example, a Canadian team toured Britain. A similar story unfolded in New Zealand – the most Scottish of all emigrant societies – where Scots formed football clubs and leagues from 1880 onwards. But they soon gave way to a passion for rugby. In South Africa, the game had been played in ports and settlements from the 1860s; the local FA was formed in 1884. The game had growing popularity among British working-class settlers and among Indians (imported initially as indentured labour). In time, however, the whites turned to rugby, encouraged by the schools system, while the native Africans turned in ever-growing numbers to football. There – and elsewhere – football was to emerge along the fissures of local racial divides. In the USA, efforts to establish soccer were thwarted by the simple fact that a different brand of football had already taken root in colleges and universities.

It was a curious fact that Association football did not become the national passion in societies which were white settler colonies, or in the USA. Of course large numbers of boys and men did indeed play the game in all those countries. Yet it failed to develop that widespread and passionate following, among players and spectators, which was so striking a feature of the game in Britain, Europe and South America. Other football games blossomed.

The English FA was anxious to encourage football throughout the English-speaking dominions, and at first sight it seemed natural that white-dominion societies, with their regular infusions of British immigrants, should readily take to the social and recreational pursuits of the mother country. The FA sent out touring teams to the dominions, led most notably by the Corinthians, who visited South Africa in 1897. But these and other efforts failed to produce the desired results. Though football survived and grew, it did not develop anything like the popularity witnessed elsewhere. Clearly the growth of sport in any society is a complex phenomenon, made possible only in part by external encouragement. Football had taken root and rapidly established itself as a mass spectator sport in the cities of Britain, Europe and South America (where football's simplicity made the game ideally suited to an urban environment). If football was essentially a game of the new urban and industrial masses, the USA seemed to offer most promise. With its great cities housing social groups similar to those which came to follow football in Europe, the USA seemed ideal for football. But the football which America adopted was not the Association game, but the native variety which had begun to emerge in the same years as the distinctive national winter game, just as baseball came to parallel cricket as the American summer sport. Where indigenous sports evolved from the distinctive cultural roots of a region, it proved impossible to dislodge them by more artificial importations of games from abroad (as the crude efforts to import football into the USA in the 1960s and 1970s so clearly showed). Soccer did take root in certain American cities, though never as a serious competitor to local American football. St Louis, for example, became the soccer centre of the USA in the 1880s, thanks – again – to the efforts of British immigrants and the later work of ex-professionals. Only where football struck a resonant local note in the host society, as it did so obviously in Europe and South America, could the game develop the healthy local roots so vital for the game's future.

In the white dominions of Canada, South Africa, Australia and New Zealand, as in the USA, football failed to establish itself as the pre-eminent local game which enraptured armies of spectators and became the first and only game for young men to play. Though local teams and associations were founded, the game was never able to compete with other more popular sports. To a degree this might be explained by the unique combinations of climate and urban settlement in each particular country. But in the case of Australia and the USA, the key resistance to football came from the fact that local sports had already become firmly entrenched before the Association game could take root. By the 1890s the reputation was already established that:

> Australian natives are too inclined
> To honour muscle at the expense of mind.

But the games they had come to honour were their own distinctive ones, making the task of pioneering football almost impossible. In this rapidly expanding frontier society (even in the cities which, in some cases, had begun to challenge British cities for size), there were both unconscious and deliberate forces resisting the introduction of British institutions. This was particularly true of the emphasis upon rural, outdoor values, upon manliness and *camaraderie* which found an outlet in recreational pursuits other than those adopted by the British working class. The key element, however, was timing, as Asa Briggs has noted in the case of Melbourne, where the emergence of spectator sports, 'predated the rise of the football leagues in England and the general provision of working-class entertainment for leisure'.

A similar situation prevailed in South Africa where rugby football, introduced direct from Rugby School in the 1870s, took firm hold and proved unshakably rooted and resistant to the threats from other sports. Football clubs were established, but with limited success, though one contemporary noted in 1990: 'From Maritzburg and Durban the dribbling game has extended all over South Africa – even to the Kaffirs of the Orange Free State.' Clearly, football had developed a certain following. In time, it was to become the game of the indigenous people; a game they were allowed to play in isolation, in the knowledge that the increasingly racist white society enjoyed other, separate sports. At play, as in life in its broader setting, black and white South Africans conducted their lives in distinct and separate spheres.

There were then good reasons why football should not prove contagious in the white Empire. More difficult to explain, however, is the failure of football to develop in the non-white Empire. These were the years of Britain's grab for empire, especially in Africa, and yet the indigenous peoples of those parts of the world which fell to her imperial control failed – at first – to adopt the British national game. Of course the transplanting of a sporting ethos was part of the Anglo-Saxon mission to import 'civilization' around the globe. Sports, disciplined recreations, vigorous games; all were part of the ideology of late Victorian and Edwardian manliness which was itself proof of British superiority. In time, perhaps, native peoples would rise to levels of equal competitors. For the foreseeable future – and certainly in the early years of settlement – they must watch and learn; seek to imbibe the important sporting lessons: of fair play, of team play, of selflessness and courage. These were the qualities of the imperial class (of both master and man) and not the attributes of native peoples.

The new empire in Africa was of course quite unlike Europe or South America, particularly in the absence of major cities. But where cities grew – and in some places they grew quickly and to remarkable size – the games of urban people took root. But in large parts of colonial black Africa, it took the urban growth and schooling systems of the twentieth century for mass sports to develop. Today football is enormously popular in Africa, both as a game and as a spectator sport, but in the years when football became a world phenomenon the necessary urban and educational base for the game simply did not exist. There is, additionally, the beguiling though unprovable similarity between the British imperial mentality towards the emergence of mass recreations among their subject peoples and that of other European powers we have examined. There were sound political and social reasons for discouraging football crowds and these may well have underpinned the British attitude towards the game in their possessions. In Europe and Latin America, moreover, football took off as soon as local people gained control of British clubs. In the colonies they were never likely to belong to them. Furthermore, the leading servants of the Empire – its senior administrators, judges and military men – belonged to that social class which at the time was rapidly turning away from football in direct proportion to the rise of the working-class game. By the turn of the century, with isolated exceptions, football had a plebeian and a professional social gloss. Football was seen by many contemporaries to reflect working-class culture. Why should the rulers of the Empire, who had so little in common with the lower class at home, concern themselves with the social institutions of working men? Football was the people's game, the game of 'the busy classes', and the imperialists were happy to let them get on with it. The games which thrived in colonial society were those of the colonial elites.

From one society to another, once imperial control gave way to local political involvement, social and recreational life began to change. The development of local, rather than imperial, political activity led, among many other things, to the emergence of new forms of recreational life. They emerged from what had gone before; from the games and pleasures of the former governing elites and from frustrated efforts of the governed to enjoy the new mass spectator sports. In the former Turkish Empire, in the former British possessions in Africa, political independence heralded an explosion of sporting activity. Football – though only one of many newly popular recreations – thrived in the changed political atmosphere. After all, this is what had happened in Britain in the 1880s, when the nation had been transformed by the granting of national and municipal democracy (women excepted). All this is not to make the simplistic point that football was a function of political democracy. It is to claim, however, that the evolution of a wider democratic sensibility, which conceded the leisure and social rights of ordinary people, was a crucial element in the emergence of mass recreations in modern society. In the 1880s, the 'take-off' years of mass football, such social rights proved invaluable. Contemporaries were in no doubt of the links between emergent democracy in advanced industrial societies and the rapid flowering of mass games and sports. But the popularity of football – its ability to galvanise millions, to represent the coarser passions of regionalism and nationalism – was too good to overlook for those politicians looking for a short-cut to fame and national glory. As football established itself around the world as an enormously attractive spectator sport, in the course of the twentieth century, the game spread in its mature form and was often sustained and encouraged by the most tyrannical of regimes. Time and again, the game of the people was hijacked by dictators keen to associate themselves with footballing success for domestic political advantage. Any number of South American generals, for example, could be seen close to their successful team enjoying its finer moments to the plaudits of the politically repressed crowds. The game which was born in the days of emergent democracy was to be put to use by some remarkably gruesome regimes.

From the first days when modern football became a mass recreation in Britain, the game had obvious international potential. In the complicated process by which football became a world game, British influence was central; the pace, style and very fibre of the game's development was British. But after a certain point, football became locally infectious and self-generating; the local game evolved along particular national lines which in turn often came to overpower the game's international characteristics. In the inter-war years, football expanded further round the world, and international contests, led by the Olympics and the new World Cup, gave football an added internationalism. This development of football as a global game entailed social changes no less fundamental than those which had made possible the rise of working-class football in Britain. But who among the handful of gentlemen who founded the FA in 1863 could possibly have envisaged that within fifty years football would have become an international game?

6 The Insular Game, 1915–39

It seems odd – insensitive and irrelevant – to discuss the impact of war on the development of sport. In the face of the suffering and privations of 1914–18, what happened to football might seem a matter of marginal interest. Yet, as before, the game held up a mirror to the changes in society at large. Though the story of the game itself was a minor detail in a history of titanic events and changes, the game provides a revealing entrée to the broader history of social change in those years. Football, like other forms of social recreation, underwent profound changes in wartime, both in Britain and throughout the world. Between 1915 and 1919 organized domestic football was put into cold storage, although military teams took the national game around the world to the various theatres of war. The most famous games were those Christmas kick-abouts played in no-man's land between opposing troops; they remained among the most vivid and poignant images of the war itself. Yet whatever else those simple games represented, they surely spoke to the universal commitment to that particular game. It was an instinct, in that first lull in the fighting, to turn to the game which, before 1914, had brought so many millions together in contests of a different kind.

The game in wartime had its bizarre moments. There were numerous incidents of footballs being kicked over-the-top, in the hope that the men would follow with sporting enthusiasm. Some attacks were led by men kicking a football, or a rugby ball. Surviving footballs used for such attacks took their place among military souvenirs as symbols of the qualities and character of the men involved. Though senior officers initially railed at the idea, it was clear that football among the troops could serve a useful purpose. In the course of the war, thousands of footballs found their way to the men in the services – on all sides. British footballing organisations provided soldiers with footballs, so too did the French sporting press and the German authorities. Providing football equipment was a cheap and universally recognised way of keeping POWs happy and fit at relatively little cost and trouble. The imagery of the game – its orderly conduct, its necessary manly virtues, its heroes – all were used by the major combatants to promote the war and to convey a sporting imagery of combat which, however much at variance with the reality of life at the front, was thought to be appropriate propaganda. Even when the war was over, the sporting imagery flickered across the national memory.

> If the first 100,000 British soldiers in the war had not been sportsmen (said a speaker at a rugby dinner in 1919), they would not have known how to take defeat and eventually turn back the Germans.

A host of sporting clubs erected memorials to former players who died in 'the Great Game'.

In Britain itself, the game inevitably languished, its teams and spectators locked in a struggle of a different order. Despite the contribution made by football to the initial war effort and recruitment, there were many who frowned on the game, refusing to forgive the footballing fraternity for continuing to play after the outbreak of war. Following the resumption of peacetime football, this hostility continued, accentuating still further the social divisions in the spectator sports. Few of football's critics remembered (or even knew of) the enormous contribution made by men in the game during the war years. Instead, the 1920s were marked by a pronounced swing away from football inspired by men and institutions who came to view football as an 'unpatriotic' game. As early as 1914, 'everyone drew attention to the magnificent way in which rugby players had joined up and gone to France. Nobody pointed out that the Amateur Association player had gone just as quickly and just as eagerly. The thing that all people seemed to remember was that professional football was still being played . . . There can be no doubt that the patriotism of the rugby player was generally considered to be much more marked than the patriotism of the Association player.'

One consequence of this distorted and distinctly upper-class view was that the public schools – and grammar schools – changed to rugby in great numbers. By the mid-1920s a string of famous schools had abandoned football for rugby, often to a crude public acclamation of 'the rugby spirit'. This had its bizarre moments. No rugger player, intoned *A Manual of Rugby Football for Public Schools*, should let his socks slip round the ankles.

> No player who is too slack to go to the trouble of finding a pair of garters is worth his place in any team.

The team was paramount; the individual important only to the extent that he fitted into the team. In 1919, *The Times* reported, 'There was much talk of making rugby the winter game in all our public schools.' In fact the origins of this swing away from football lay in the pre-war changes in the game, and could be best seen in the split within the ranks of the FA on the question of amateur status. The overall result after 1919 was a sharp decline in the number of ex-public-school and Oxbridge footballers, and a corresponding rise in the number of Rugby Union teams. Football had of course been markedly working class before the war; after 1919 this tendency was even more pronounced, and many of the criticisms levelled at the game in the inter-war years were often a mask for complaints of a more fundamental social nature. After the war football became ever more plebeian, boisterous, lucrative and professionally dominated, attracting to itself ancillary betting industries, all of which appalled the gentlemen who had played the game at public school. After 1919 it was difficult to see in football the old public-school virtues of selflessness, independence and the amateur 'sporting' mentality, and much easier to find those qualities in Rugby Union.

Even those public schools which remained loyal were repelled by the increasing emphasis on professionalism. In truth, the professional game was only the elite version of a national game which, at its base, embraced millions of boys and men. But the march of a professional spirit was undeniable. It seeped into every level of the game and it was almost impossible for a talented youth to play in school or factory without coming to the attention of scouts who travelled the country in search of talent. Furthermore, there were few among the millions of weekend footballers, especially among working men, who would have refused the opportunity of turning professional. Thus in direct ways the professional game became the norm against which millions of footballers, who would never receive a penny for their efforts, gauged their own performances. They were aware of the game, of its standards and its excitements, because they also watched it. And of course they read about it in that flurry of national, local, and special newspapers which gave such prominence in print to the national winter game. Here, in the eyes of its opponents, was a game greatly demeaned by encroaching professionalism. As the Dean of Durham wrote to *The Times*: 'In old days a boy who had been accustomed to such games as the Field Game at Eton or the Harrow game naturally passed without any effort in the Universities of Oxford and Cambridge to Association football; but at the present time one school after another seems to be adopting rugby football partly, I am told, if not mainly, because rugby football is not so tainted as Association football by professionalism.' How to define 'amateur' was a problem which plagued footballing authorities for years. A strict, unbending stance against payment of any kind was bound to lead to problems (similar, in fact, to those faced by Rugby Union in recent years). It was a complex issue, made worse by residual snobberies and pretensions (not ended in fact until the term 'amateur' was removed in 1975. The year before was the last year of the FA Amateur Cup).

Amateur football thrived of course, including a number of 'gentlemen' teams, but the growth of Rugby Union was achieved at the expense of middle-class football and clearly owed its inspiration to social rather than sporting factors. Earlier hopes that British football would become the classless sport faded and football continued to mirror a socially divided society.

Determined efforts were made within the FA to save the public schools for football, but in many respects they were not needed, for peacetime brought an unprecedented upsurge in interest in the game. By any criteria football after 1919 enjoyed an amazing boom, as men turned their backs on the austerities of the war years and returned to their old recreations. The economic conditions of the new peace were, moreover, appropriate for the expansion of football for, after a brief post-war economic buoyancy – a transient hint that conditions were returning to normal – the country slithered into a series of depressions which were to characterize Britain until World War II. From depression and unemployment there emerged new generations of footballers who sought in the game the material rewards unobtainable in industry. For their part, the fans saw in their local teams a touch of colour and a source of pride which eluded them outside the stadium. Football had been born of rising prosperity; in the inter-war years it was nurtured on hardship.

It was in these years that poor but talented Scots continued to trek south to the football clubs of England. Dozens travelled from the coalfields, the shipyards, the steel works to find on English football fields a livelihood denied them in their homeland. In the process they enriched the English game, much as their predecessors had done before 1914. It was always assumed that the very best would inevitably move south, lured there by the greater wealth and seductions of the big English clubs.

Enthusiasm for football at all levels was greater than ever; there were more players, more clubs and many more spectators. English professional teams grew in numbers and Divisions One and Two were forced to expand to twenty-two teams each. In 1921 Division Three was formed, largely from southern teams, and in the following years Division Three North was launched, thus providing the four professional divisions which, with variations in size and location, have remained the basis of English league football. There were similar changes to the leagues in Scotland (where the main league had, unlike the English, continued to function throughout the war). The simple growth in registered football clubs was remarkable. By the end of the 1930s there were perhaps 10,000 clubs affiliated to their county associations. In the 1920s, the northern and midland teams of the premier English division continued to dominate the game. Indeed in that decade London and the south were represented in Division One by a maximum of four clubs. A similar pattern was clear in FA Cup competitions where, in the first ten years after the war, only Spurs (1921) and Cardiff (1927) took the trophy away from the northern and midland teams. Despite the expansion of football throughout England as a whole and even allowing for the emergence of superb professional teams in the capital, the centre of footballing gravity remained firmly located north of Birmingham – as it had been since the mid-1880s. In terms of peaks of footballing excellence, this was to change in the 1930s.

Crowds at professional games were enormous; bigger than ever, often restricted solely by the physical capacity of the stadiums. What we will never know is how many of the spectators packed into those arenas could see anything at all. It was little short of miraculous that more serious accidents and disasters did not occur. Paying an average of 1s entrance, the fans turned up in their millions. Time and again, games drew crowds of 60–70,000 plus, to stadiums which today are allowed perhaps half that figure. Almost 50,000 at Partick Thistle, a similar figure at Fulham; 75,000 at Spurs, 78,000 at Old Trafford. Thirty-six major clubs recorded their record crowds in the years between the wars. Of course the stadiums themselves were greatly improved; modernised, developed and enhanced from the basic grounds of the late century. It was surely no accident that the greatest architect of football grounds was the Scot, Archibald Leitch, who built Parkhead, Ibrox, Hampden, Old Trafford, Highbury and Spurs' new stadium. These structures and styles remained basically unchanged until the 1960s.

It was fitting that the expanding national game should find a new appropriate setting for the annual finales to the season, the London and Glasgow Cup finals. For the first three years after the war the English Cup final was homeless; Crystal Palace was still used as a War Office depot, so Stamford Bridge was used as a temporary venue. But in 1923 a splendid new stadium was built at Wembley. Originally part of the Empire Exhibition, and built in 300 working days for the then staggering figure of £750,000, Wembley stadium was completed in April of that year. Tested for strength and safety by gangs of heavy-booted workmen and a battalion of soldiers, Wembley was ready for its first Cup final four days after the stadium was completed. But no physical tests or predictions could have envisaged the staggering scenes which followed on that first Wembley Cup final on 28 April 1923, played between West Ham and Bolton Wanderers. Officially, 126,047 people passed through the new turnstiles; unofficially, just as many climbed over them – and over any other obstacle in the way. As the unnumbered thousands spilled on to the playing area, police reinforcements were rushed to Wembley from all parts of London, but by the time the king arrived, a game of football was out of the question; not a single square foot of playing surface was visible. Gradually, order was restored to the milling crowd. Mounted police, aided and encouraged by the players from the competing teams, slowly moved back the human tide until the pitch had been cleared, though even then spectators formed a human touchline (and often kept the ball in play). Those unprecedented and unrepeated events of the tumultuous hours before the match were captured by Sir John Squire who kept a running diary of the scene before him:

1.10 – What a sight. This is two hours before the start, and except for a few reserved seats there doesn't seem to be even standing room for a person more. A vast, elliptical basin. A hill of people all around, and a clean rim far up, cutting the sky . . .

2.15 . . . There isn't room for another soul, and yet they are still pouring in through the entrances . . . the crowd has burst in. They are all over the ground now . . .

2.36. – Our citadel has been stormed and there are thousands of them, all covered with favours. They force their way through us, press in on the track and spread over the field: nothing but people . . .

Amazingly, few people were injured and no one was killed. Bolton went on to win the Cup, though they were lucky even to get into the stadium, for their arrival was as bizarre as that of any of the non-paying spectators. Caught in a traffic jam, 'we left the motor coach, made our way across some fields, crossed a railway line and, at the outer barriers of the Stadium, came upon a man with a spade who was digging a hole under the fence. Through the hole he went; we followed. As we climbed another fence we met a policeman, who grinned, and Rob Wilton-like, said, "You're wasting your time . . .".'

Such scenes could have been predicted, not least because they were already familiar in Glasgow. From the opening of Hampden Park in 1903, vast crowds had flocked to that most up-to-date stadium. Though technically the home of Queen's

Park, the oldest of Scottish clubs, Hampden became the venue for set-piece internationals and local Cup finals. Expanded gradually between the wars, by the late 1930s Hampden regularly filled with up to 140,000 people. Again, the attendance was certainly under-recorded and tens of thousands were locked out. It remained the world's biggest football ground until post-war safety regulations intervened and the opening of Rio's Maracana took the title. Today, its capacity is a fraction of its pre-war record.

The Cup final and international crowds in Glasgow and London were only the most spectacular of a string of remarkable crowds which characterised football between the wars. Money simply poured into the game. Football in the 1920s was even more lucrative than before the war. In 1928, for example, the first £10,000 transfer was completed, while the growing band of professional footballers earned higher wages than ever before (though rarely guaranteed the decent long-term conditions of employment acceptable in other industries). New ancillary industries prospered on feeding upon the game's public prominence. Periodicals and comics provided schoolboys with galleries of pictures of the latest teams and stars; indeed schoolboy comics competed to outdo their rivals in the lavishness of their offers of footballing 'gifts'. But perhaps the most striking impact on the young was made by the new craze for cigarette cards, many of which depicted current footballers. The war and mobilization had transformed cigarette smoking into a ubiquitous social pattern and created a major industry. Figures for smoking reached new heights and in order to capture the interest of a potential, future market the cigarette companies created the vogue for their cards. The sole acquaintance which many boys had with the great football stars of the inter-war years was through the pictures on these cards, which they collected with religious zeal from their smoking elders. Cults and marts developed around the cards and for many boys they became a substitute for football itself; a boy could in fact build up a detailed picture of the game simply by collecting them.

Of all the commercial by-products of football, gambling was by far the most prominent and most important. Betting on the results of matches was as old as the game itself – as football's social enemies were always swift to point out. Of course gambling had been common in a host of recreations since time out of mind. Horse-racing and prize-fighting had been inextricably linked to gambling for at least two centuries. Betting on football had been well-organised, though largely illegal, before being effectively taken over before 1914 by the major newspapers who organised 'competitions'. But the major breakthrough came in the 1920s with the invention of the football pools. So influential did the pools become that many people thought that football's post-war boom was due solely to their attractions. It is also clear enough that many more people were interested in football pools than in football itself. But from the first, football's senior management took a severe, moral line against gambling, as indeed did politicians. In part, fears of corruption and game-rigging lay behind much of the opposition. More fundamental still, however, was a deeper, puritanical distaste for gambling *per se*. It was a debasement of the sporting ethic, and a corrosion of the ideals of fair play, which still inspired so many of the older men controlling the game's destiny. Not surprisingly, the FAs did their best to resist or control gambling on football. They sought to keep such betting out of football grounds and even to inhibit the development of the pools themselves. Before 1914 a similar gambling system had been developed, requiring the sending of circulars through the post, but so determined was the FA to eliminate it that they tried first to recruit the help of the Postmaster General (in 1909) and later in 1913 to introduce a prohibitive bill in the Commons. Such a bill was finally enacted in 1920. The pools were designed specifically to circumvent the restrictions of the act by collecting the sum wagered during the week following the games. The pools system which came into being in the 1920s, mainly a fixed-odds system, boomed in the 1930s.

The FA's resistance was not totally unrealistic; there were sound reasons for official alarm about the risks of gambling, particularly about the dangers of bribery among poorly paid players. They also worried that betting could lead to crowd disorder; if a game swayed in the wrong direction, crowds with money on a different outcome might take things into their own hands. Indeed in 1936 the FA complained that crowds often barracked a team who seemed about to upset the expected result. The FA even suggested that 'Many people gamble on Football Coupons with money they can ill afford to lose.' Such moral objections predictably made no impression on the public who turned in their millions to the pools, transforming them into a major industry within a few years. By the mid-1930s sixteen-and-a-half times as many people gambled on football as watched it, pumping some £800,000 a week into the new companies, led by Littlewoods and Vernons in Liverpool. An estimated five to seven million people were spending £30 million a year, and the graph of this spending could be traced by the sales of 6d and 1s postal orders at the Post Office. It was, from the first, a source of intense irritation to the anti-gambling lobby that the whole system was made possible and kept in place by the state-run postal services. The pools actually attracted only one fifth of the amount of money spent on horse-racing, but unlike the turf the pools seemed eminently fair, providing even the humblest gambler with the illusion that he could scoop a fortune. Sums as high as £22,000 were paid out to successful toters, while the overall turnover was sufficiently high to give employment to some 30,000 people (mainly women). So lucrative had the pools become that some of the promoters soon found themselves with surplus capital they could not use within the pools system. As a result, two of the major firms branched out into the mail-order business and opened retail chain stores in a number of towns.

These economic by-products of football quite clearly owed little to the game itself (and gave it little in return), but the pools were able to become such a nationwide concern because the game they fed upon was the national sport. Throughout this remarkable growth of the pools, with their handsome profits and appeal to all social classes (thanks to anonymity), the footballing authorities resisted the inevitable. It was to be many years after World War II, many years and many millions of pounds after the formation of the pools, before football's authorities reconciled themselves to the pools and began to tap their funds for the benefit of the game itself. In an unusual way, the pools helped to confirm football's status in British society; they widened even further the national interest in the game and gave many millions of people, who would otherwise not have taken an interest in it, a personal, albeit distant, commitment to the weekly progress of matches. Ultimately the pools were to become an institution in their own right and, in a bizarre twist to their history, even continued to function, thanks to the impersonal genius of a computer, when bad weather stopped football itself. For many people, the pools transcended the game, though others tended to see them as part of the overall corruption of professional football. In 1937 *The Times* complained: 'The pools, the transfer system and the amount of money involved in the gates have turned football into something like a national industry.'

The financial ramifications of the game were clear proof of its buoyancy. And therein lay a problem which was to characterize football throughout the inter-war years (and into the 1950s). So successful and expanding was the domestic game that it had little need to pay attention to the game abroad or to look to those parts of the world where it had been exported by expatriates. But in these years football abroad was equally buoyant and yet it was simply assumed by the British that the continuing health of their insular game would forever guarantee the superiority which had existed before 1914.

For most of the inter-war years British football effectively cut itself off from football in Europe, concentrating instead on cultivating contacts with parts of the world where football was insignificant and insecurely based. To a large extent the origins of this attitude were blatantly political. In 1919 the FAs took a firm stand against playing Germany and Austria, countries where the game was expanding dramatically. Unhappily, the former neutral countries refused to operate such an embargo and were soon joined by the French, Belgian and Italian authorities. Thus isolated, the British FAs accordingly withdrew from FIFA – the international forum for the expanding game of football – in 1920. Two years later the FA agreed to play football with the former neutral powers, but continued the embargo on games with the former enemies. Six years after the end of the war, in 1924, the British authorities agreed once again to rejoin FIFA but in their dealings with the international body, both as members and as distant observers, they reacted tetchily to alterations in what they considered to be *their* game. 'We have long established Laws of the Game and Rules of the Associations which are suitable to our wishes and requirements,' the FA secretary wrote to FIFA in 1923. 'In some respects these do not appear to be suitable or acceptable to some other national associations. We do not desire to interfere with the action of other associations who do not agree with our Rules, nor do we desire that they should interfere with ours.' The correspondence we have between the British – especially the English – and their European colleagues makes for unhappy reading. Letters were curt to the point of rudeness. European associations were accused of being fairly new foundations, 'and in consequence cannot have the knowledge which only experience can bring'. Worse still, were the dealings with footballers further afield. A reply to a Uruguayan invitation to play in the first World Cup concluded, 'I am instructed to express regret at our inability to accept the invitation.'

In their unhappy relations with the international authorities, the British displayed hauteur and aloofness. Difficulties between the two sides were never fully resolved, for one source of friction was simply replaced by another. As time and events rendered pointless the refusal to play the old wartime adversaries, the status of the amateur footballer was produced as the chief objection to the international conduct of football. No sooner had the British rejoined FIFA than they took exception to the prevailing definition of amateur status, typically taking a more rigid view than anyone else in European football. After protracted arguments, centred in particular on the Olympic Games, the British in 1928 once more withdrew to their island retreat, not to rejoin FIFA until 1946–7. The end result was that between the wars, while football was making rapid progress throughout Europe and South America, when the Olympic and, after 1930, the new World Cup games offered football new international horizons, British football was a member of the international footballing community for a mere four years (1924–8). For the rest, the British FAs took umbrage at the refusal of other less experienced bodies to accept the lead of the people who had given football to the world. Turning their back on the world, the British authorities could nonetheless pride themselves on the health of the game at home, and try to cultivate sporting contacts with more appreciative and congenial countries, notably our cousins in the white dominions. National teams did of course play against other European teams but only infrequently. Altogether the England team won thirty-four games, drew four and lost only seven international matches in the inter-war period. Not until 1929 was England defeated abroad (and then 4–3 in Madrid), and the game had to wait until 1953 for the first English defeat at home. There seemed little reason to feel alarmed at isolation.

In fact the Foreign Office, no less, had begun to complain about some of the poor teams playing in Europe. If football was to be part of the broader British cultural drive, to 'fly the flag', what was needed were excellent, not weak teams. It was clear enough that sport had become part of the drive to foster good relations and promote British interests. But football's guiding bodies did not see it in that light.

They did, however, spend a great deal of time and effort in attempts to cultivate football in the dominions. In the years when only forty-five full international games were played against European teams, no fewer than 124 representative games were played in extensive tours of South Africa, Australia, New Zealand and Canada. It must have been comforting to win all but three of them, although it was already apparent that football had not developed local roots in the dominions despite (or perhaps because of) continuing British emigration. In fact the footballing tours of the white Empire were viewed more as missionary work and were backed up by advice and financial assistance from London. But mass sports cannot develop strong local roots simply through the efforts of interested outsiders; and many of the overwhelming victories in the dominions may well have been counter-productive and actually helped to inhibit the development of local football.

An indication of the British preoccupation with their own game to the exclusion of international football can be gauged from the fact that the FA spent as much time considering the ramifications of the Irish troubles as they did on international affairs. The partition of Ireland placed the FA in a politically embarrassing position, for two footballing bodies emerged. The substance of the debate (which continued to World War II) was firstly about the respective titles of the two bodies, and later about which teams should be able to call upon Irish players for their international matches.

With or without the split, English football continued to exercise a dominant gravitational pull over football throughout the British Isles. The English professional game continued to lure players, coaches and managers from the whole region. It was in essence a free market in which higher wages, greater opportunities and more varied, related prospects benefited the English game at the expense of their neighbours. It was an unconscious and seemingly uncontrollable tradition that

England drained Scotland, Ireland and Wales of their best footballing talent, as had been the case since the inception of professionalism. Between the wars English managers regularly headed north to watch the professional and amateur teams of Scotland, just as surely as American boxing promoters turn to the black ghettoes for their manpower. In this period the Scottish impact on English football was inescapable and there was scarcely a successful English team without its quota of key Scottish players, trainers and managers. A brief glance, for example, at the composition of Championship-winning sides between 1920 and 1939 confirms this pattern, for not one of the nineteen successful teams played without a Scot. Indeed in two exceptional cases Scots formed an absolute majority of the teams. The Newcastle United team of 1926–7 won the title with seven men from Scotland, led by the incomparable Hughie Gallacher, their tiny but abundantly talented centre-forward. Nine years later, Newcastle's rivals, Sunderland, took the Championship with eight Scots in the team (but spearheaded by the talented local pair, Raich Carter and Bob Gurney). Sunderland also had a Scottish manager. One could similarly trace Scottish infiltration, even dominance, through all levels of English professional football.

While the Scots were the most obvious single group, English teams turned for players to any region of Britain which seemed to offer ideal conditions for breeding footballers. Almost without exception, this involved searching in working-class industrial areas. In the inter-war years, and from 1945, large numbers of footballers were discovered in the poorer areas of Northern Ireland, the north-east of England (perhaps football's most fruitful breeding ground), industrial Lancashire and the midlands. Indeed one Arsenal manager in the 1920s specifically searched for footballers in the drab streets of the Shankill and Falls Road areas in Belfast. A brief analysis of the social and geographical origins of English footballers of the period reads like an introduction to a study of urban depression. In addition to the sprinkling of Scots and Irish, the Liverpool team of 1921–2, for instance, boasted men from Bolton, St Helens, Bootle, Liverpool and Middlesbrough. At heart, this simply confirms the story of football since the 1880s; that the game's dynamism, its training grounds and the bed-rock of its support lay in the industrial heartland of Britain.

Not only were English clubs able to drain the rest of the British Isles, but the dominance of the English FA guaranteed for English football a totally unjustifiable advantage over its rivals in Scotland, Ireland and Wales. The dominance of the English FA and the intransigence of the Football League (which normally refused to place any interest before that of league football) gave English national teams an enormous advantage in home international matches. Nonetheless, the strength of Scottish football can be gauged by Scotland's performances against England in these years. Despite all the disadvantages, of the twenty-two games the Scots won eleven, lost seven and drew four. Thus while English football remained generally supreme in games in Europe and the dominions (with the occasional upset generally put down to the freaks of foreign climate) it was less successful when faced by Scotland which, in any case, provided the talented core of the English game.

Contacts with European football increased in the 1930s when continental tours became an annual event for England teams. But football in Europe was severely troubled by the political problems of the decade, and touring football teams, along with many other sporting organizations, travelled and played along guidelines laid down by the Foreign Office. Recently opened Foreign Office files reveal a marked degree of political involvement in the affairs of non-political sporting bodies in the 1930s. To a degree it is easy to understand official Foreign Office concern. In the fascist states of Germany and Italy, sport had become a crucial means of political and national expression; victories were trumpeted as political triumphs for the local nationalist system, which in their turn placed enormous emphasis on physical prowess and achievements as expressions of national character. After a fashion of course a similar ideology had underpinned the older British urge to implant athleticism throughout the world. In the 1930s, however, the stakes were more overtly political. It seemed all the more important to be represented abroad by winning teams and supreme athletes. It was becoming ever clearer, in the course of the 1930s, that politics could not be easily divorced from sporting contests, but in the 1930s the degree of direct political interference in the conduct of sport was remarkable.

The FA were given instructions stating which countries they should visit, and which they should avoid. Naturally the Foreign

Office appreciated the propaganda value of football and made it clear to the footballing authorities that good performances were expected of visiting teams in diplomatically sensitive countries. Foreign Office mandarins felt, for instance, that it was imperative that the international teams should give good account of themselves in Nazi Germany (though they also insisted that they should give the Nazi salute before the match). Admittedly the fascist regimes were extremely keen to use their sportsmen as substance for their ideological claims of racial superiority, and it was difficult for their opponents not to rise to the challenge. But the Foreign Office response to matches against Nazi Germany was only a more elaborate version of their interference in sporting events. As if this were not enough, in public the government presented a totally different face, and spokesmen openly denounced the idea of political interference in sport. In 1935, for instance, when Germany was due to meet the England team in London, the TUC (among the first British organization to appreciate the threat of Nazi Germany) asked the government to ban the game from fear of an invasion of Nazi thugs disguised as football fans. Sir John Simon for the Home Office tartly replied: 'I do not think that interference on the part of the government is called for . . . Wednesday's match has no political significance whatever . . . it is a game of football, which nobody need attend unless he wishes, and I hope that all who take an interest in it from any side will do their utmost to discourage the idea that a sporting fixture in this country has any political considerations.' It was, of course, political bluster. Like it or not, the game clearly did have political implications. Moreover, we now know that other government departments clearly realised that fact. Nor were the visiting Germans unaware of the significance of the game. They greeted the fans at Tottenham's ground with the Nazi salute, while the Swastika fluttered alongside the Union Flag on the stadium roof. Contrary to TUC fears, the match passed off without incident, and the Germans were given a rousing reception by the crowd. Doubtless the German authorites in Berlin regarded the episode as a highly successful business, despite the English victory, 3–0.

While British football's contacts abroad were limited, the game was fast developing its international structures. It had, for instance, rapidly become one of the highlights of the Olympic Games, after 1908. Won by England both in 1908 and 1912, the

Olympic football title was the sole international one in football
until the establishment of the World Cup in 1930. But in two of
the inter-war Olympics, those of 1924 and 1928, English
football refused to participate because of the dispute about
amateur status which had led to its withdrawal from FIFA, and
the title fell to Uruguay. Those who looked beyond the British
Isles, and those watching the development of the game in other
key parts of the world, could see the dramatic improvements
around the world. It was clear from the quality of football
played in the Uruguay World Cup that football was making
rapid progress around the world. In addition, international
tournaments proved to be highly prestigious and lucrative
ventures which competing nations approached with a
frightening and escalating determination. To provide
professional football with an international equivalent to the
Olympics, FIFA launched the World Cup in 1930. Played in
Uruguay, the first competition was won by the host country,
nicely rounding off their two previous Olympic victories. It was,
however, a tournament marred by controversy, and by some
remarkable antics by players and referees; an omen of what lay
ahead. But the crowds were huge – the final attracted 90,000 –
and outbursts of nationalism flared in all competing South
American countries.

The 1934 and 1938 contests were both won by Italy; by teams
who were rigorously controlled by the governing fascists, and
who were expected, like their German counterparts, to bring
honour to the regime through their play. Not surprisingly, the
Italians reflected their government's style and brought to
international football a toughness which in no small part helped
them to capture the trophy. The Italian team was managed by
Pozzo who, as we saw, had learned his football in Manchester
before 1914, but his skills and the efforts of the team were
unscrupulously manipulated by the regime for their own
glorification. It was not the last time a dictatorial regime took
advantage of its sporting teams to share in the reflected glory.
But it all assumed that the people liked what they saw; that the
populace approved of team's sporting success. Sports had
become enormously important, not simply where it had always
thrived – at the local level – but now on the national and
international stage. The people's game had become a reflection
and a manifestation of national status and aspirations.

The introduction of the World Cup saw the beginning of that xenophobic and often strident and unpleasant nationalism which has gradually come to dominate international football. Within the British Isles of course footballing patriotism was nothing new, for it was annually aroused by the England–Scotland games where the Scots could normally flaunt their superiority over their political masters. But the European tensions of the late 1930s were qualitatively different, for they were ideological as well as national. World War II helped to give added emphasis to patriotism on and around the football field, particularly in games between former combatants. But before 1939 the ideological pace was clearly set by the fascist regimes for whom sport was a living proof (or refutation) of their ideology. It is nonetheless true that political and national considerations were regularly invoked in British football as well.

By the eve of World War II international football had already become overtly 'political'; since then, the political importance of the game has increased only by a matter of degree. International football furthermore was an increasingly violent sport; the violence which was the basis of the Italian success of 1938 was only an extreme version of a common phenomenon. Football had of course traditionally been a rough game, and the evolution of tight discipline and regulation within the British game had never removed (nor was it intended to remove) the emphasis on physical contact and controlled aggression. Older observers even claimed that men were sent off the field in the 1920s for offences which were the stock-in-trade, years before, of the Old Corinthians. Indeed the robustness of football was (and is) perhaps one of the game's great attractions. British football before World War II, while characterized by the emergence of thoroughbred professional teams led by Huddersfield and Arsenal, was, in keeping with tradition, a rough game. For every skilful and diminutive idol of the crowd, there was a great bone-bruising specimen, able to stop anything human. To some extent the emergence of these physically powerful 'stoppers' was a function of tactical changes within the game and the need to build an effective defensive structure around one 'stopper'. Such a man was Frank Barson, a tough, fearless giant who survived four broken noses and two back injuries in the process of shoring up the defences of Barnsley, Aston Villa and Manchester United. Men like Barson – and there was at least one in every team – remained the backbone of the British game.

Notwithstanding the ancient tradition of violence, during the 1920s and 1930s there were regular squeals of alarm from the press about the rise of violence in football. Many complaints, however, stemmed from a confusion between unfair play and roughness. 'Gamesmanship' was a relatively new phenomenon, reflecting the rewards and tensions of the professional game; roughness was, and always had been, integral to the game. 'Unfair play should certainly be dealt with, but why rough play?' asked C.J. Burnup, a former Corinthian, in 1922. 'In my days I never heard of a team complain of rough play.'

Throughout the twentieth century the FA had been at pains to keep football's innate roughness within acceptable bounds, but their determination often outstripped their sense of fairness. Consequently, a system of discipline evolved which was both arbitrary and, for many years, quite contrary to the spirit of justice. Footballers, with a weak union and with few alternative means of employment, were effectively controlled by a system of work discipline which would have proved intolerable to any other group of workers. Despite the arbitrary manner in which footballers were fined, suspended and banned from their work – and that without real redress or even representation – there was quite obviously no effective deterrent to 'bad behaviour' on the field and footballing incidents were a weekly event. Commentators with short memories, however, considered such scenes to be a new sign of the inevitable decay induced by money (as of course they still do). In January 1937 *The Times* went so far as to run a leader on the subject, entitled 'Not Football'.

> The most cursory reading of newspaper reports on Monday mornings is profoundly disquieting to all who love Association football as a game of skill. Again and again that unpleasant word 'incident' has a way of cropping up, reports of matches resound with stories of free kicks, and crowds seem altogether too vocal and biased in their opinions on the conduct of the referee ... The unforgivable sin in any game is the cold-blooded and intentional foul, and it is unfortunately true that the modern game of professional football is all too full of it ...

What was new in the 1930s, however, was not so much robust play as a sense of professional determination which generated an unwelcome sense of gamesmanship.

   The greater sense of professionalism stemmed largely from the work of a new breed of managers of the bigger teams who sought to bring their teams to new peaks of fitness, skill and achievement, and who sought to ensure a continual flow of talent into their clubs through effective nationwide scouting systems and careful transfer policy. The precise qualifications for management were (and are) unclear; distinguished managers often emerged from mediocre and unpromising players. One such man was Herbert Chapman who retired from an uneventful playing career to become one of the most distinguished managers of all time. Chapman's managerial career began under a cloud, for he was in charge of Leeds City when they were expelled from football in 1919 for gross irregularities. To add insult to injury, the Leeds players were publicly auctioned – the most unpleasant but revealing reminder of their peculiar 'slave' status. Neighbouring Huddersfield, themselves in a parlous state and only kept viable by the determined local fund-raising drive, absorbed some of the Leeds players. With virtually nothing to lose, Huddersfield also decided to take on Chapman as manager, little knowing that he would steer them towards the Championship of Division One in three consecutive seasons (1923–6). As if this were not enough, the revitalized team were runners-up in the next two seasons, for although Chapman left the club in 1925, his firm control, rigid discipline and unremitting emphasis on teamwork laid the foundations for continuing success.

   On leaving Huddersfield, Chapman moved south to Arsenal where his success was even more staggering and where he helped to create a new centre of footballing excellence, deflecting much of the traditional limelight from the midlands and north. Chapman's translation south coincided with a major change in the rules of English football; a change which forced managers and players to recast their attitudes to and preparation for the game. In 1925 the off-side rule was changed to its present form, in which a player is deemed to be off-side if, when the ball is played, fewer than two opponents stand between him and the opposing goal (it had previously been three). Tactically, the result of this change was a dramatic increase in the number of goals scored. In order to staunch this goal-scoring spree, the 'stopper' centre-half was devised. This in its turn led to tactical plans to by-pass the huge men who came to dominate the centre of the pitch. Herbert Chapman at Arsenal first mastered the new techniques and rapidly moulded a new team around the new features of the game.

Until the post-war years, Arsenal had enjoyed only moderate success, though just before the war, thanks to the enterprise of Sir Henry Norris, a London businessman and politician (and despite the opposition of other north London clubs and local residents), a new stadium had been opened at Highbury. By assiduous back-stage political machinations, Norris succeeded in getting Arsenal elected to Division One in the post-war reorganization. But his main coup was to persuade Chapman to leave Huddersfield. Chapman proceeded to create a new Arsenal team by careful though expensive purchases, detailed tactical preparations and a new emphasis on physical fitness in which he used every available piece of modern electrical equipment. In all this he was greatly assisted by his trainer Tom Whittaker, the forerunner of the modern trainer, who made it his task to know each player's physical and personal peculiarities and to treat them accordingly. There was, however, a price to be paid for Arsenal's success, surrounded as they were by older clubs who resented their success, and it was paid by Sir Henry Norris. He was banned from the game for a series of irregularities. But in the teeth of rigid rules and considering the game's increasingly high stakes, it is difficult to envisage the creation of a new, successful professional team such as Arsenal without infringing the spirit, if not the letter, of football's laws. Much of the trouble which Norris faced stemmed from rules designed to keep professionalism within limits by careful control of transfers and payments to players. Such rules were, again, counter-productive and the inevitable result was widespread 'illegal' payment to footballers – and exile for those men who were discovered. As the game's commercial importance grew, the absurdity of such rules, which were in effect a ceiling on footballers' earnings, became manifestly unfair and inoperable. But the worst excesses, of intransigence on the one hand and 'illegality' on the other, were only finally controlled in the 1960s with the removal of the maximum wage and the granting of a percentage of a transfer fee to the players involved.

Norris had laid the foundations for Arsenal's success but he was unable to enjoy it when it fully materialized in the 1930s. That decade belonged to Arsenal. They won the Cup in 1930 and 1936 (losing in the final in 1927 and 1932) and were Division One Champions in 1931, 1933, 1934, 1935 and 1938. Once again, however, it was an English team which hinged on a Scot, in this case the footballing genius of Alex James. Time and again, the familiar pattern repeated itself; of Scots bred and educated in the coal mines, the heavy industries and the sheer deprivation of their industrial homeland finding their way south, into all sorts and conditions of English football. And wherever the English game was played best – wherever there was a successful English team – there you would find a Scot (more likely, more than one) at the heart of their footballing success. There were other, periodic reminders to the English of the footballing passions to the north. When Scotland played at Wembley, armies of Scots rolled south for the occasion. In 1934, fifty-two trains carried 23,000 passengers to London for the game. In Glasgow, the crowds for the return games were the biggest ever witnessed; almost 130,000 in 1931. In 1934, in the midst of depression, prices to Hampden were reduced and 134,710 turned up. In 1935 it was calculated that almost 200,000 managed to get inside. Under such pressure, the Scottish football authorities introduced tickets; all 150,000 were sold. Though receipts were £20,000, the players received £6 each. Similar crowds packed into Hampden for a host of Scottish games between the wars. On New Year's Day 1939 118,577 were there to watch a Rangers–Celtic game. However we look at the game between the wars, it offers remarkable images; of a buoyant, thriving national sport, able to draw unprecedented crowds, a game fuelled at all levels throughout the mainland by a passionate Scottish commitment, and serviced by contingents of talented Scottish players.

Arsenal's amazing run of success in the 1930s had repercussions through all levels of the game – both amateur and professional – for it clearly pointed to the need for, and the rewards of, a professional attitude to the physical and tactical preparation of football teams. One obvious result was the encouragement of further, more elaborate scouting and training among schoolboy players. Often, however, the clubs found themselves unable to entice promising youngsters to their clubs by legal means and even today illegalities dog the approaches of many professional teams to schoolboy footballers.

Schoolboy football had long been viewed as a vital element in the national game, and as early as 1901 efforts had been made to encourage the development of football in schools. Games in elementary schools had been sanctioned as early as 1906, and by 1914 there were schools football associations in England, Wales and Scotland. The number of footballing schools grew throughout the inter-war years, though at first a disproportionate amount of effort had gone into the unsuccessful attempts to keep the public schools within the fold. More important, in the 1920s football in elementary schools was brought under local FA jurisdiction, and county FAs were given control over school football in their areas. When, in the mid-1930s, determined efforts were made by government and private bodies to provide the youth of the country with improved facilities for physical education, the FA's schoolboy network was perfectly placed to capture even more boys for football. As late as 1939 the FA was continually trying to widen and improve its hold over the country's footballing youth, a policy continued after the war. By 1968, more than 14,000 schools played football.

Of all the changes in British social life in the 1930s, the wireless and the cinema must surely rank among the greatest. Broadcasting in particular changed the course of entertainment for it brought all aspects of society into people's homes. Initially, the BBC faced enormous and fundamental resistance from the press, who feared that their monopoly of information would be destroyed. Newspapers particularly resisted the broadcasting of sporting events, an area in which they held a unique and remarkably influential position. They objected, for example, to live broadcasts of the first half of football matches and resisted demands for a better football results service. In the event, radio tended to complement rather than replace newspapers, as one contemporary noted: 'It would be interesting to know if evening papers ever noted that those coming away from a Cup-tie or a Derby seem just as keen on reading an account of what they have just seen as anyone else.'

The first sports broadcasts were transmitted in January 1927 (the first football match, a Cup-tie, going out on 29 January). But effective outside broadcasts lagged behind studio broadcasts because of the technical complications of outside work. Moreover, a new breed of men, the sports commentators, had to be trained, for until the rise of radio there had been no need for a coherent running commentary on a fast-moving event, and the BBC had the difficult task of creating this new skill. Sportsmen were often found to be unsuitable and Gerald Cock, head of outside broadcasts, had to mould men to the work. George Allison, later manager of Arsenal, was an early success, but on the whole the most successful BBC commentators were internal creations.

Within ten years of the establishment of the BBC the size of its audience was staggering. In 1927 there were 2,178,259 licence holders; by 1939 this had risen to 9,082,666. In 1935, ninety-five per cent of the population could listen, on cheap wireless sets, millions of them bought on hire purchase, to BBC broadcasts. The market was practically universal, but football's authorities, like the press, resisted this remarkable innovation, fearing that radio would undermine all spectator sports. The Football League frequently banned broadcasts of league matches, though the FA was thought to be more co-operative. It was noticeable, however, that 'The less popular the sport the more willing were its sponsors to have it "advertised" by radio.' There was a pronounced bias, at least initially, within the BBC against broadcasting professional games. Much more time was devoted to amateur football and rugby. But as the working-class radio audience grew, as demand increased for an adequate coverage of the national winter game, the BBC was forced to respond. And for those unable to afford their own radio set, the nearest radio shop provided games' progress and results.

Radio had a seismic impact on the social and cultural life of the British people (and of many other people around the world). It clearly widened the interest in sport for, like other pleasures covered by broadcasting, it was brought into people's front room. Nor was there any evidence that sports broadcasts in these years undermined attendance or playing figures. Even later, when TV had a far more dramatic impact on the fortunes of spectator sports, it would be naïve to see the effect of broadcasting as totally bad or totally beneficial. Certainly up to 1939 radio coverage of football (and the results service which, in harness with the pools, became enormously popular) generated further interest in football, apparently without undermining the game's spectator appeal. Indeed BBC coverage of football expanded the game's hold in Britain by creating an interest in the players, teams, competitions and results among many thousands who would never have watched the game. It could in fact be argued that broadcasting reinforced football's national status though, again, many of the game's social opponents considered this (rightly in some respects) to be due largely to the financial rewards surrounding the game.

Relations between football's authorities and the BBC were never easy, however. There was a fear among the clubs that radio would undermine attendances, despite the weekly statistical evidence throughout the 1930s. But football had more to offer than the simple reporting of live games; it was a topic of endless fascination which spawned a host of radio programmes by men in the game – and all without any noticeable reduction in the game's popularity at the turnstiles. Gradually, this fact was accepted. During the war, and as part of morale-boosting campaigns, football was allowed more broadcasting time than any other sport.

Football was courted by other new broadcasting developments. The first – largely experimental – TV broadcasts of the game took place in 1937, but it was film and cinema which made an even bigger impact. The weekly newsreels shown in British cinemas invariably devoted a slice of their time – upwards of thirty per cent – to football matches. But they could never compete with the excitement of a live radio broadcast. Indeed it is a sign of radio's contribution to the game that its most famous sports broadcasters became celebrities in their own right.

British football on the eve of World War II was in a remarkably healthy state. It was watched by more people than ever before and it was played by more men and boys than ever before. The FAs sat astride a truly national organization which embraced schoolboys on the one hand and Cup finalists on the other. The game could boast of teams of unprecedented excellence, with national annual finals at Wembley and Hampden which were unrivalled throughout the world. With such success at home – with packed stadiums, armies of satisfied listeners huddled close to their radio sets, with millions ticking their football pools weekly and with the press replete with footballing interest – why bother too much with football abroad? British football appeared to be in little need of help, challenge or co-operation from any quarter, though English football simply could not manage without the Scots.

One year before the outbreak of war, in October 1938 (a mere three weeks after the Munich agreement), the English game celebrated its seventy-fifth anniversary by defeating a combined European team 3–0. But in that same year the Italians (without British opposition) were making their way to a second World Cup victory. Characteristically, English football was celebrating its birthday with a splendid feast while the rest of the footballing world was doing battle for the World Cup. Whether that trophy was worth the winning remains a moot point. For our purposes, however, the absence from the World Cup symbolized an insularity which was part of an even wider isolationist malaise within the country as a whole. This insularity had firm historical roots, for it originated in the early ascendancy of the British game and its undoubted superiority up to 1914. Throughout the inter-war years football in the British Isles never questioned the belief in inherited superiority; an attitude compounded by administrative isolationism and shored up by domestic buoyancy. It was to be many years before the reality of football abroad and the relative decline of the domestic game were fully appreciated. But in 1939 there were more pressing matters to attend to. Twenty years after football had begun to pick up the pieces after World War I, the game was, once more, put on the shelf.

7 Leisure in Austerity, 1939–52

The country had begun to prepare for war long before the Prime Minister's announcement of 3 September 1939. By then, three-and-a-half million people had already been evacuated to less vulnerable parts of the country (a process which pitched together social classes and groups which had previously remained virtually ignorant of each other's existence). Once at war, the face of Britain changed rapidly. Social life, from sports to the cinema, was instantly frozen; the night lights were extinguished and the BBC went over to emergency wartime broadcasting. Thousands of miles of beaches, so recently the summer playground of holidaying millions, were hastily defended with barbed wire and gun positions. Shuttered and uneasy, Britain slipped into the 'phoney' war.

However 'phoney' the next few months, there was no doubt about the nature of the impending hostilities. This was to be a war fought as much at home as abroad; the home front would be as embattled as any foreign field. The nation began to prepare itself for a war on its own doorstep. As the king warned on the first day of war, 'There may be dark days ahead, and war can no longer be confined to the battlefield.' For all the early confusions, the government had learned the lesson of 1914–16 when the war had been fought virtually on a part-time basis. In 1939 there was no mistaking the resolve to harness every aspect of the nation's material and human potential to fight a total war; it was to be a people's war, and the people had to brace themselves for war effort of the most comprehensive kind.

Conscription had begun as early as May 1939 for men aged twenty to twenty-one, but on the first day of war a new act rendered all men between the ages of eighteen and forty-one liable for military service, and although recruitment proceeded slowly, it made major inroads into the male population. Even had there been no formal restrictions on organized sports, this steady absorption of young men into the armed forces would have been sufficient to undermine the country's ability to play and watch sport in any significant way. In September 1939 (as in 1914), private organizations rallied to the war effort without governmental prompting. There was, after all, a very imminent threat of aerial attack and invasion. Accordingly, in the first week of the war representatives from the FA and the Football League meeting in London decided to suspend all football, with the exception of that played in the armed forces. The Scots refashioned their leagues, making them local and regional but, like the English, they soon faced difficulties about absent players – and spectators. Older men were doubtless conscious of the antagonism directed against football for continuing during World War I, and they were anxious to avoid a similar reaction. The winter of 1940 was terribly severe. Grounds were too hard to play on whatever the political problems. But the end result of private initiative and governmental policy was that, whatever else weighed on people's minds, millions of fans looked forward to a bleak, gameless winter for the first time in more than twenty years.

Those men responsible for galvanizing the nation's resources and manpower for the war looked on the nation's sporting facilities and potential with some interest. In particular, professional football held enormous and immediate potential for the early war effort, for it employed large numbers of healthy young men, expert in the much-needed skills of physical recreation. There was, moreover, a great deal of equipment and physical space available for mass military training in the hundreds of football stadiums dotted around Britain. In 1939, football's authorities again put the game's unique and nationwide facilities at the disposal of the War Office. Coaches, trainers and masseurs, to say nothing of hundreds of professional footballers, were ideally suited to the pressing need of knocking a conscript army into sound physical shape, as the War Office immediately recognized.

Footballers rapidly established themselves as the backbone of physical training in the armed forces, beginning their army careers at Aldershot whence they emerged as sergeant instructors APTC. Commissions were given to a number of famous footballers who became specialist officers in physical recreation, while a further batch of forty footballers formed the spearhead of new NCOs in the RAF Physical Training School. In all this, the FAs co-operated with the War Office but, not content simply to work within the armed forces, the FAs, in co-operation with the Central Council of Physical Recreation and the government, set up a number of training centres, under the supervision of coaches, to prepare youths before they were conscripted.

Not surprisingly, the clubs were rapidly denuded of their players. Some clubs encouraged their players to join up *en masse*; Arsenal, for example, was eventually left with only two of its forty-two professionals – the rest were in uniform. Symbolically Arsenal's ground was converted into a Civil Defence fortress, though the fate of other stadiums was more unusual. Twickenham was converted into allotments and used by the Civil Defence, while at Wimbledon the tennis courts were used for Home Guard drill. Surrey's Oval cricket ground (once the venue for the Cup final) became a POW camp. Nothing was sacred and even Epsom was turned over to the military.

The ban on organized football was soon lifted. The phoney war gave way to something of a different order; a more considered appreciation of the long slog that lay ahead and the need to prepare for it. Unlike World War I, it was now widely accepted that morale and public spirits at home would be vital to the armed conflict. Discussion with the Home Office persuaded the FAs to launch a revised programme of football, based on reorganized local leagues using makeshift teams, but it was strictly on the understanding that matches were not to interfere with local industries or recruitment, and that teams would have to travel no further than fifty miles. Crowds were limited by ARP regulations to an eighth (later a quarter) of pre-war capacity, and on 21 September 1939 the stunted national game was set in uneasy and unusual motion. Not surprisingly, the games failed to attract their usual following. Wartime propaganda had warned of the dangers of mass gatherings, while many would-be spectators stayed away from fear of not gaining admission to the restricted grounds. Many young men were of course already in the forces; many more were working overtime on Saturday afternoons, while the weekend offered the sole opportunity for parents to travel to see evacuated children. But despite all these problems, football got under way, encouraged by a government which, anxious to keep civilian morale high, appreciated the therapeutic value of football in the cities. Indeed during the war, the sole sporting event to be graced, in a formal capacity, by Winston Churchill, was a football match; a clear indication of the value he placed on it.

The quality of football inevitably declined. Professional clubs fielded teams which were the most motley assortment imaginable; youths and local part-timers, visiting soldiers and airmen (often ex-pros) and even spectators plucked from the terraces at the last moment to make up the team. In one match Norwich City allegedly played against Brighton and Hove Albion; the visitors were made up of five Brighton men, two Norwich reserves and the balance made up from soldiers who had arrived as spectators. In 1940 Manchester United entertained a depleted Blackburn side at Stockport (United's ground having fallen an early victim to the blitz). Four spectators were recruited to complete the Blackburn team (the only criterion of selection being the correct size of feet to fit the available boots). One of the volunteers, 'Little Hallam', could scarcely play football, regularly miskicked and was periodically flattened by the opponents who won 9–0. But for Hallam it was a sweet moment. 'It was something to have worn the colours of one of the most famous clubs in football history for an afternoon.' On another similar occasion, Millwall's fifty-year-old manager turned out for the team. Equally unusual in 1943, Stanley Mortensen, later to be a prominent English international, made his international debut at Wembley – for Wales. Matt Busby, quickly drafted into the army as a sergeant-instructor, played for Reading, Aldershot and Hibs. Towards the end of the war, he managed army teams playing to entertain the troops close to the front lines in Italy. At home, the game became a topsy-turvy sporting world in which the sole aim was to send eleven healthy men on to the pitch.

The long-suffering fan, accustomed to high-quality football before the war, found little to savour in such scratch games though the scoring rate rose dramatically and there were unexpected surprises when famous stars, passing through on military duties, turned out for the local team. Indeed the ex-pros played more football than ever before. Denis Compton later recalled: 'Cup finals, League South matches, and army representative games followed one on top of each other in a seemingly endless stream.' New teams, competitions and leagues were devised to provide football for different groups and occasions. Sunday football was sanctioned for hard-pressed industrial workers – and formed the first effective breach in seventeenth-century restrictions governing sports on the Sabbath. Matches were devised for different age groups, for Civil Defence organizations and charitable causes. Municipalities opened up restricted park space for footballers in the cities. There was in fact a wide range of football to choose from, though it lacked the regularity and national press coverage which gave traditional rivalries their edge. The game continued, thanks to the Board of Trade which provided coupons for football equipment and for the manufacture of footballs (a particular problem following the fall of Malaya and the resulting rubber shortage). Football was fragmented and impromptu though, revealingly, it is thought that handshakes after the game first originated in these troubled years.

If the old professional teams were unrecognisable and generally poor, the military teams were remarkably good, not surprisingly since they had the pick of the former professionals to choose from. This was a feature of military teams that was to last, thanks to National Service, into the 1950s. The military teams were virtually international, the consequence of which was the development of a superb English national team, accustomed to playing alongside each other in the forces. The Scots, Irish and Welsh, however, were rarely given a national base within the armed forces and the result was the dramatic superiority of the English over the others in home internationals (in 1944 England beat Scotland 8–0).

Throughout the war football for civilians remained on an ad hoc basis but gradually, thanks to the progress of the war, bringing greater security at home, coupled to the need of the civilian population to break away from the monotony of industrial life, the crowds came back. By the end of the war, as the limits on size were raised, crowds of up to 60,000 gathered to watch matches. Happily for the pools addicts, business continued; in November 1939 the leading pools companies had merged to form Unity Pools and to avoid extra cost printed their coupons in the newspapers.

During World War I the FA had adopted the policy of giving the Association's funds towards the war effort. By the end of the war it had consequently been perilously close to insolvency. World War II, however, brought a more realistic attitude towards the game and towards its earning power. Both the government and the FA appreciated the social and morale-boosting value of football, and the growing crowds at wartime matches presented an ideal opportunity to raise income for various wartime causes. From the early days, proceeds from the game were earmarked for Red Cross and St John's funds, and by 1943 football alone had channelled some £55,120 into their coffers, while in the course of the war sport in general gave the two organizations some £3 million. Anxious not to lose its control over the footballing nation, the FA diverted much of its energy into making provision for football within the armed forces, and even supplied money and equipment for the 100,000 British POWs abroad.

Between 1939 and 1945 Britain became a remarkable (for her) polyglot society; a social crucible and entrepôt for hundreds of thousands of men from all over the world who were deposited on the offshore island firstly to defend Britain and later in preparation for the invasion of Europe. Socially the results were fascinating, for each national group introduced their distinctive and often unknown social and recreational habits into the host country, returning home with memories of and an interest in distinctively British ones. To many visiting troops, football and cricket symbolized the host country, and thousands of them adopted the games for the duration of their stay. By 1940, for example, there were eighty-four Canadian football teams in the United Kingdom, and the game was also played by thousands of European soldiers in temporary exile. West Indian cricketers, American baseball players and American footballers brought a variety and fizz to the social life of a beleaguered country. In September 1942, for instance, a baseball match was played on the Oldham Rugby League ground between the New York Yanks and the Californian Eagles – a bizarre setting for that game. Cricket continued to dominate the summer, but during the war it attracted a different and at times bemused audience – including a Russian general. Football, particularly the wartime internationals and Cup finals, similarly attracted the exiled European monarchs (of Norway, Greece and Yugoslavia) and thousands of Allied troops, prominently headed by General Eisenhower. Football's old virtues once more came to the fore, for the game was ideal for entertaining crowds cheaply. It was also a perfect tool (as educators had discovered in the late nineteenth century) for keeping large numbers of men fit, with a minimum of expense, equipment and space. Once more repeating the pattern of World War I, military, notably naval, teams, took the game of football to different theatres of war, creating a local interest in football which flourished in the post-war years. Football in Malta, for instance, had long depended on the Navy. In 1942 Reuters received a telegram from the besieged island: 'Please repeat Saturday's football results – heavy bombing interfered with our reception.'

The game was played by scratch teams and by teams of drafted professionals, in most parts of the world. It entertained tens of thousands of troops who found themselves uprooted from their familiar routines and pleasures. It once again proved itself to be the most popular of games; easily played in the most diverse conditions, adaptable and yet appealing to throngs of men. The fact that military authorities set aside such important facilities – including transport of the players and equipment – in times of scarcity, speaks to the game's undisputed importance.

In that all-consuming struggle between 1939 and 1945, no single section of the community can with justice be singled out for extra praise for its war work. All sections of the community played their part, often under the most trying of circumstances. But they needed moments of pleasure; brief respites from the grind that became their daily lives. Yet historians have paid relatively little attention to the role played by mass recreation in keeping the nation happy, fit and ready for further efforts. It is, however, perfectly clear that popular recreations played an invaluable part in maintaining high spirits and morale. At the time no one was deceived into believing that social life continued uninterrupted, but the national games of football and cricket bravely struggled to maintain a semblance of business as usual. This view was well put by *Mass Observation* in 1940:

> In a society where things like sports and jazz are just as important as politics or religion, it might well be thought that first-class sportsmen were as important to the community as say watchmakers and curates who are in reserved occupations.

> Sports like football have an absolute major effect on the morale
> of people, and one Saturday afternoon of League matches could
> probably do more to affect people's spirits than the recent
> £50,000 Government poster campaign urging cheerfulness.

This attitude, widely expressed among men in authority,
represented a major sea-change since the last great conflict
twenty years earlier. Then, authority and the press had
periodically thundered against the frivolities of public pleasures.
Enjoying oneself at home seemed an affront to those millions of
menfolk glued in the trenches. Now, few doubted that the
domestic war effort – crucial for the military conflict – would
not succeed unless the people relaxed occasionally. All work and
no play made Jack (and Jill) not so much dull as inefficient.

The national games outside the armed services still needed
their administrators of course; though the young players had
been drafted into uniform, older men were left to play their own
part. Football was able to continue as a national game largely
owing to the remarkable efforts of small groups of older men
who were determined to keep the game's organization alive in
the teeth of government restrictions on labour, travel, crowds,
equipment and clothing. It was – and is – one of the remarkable,
untold stories; of groups of committed men, lovers of the game
(and players in their youth) who devoted all their spare time to
organizing and managing football through good times and bad.
Of course the same was true of all other sports, all of which
relied on their unsung and generally unknown administrators.
The success – survival – of the national games needed much
more than the players who were household names.

The hardships of everyday life did not end with the cessation
of hostilities. The fighting ended, but the restrictions and
privations continued. Peace in 1945 was bleak and forbidding.
The new Labour government presided over a country in the
grips of severe economic and social dislocation, for the war had
drained the nation's energy and financial reserves, had
undermined the industrial plant and sapped the nation's
economic strength. Yet the war had raised expectations. People
who had been deprived of all but life's necessities for the best
part of six years expected peace to bring more than merely the
end of fighting. The war-weary British people were anxious for
an improvement in their economic and social lives. Such hopes

were, for most, to remain unfulfilled until the mid-1950s, because wartime rigours were of necessity continued into peacetime, as the country struggled to overcome the major residual problems of a war-taxed society. With domestic capital run down by £3,000 million, overseas investment by £1,000 million, debts running at £3,000 million and exports cut by two thirds, any government elected in 1945 would have been faced by massive problems of reconstruction. The Labour government, however, had even greater problems, for, spurred on by its overwhelming electoral victory, it was determined to reconstruct post-war society on a new, socially equitable basis, a vision which was to meet with dogged resistance and which was to compound the government's political difficulties in putting the country back on a stable basis. Labour's social improvements, wrought primarily through the ambitious new Welfare State, did not really begin to take effect until after 1948. Though most of Labour's ambitions hinged on detailed legislative and administrative intrusion into what had, before 1939, been private preserves, they also inherited the amazingly intrusive wartime state system. The result, in Arthur Marwick's words, was that 'life under the Labour government was in large measure determined by wartime rather than post-war legislative developments'.

It was clear enough that little could revert to its pre-war mode, in the short-term at least. But it was equally clear that the British people longed for a return to the normal lives they had last enjoyed six years earlier. Social and recreational life could not immediately revert to its pre-war patterns, although the arrival of peace, the return of demobbed soldiers and the easing of wartime restrictions unleashed a widespread and palpable desire for pleasure and recreation. The British people were desperate for entertainment and pleasure. Here was a climate in which all the old mass pleasures could flourish – despite the persistence of austerity.

It was, then, not surprising that, in the first five years of peace, football, the national game, enjoyed its greatest ever boom. As the ex-pros changed their PT sergeants' uniforms for demob suits, they drifted back to their welcoming clubs after six years of nomadic football. Six years in the life of a professional athlete is of course a long time and many of them had passed their peak of talent without ever having been able fully to show their skills.

The players' union, however, was not prepared to return to the conditions of employment of 1939 and, after determined agitation by the union, in 1946 the Football League reluctantly increased the wage limits of £8 (winter) and £6 (summer) to £10 and £7 10s.

Set against the enormous drawing power of football teams and the clubs' resulting income, these wages (which, it has to be stressed, were maximum and not average) were scandalously low. Footballers, however, seemed to find them acceptable partly because their weak union was in no position to insist on better terms, but mainly because, by comparison with their friends and family, such wages seemed a handsome reward. From the early twentieth century the illusory comparison with the wages of contemporaries had been instrumental in persuading generations of working-class footballers to accept wages which bore no relation to their market value. When in 1911, for instance, a male worker in industry might expect to draw £2 13s 9d a week a footballer could earn up to £5. In 1920 the players' union had forced wages up to a maximum of £9; in disgust many players quit the union and the League consequently felt justified and able, in 1922, to reduce the wage limits to £8 and £6. Furthermore, the players who had led the union agitation were faced by open discrimination, particularly about international honours. These were of course the years of arbitrary wage cuts in industry at large and the football mandarins apparently saw nothing wrong or unusual in taking political and economic advantage of the men whose efforts kept them in office.

Throughout the years of depression, the wage limits of 1922 remained intact. Again, comparisons with the £3 weekly industrial wage of 1924–38, for a forty-six-hour week, put the footballer in a favourable light, particularly since he could often work locally in the summer. But in 1945 the Professional Footballers' Association began to press for a rise in wages, which had remained static for twenty-three years. Indeed disgruntlement with wages had led to a sharp rise in union membership, from 434 in 1929 to 1,900 in 1939. By any standard, the footballer was in need of a new deal; in manufacturing industries, for instance, wages had doubled between 1938 and 1945. But before major changes were implemented both in the level and structure of footballers' pay, the union had to threaten strike action and take its case to arbitration. The minor concessions won after the affair, however, were only stepping-stones towards a more equitable pay structure for footballers, and they had to wait until 1961 before economic and social justice was finally wrenched from the authorities.

The reluctance to pay footballers a fair wage is difficult to explain. Certainly in the immediate post-war years there was no shortage of money in top-class football (where wages were most obviously an inadequate return on a player's drawing power), for the stadiums were regularly packed. Entrance fees were, admittedly, low, but so too were the clubs' overheads of travel and expenses. Nor was the money invested in the football stadiums, which remained in their early twentieth-century condition (adequate by the standards of 1914 but crude and often dangerous in 1945). Indeed it was only the decline in attendances in the 1950s which forced the management to look to their rusting girders, crumbling terraces and medieval lavatories. It is also true, however, that in the late 1940s the government and a parsimonious Civil Service refused the necessary permission for ground improvements. Material was scarce for every form of post-war reconstruction, from housing to industrial plant, and it seemed wasteful to grant licenses and material for shoring up football stadiums.

The years after the war accentuated the sharp contrast between football's commercial health and its Scrooge-like image as an employer. The game abounded with tales of stars, returning from playing before tens of thousands of people, forced to stand in the corridors of trains' cheapest class. People flocked to professional games as never before; the post-1919 boom paled into insignificance. Stadiums were regularly crowded, often to dangerous levels; in many cases the record attendances at individual grounds belong to these years. Indeed the all-time peak of football attendance came in 1948–9 when more than 41 million people filed through the turnstiles. Annual attendances were staggering:

1946–7	35,604,606
1947–8	41,259,130
1948–9	41,271,424
1949–50	40,517,865
1950–1	39,584,987
1951–2	39,015,866

At the end of the first post-war season (which was a replica of the cancelled 1939 fixtures) all but six of the professional clubs made profits, led by Stoke City with a (then) thumping £32,207. Football was not alone in enjoying this post-war bumper harvest of pleasure-seekers. Wherever we look, a similar story unfolds. Cricket crowds were unprecedented. The wonderful summer of 1947 saw three million people flock to cricket grounds. Much the same was true of all other sports – major and minor; from the dog-tracks (45 million in 1946) to speedway (300,000 a week in 1946). And similar examples could be cited from one sport to another, from boxing to athletics, from tennis to horse-racing. Even fox-hunting boomed (with 190 packs in 1953). For those with a more active bent, cycling clubs were healthier than ever. Dance halls – 450 by the late 1940s – and of course the cinemas, lured people in their millions. And, because millions more were entitled to holidays with pay (the 1938 Holidays with Pay Act had been delayed until after the war), millions flocked to their favourite seaside resort; that lemming-like rush to the water's edge which had characterized the British people for a century past. Now, the numbers were staggering. In 1949, 30 million people went to the seaside. Resorts were heaving with visitors; photographs of the summer beaches in the late 1940s show scarcely an inch of available space. Resort after resort recorded their best tourist figures in the post-war years. Football's popularity in the late 1940s was, then, part of a much broader outburst of pleasure-seeking, as the British people returned to their traditional pleasures with a vigour and on a scale never witnessed before.

Not surprisingly, football was strengthened after the war. Excluding football in the armed forces, universities and public schools, in 1949–50 there were an amazing 31,219 registered football clubs. While there were some 500 clubs which employed professionals (numbering some 7,000 in all), more than 30,000 were completely amateur. They too shared in the boom after 1945 and attendances at their games rocketed. In 1946, 1947 and 1948, for instance, the crowds, at the Amateur Cup finals doubled the pre-war figures and the English FA was forced to transfer the game to Wembley, where, in 1949, 95,000 people watched the final.

These crowds brought serious problems of industrial absenteeism in the major cities. Though the Labour government was ever anxious to goad the workforce to greater productivity, 'national interest' usually took second place to football. In February 1945, for example, the *Manchester Guardian* noted that 'The problem of "footballing absenteeism" has been particulary serious in Birmingham this week.' In fact this 'problem' flitted from city to city, depending on the fortunes of local teams. The same problem plagued Manchester as late as 1951 (though the pattern was to last to the present day). Anxious to clear a back-log of work in the Manchester docks brought on by a strike, the Docks Board ordered local dockers not to watch a game between Manchester United and Birmingham City. The dockers, predictably, left work for the stadium and the Board's contingency plan for importing dockers from Fleetwood was thwarted when they found the Fleetwood men to be watching a match in Blackpool. Midweek football was particularly troublesome and the government, after trying to ban it, was forced to relent and instead sanctioned the staggering of working hours in affected areas.

Football of course was itself an industry. The takings for the 1947–8 season topped £4 million, while the pools, restarted in their separate form in 1946, took on the trappings of a distinct and major industry. Their income rose amazingly: £20 million in 1935; £44,450,000 in 1936; £50 million in 1939. In December 1946 alone the pools companies presented no fewer than 24,309,137 postal orders to the Post Office, suggesting an average of 7–8 million punters each week. By the early 1950s the pools and related gambling concerns had become the nation's seventh largest industry, employing some 100,000 people. By 1948 the pools paid £12½ million in taxes and £2 million into the Post Office. Such economic power eroded the 'moral' opposition to the pools and gradually both government and football authorities came to view them as economically vital. More than that, the pools had become a form of social activity which drew people together, to discuss, plan their strategy and pool their money – and winnings. They were also, in the words of a recent historian of the pools, 'the working-class equivalent of *The Times* crossword, testing knowledge as part of working-class culture.' Moreover, unlike so many other formal pleasures, the pools enabled women to take part.

In the late 1940s football expanded in all directions, notably among the young. The game had of course been enormously popular with the young throughout the century, but hitherto had generally lacked the incentives of competitions and trophies. After the war this changed, and County Youth Championships, International Youth tournaments, Youth International Championships and later the Youth Cups provided a clearer framework for the development of young footballers – and of course gave the professional clubs a new opportunity for assessing future talent. In addition, football authorities were anxious to introduce the young to up-to-date coaching. In part this new emphasis on coaching was derived from the pioneering tactical and 'scientific' work of the professional clubs in the 1930s. But the war too had played an enormous part through the military preoccupation with physical fitness (in its turn to remedy the genuinely debilitating effects of urban life), and the efforts of hordes of highly trained PT instructors. Wartime experience confirmed the value of a controlled, professional approach to recreation and the post-war reconstruction of football – along with most other sports – made full use of these lessons through peripatetic professional coaches who visited schools and youth organizations. Ultimately this innovation was to culminate in the sophisticated coaching schemes of the present day and the even more elaborate courses for training coaches – all of them operated by the parent FAs.

Before these improvements could make themselves felt, indeed before the post-war game had begun, British football was given what ought to have been a healthy jolt by a visiting team; a reminder that football abroad had progressed to an unexpected and amazingly accomplished level. In November 1945 Moscow Dynamo – the team whose foundations were laid by British workers in pre-revolutionary Russia – made a tour of Britain, in the process revealing a degree of professional excellence and ruthless competitiveness which alarmed observers. Dynamo (who were in fact a national Russian team) bore no resemblance to the scratch team set up by the Lancashire textile men in the 1880s. The Russians came to Britain as allies, but they also came as the sporting representatives of an assertive Stalinist Russia. They were a totally unknown quantity, neither amateur nor professional, but nonetheless able to draw enormous crowds wherever they played (a hint of the hunger for the game at the end of the war). Their first game, against Chelsea at Stamford Bridge, was watched by 82,000. Not surprisingly, the FA was instantly deluged with requests from other clubs anxious to play the Russians. The 3–3 draw with Chelsea was followed by a 10–1 victory over Cardiff before 45,000, a fog-bound, farcical win over Arsenal (4–3) before 54,000, and finally a 2–2 draw with Glasgow Rangers in front of 90,000 Glaswegians.

The four games proved a disturbing experience from many viewpoints. British football had been accustomed to more than fifty years of unchallenged superiority (the occasional international defeat scarcely ruffling the game's surface) and the abrasive and highly successful football of Dynamo proved unsettling for players and spectators alike. Given the havoc caused by the war in Russia, the British could scarcely take shelter behind arguments of post-war dislocation. Even before a ball had been kicked the Russians had bemused the FA with a series of fourteen conditions which they insisted on being fulfilled before they played. Most notably, they insisted on using their own Russian officials in at least one game; they took their meals at the Russian Embassy and, in good capitalist spirit, agreed to take fifty per cent of the proceeds. Many of the more technical points in their demands were difficult to meet and though all were ultimately resolved, the episode indicated the bureaucratic and diplomatic niceties which were later to reach absurd proportions as international contacts expanded, and as national peculiarities within football brought home to the founding nation the divergencies in what seemed on the surface to be a uniform game.

On reflection, however, contemporary observers were surprised by the quality of the Russian play. 'Surprise of the tour,' said the *Sunday Chronicle*, 'was not so much the results – the British teams were not yet in full-training – as the impressively high standard of the Russians' attacking play. In positional work and crisp, ground combination, they were captivating. Every bit as good as the Austrians in these arts, they reached greater heights near goal than the team from Vienna, because of stronger shooting power.' The teamwork, discipline, retreating defence, but above all else the attacking flair forcibly struck spectators, particularly the older players who had memories of the British game before 1914. It was in fact apparent to many of the game's observers that the former pupils had become every bit as good as the masters; indeed the

Russians' football had enhanced some of British football's long-forgotten qualities.

Even more disturbing, however, were the wider questions raised by the success of Moscow Dynamo. If football had progressed so remarkably in Russia since those pioneering days of British influence, what had happened elsewhere, in parts of the world more noticeably affected by the game? But with isolated exceptions, British football remained unconcerned by the lessons of the Russian visit.

Once the Russians had gone home (to become Heroes of the Soviet Union) the questions raised by their visit were soon submerged by the continuing domestic boom. The pattern of isolationist attitudes which had characterized football between the wars once more reasserted itself. But the international experiences in these boom years confirmed the relative international decline of the home game. Despite the appointment of an international manager, the English (and other British) teams began to meet serious challenges in the late 1940s. Moreover, the organization of English international teams ran counter to the needs and interests of club football – the bed-rock strength of the domestic game. The amazing teamwork and unity of the wartime English national team crumbled in peacetime as players left the forces (which had helped to perfect that teamwork) and moved back to their clubs, who insisted upon the players' undivided attention – for a maximum of £10 a week. The professional game thereafter slid into an apparently paradoxical position with, on the one hand the world's most numerous (and some of its finest) football clubs, and on the other hand a disproportionately weak national team. It seemed that the one could only be strengthened at the expense of the other and it was to be a further twenty years before the conflicting interests, of clubs versus country, were partially reconciled.

In organizational terms, the English FA decided to rejoin the international footballing authority, FIFA, from which it had been absent through most of the inter-war years. When international negotiations began in 1945 (with the English automatically invited) it seemed at first sight as if the representatives from the Allied side would repeat the mistakes of 1919. FIFA resolved that since their aim was 'to foster friendly relations between the National Associations it is not possible at present to entertain such relations with the subjects of Germany and Japan'. Fortunately, this politically exclusive mentality soon evaporated, and Germany was allowed to re-establish herself as one of the foremost footballing nations. In this, as in most other areas of economic and social life, Germany bounced back from the devastation of 1945 to European leadership within a decade. It is fair to say, however, that the antagonisms of both wars were and are periodically and tastelessly rekindled, notably by the press, whenever the British and Germans meet on the football field.

Having joined the international football circuit, it was natural that England should compete, for the first time, in the World Cup when it was played in Brazil in 1950. In the preceding years there had been clear signs of the relative decline of English international football, but nothing to suggest the weakness of the first English contribution to what had already established itself as the high point of football as an international game. A series of lame performances culminated in a defeat by the USA. This result was undoubtedly a freak, but it served to highlight a major weakness which perceptive English critics and foreign observers had discussed for some time. As early as 1945, much of the surprise about the Dynamo visit was because 'the public had been slow to realise how the game has developed abroad and how brilliantly foreign teams play'. It was thought that English football was 'at the crossroads because of the more artistic standard of play revealed abroad'. While the English game was basking in its inter-war superiority and its post-war boom, one perceptive ex-footballer turned-journalist noted, 'the foreigner has stepped ahead of us in his style of play . . . We exported the goods and lost the knack of making them'. The 1948 Olympic Games in London had provided further evidence of rising world standards – but little heed was taken. By 1950 the pattern was clear. According to Pozzo, the English-trained mastermind of Italian football, 'Continental teams can read English teams like an open book, as your players behave in International Games absolutely the same as in League games; same moves, same tactics, same tendencies – all on one pattern.'

The Scots experience was even worse. They did not compete until the 1954 World Cup in Switzerland where they were quickly revealed to be inadequately prepared. Officials were divided about whether it was a good idea to be there at all,

Rangers players were absent on a club tour of North America, there was a confusion about dates, they took no training kit and had only 13 players (instead of 22). Not surprisingly, they were eventually trounced 7–1 by Uruguay. In 1950 and 1954, the British teams had been confronted by indisputable evidence of their own relative decline. As competent as they seemed on their own patch, they now ventured abroad at risk to their sporting records.

By the early 1950s the British game had begun to face problems. On the one hand, more than 40 million people had flocked to see the season's games in 1950, but on the other, the foreign challenge at the World Cup had highlighted England's international weaknesses. Moreover, a small number of star players had quit the home game for a seductive (and in the main unrealized) promises of riches in South America. The truth behind these 'illegal' defections to Eldorado was simply that British footballers were badly paid at home, and like most other people were keen to capitalize on their skills. Paradoxically, while British footballers were in great demand abroad, the British national teams had ceased to be dominant. Football's problems were compounded further when, in the 1950–1 season, for the first time since the war, attendances showed a major fall. Admission prices rose, and the English Football League responded to demands for increased broadcasting of matches by banning it completely.

As the new decade advanced, evidence mounted that the boom period was over while at the same time the hard face of post-war austerity began to give way to the first signs of material prosperity. In 1952–3 football attendances fell by two million; in the following year by an even more alarming four million. Progressive proposals to face the rising challenge of contraction in the game and the related rise of a more prosperous society, able to divert its spare money and energies into new fields of social and recreational activities, were dismissed by the authorities, and the game struggled on, into a new age of practically universal insolvency, dwindling crowds and chronic indecision. Supporting a structure and rationale designed in the 1920s, the game lumbered into the age of the affluent society.

In many respects British international football might appear to be distinct and isolated from the domestic game's social roots. In fact it tends to reflect both the strengths and the weaknesses of the national game. When in November 1953 the Hungarians (like the Russians of 1945, former pupils of British footballing missionaries), drubbed the England team 6–3 at Wembley, there was no disputing that primacy had slipped away from the founding fathers. The game in Britain nonetheless remained extremely strong, growing in size, firmly rooted in the school system and widely popular at the informal, grass-roots of society. But despite this, it had failed to produce an adequate challenge to European and South American football. A discrepancy had developed between potential and reality. That discrepancy was born of distinctly historical factors; namely the earlier primacy which had generated marked insularity. By 1953, after the Hungarian visit to London, but, more fundamentally, in the face of a rapidly changing society which was ready to reject traditionally accepted patterns of social behaviour, it had become vital for British football to recast its aspirations and shake off its limiting insularity. It was imperative that it should involve itself more closely with the game abroad, particularly in Europe, if only to keep in the mainstream of tactical change and progress. But such a move involved a change of heart – a quality not easily found in football's administrative circles. Most managers, directors and officials, brought up in a game which had enjoyed the undivided loyalties of the fans, saw little need to look abroad. Happily, however, there were a few isolated men in powerful positions who, like their counterparts in politics in the same years, spoke up in favour of a wider view; who saw in Europe (and South America) a challenge which British football could ignore at its peril. Indeed the debate about Britain's role in a wider European community found a close parallel within the football world, where, as at Westminster, 'Europeans' found themselves for many years waging an uphill and apparently unpopular battle. Much of the problem lay in officialdom; among those (often) older men versed in different habits. The amateur directors of clubs, the stuffier officials on central committees, all found it hard to give way to a new breed of professional managers who viewed the game differently – at home and abroad. Slowly, however, the professionals began to turn the tide.

In the late 1950s and 1960s football's handful of Europeans dragged British football into the European arena – both for good and evil. The modern game, in which the British played a part in the European and even global game, was in no small measure due to the efforts of a small band of men in redirecting football's attention outward. For an increasingly prosperous and leisure-minded society, the attractions and rewards of foreign football were ever more appealing. But what a contrast this made to the dourness and austerity which had characterized British football, like British society, in the years between 1939 and the early 1950s. Football had been forced to change to fit the unusual conditions of war. In 1945 the game had been able to capture unprecedented crowds by simple force of habit and by the nation's collective urge to enjoy themselves as never before. But within five years, it was clear that the old habits, the old pleasures fashioned over the past century, were no longer adequate to the task of entertaining a rapidly changing nation. More and more people found themselves with more spare cash and more free time than their parents could ever have dreamt of. As society lurched into that first phase of material prosperity which shaped the face of modern Britain, football, like most other recreations, found itself confronting problems of adjustment on a scale and a pace it could scarcely comprehend. The game which, at the turn of the century had been given its modern direction by the rise of material well-being among millions of working men, now found itself dislocated by economic changes of an even more fundamental nature.

8 More Prosperous Times

The changes which affected the western world in the twenty years from the early 1950s were so fundamental that they served to transform the face of the world at large. What was true of Britain was also true of Western Europe as a whole – and even more so of the United States. Everywhere, the substance of material well-being – the artefacts of affluence which, today, we take for granted but which, in those years, were new and exciting – reshaped the nature of people's lives and enhanced their expectations. The economies of the west yielded ever more material bounty to more and more people. It became commonplace to speak of the 'affluent society'. The economic and technological changes which spawned that economic growth saw a massive rise in real wages and a consequent diffusion of higher standards, most notably to those social groups – working people – whose lives had been characterised for generations past by meagre surroundings and humble life-styles. Of course there were millions who remained untouched by these material improvements, notably the old and the sick, for whom the improvements around them merely underlined their own relative deprivation. In a world where more people were enjoying better standards of life, those who failed to keep up felt their poverty more acutely.

Millions of people in Britain found themselves with money to spare. They also found themselves seduced by retailers of goods the likes of which their parents could only have dreamt about. After almost a decade of wartime and post-war austerity (to say nothing of the privations of the 1920s and 1930s), it was as if the British people were let off the economic leash. There was a quite extraordinary explosion in consumer spending, as the British people found themselves with more money to spend, and a dazzling variety of things to spend it on. While the proportion of the total national expenditure spent on food remained unusually stable, the amounts spent on new forms of leisure escalated beyond all imagination. Money spent on cars is a fair index of what was happening: £90 million in 1951, £910 million in 1964. Expenditure on furniture and electrical goods rose from £526 in 1951 to £975 million in 1964. Television is another relevant example; by the early 1960s it had entered four out of five homes. By the mid-1970s failure to own or rent a set was tantamount to an admission of social eccentricity. All those items we now take for granted – vacuum cleaners, fridges, washing machines – all and more found their way into a majority of the nation's homes. More than that, ever more people were buying their own homes. Homes, especially among working people, shed their stark, minimalist look and became the place to display new-found personal prosperity in the form of a range of new household goods.

Television and private transport epitomized the change in spending patterns and in their turn came to exert their own powerful influence over social life. The cumulative effects of expanding TV-watching was the emergence of television as a pace-setter for social style and taste to a degree which at times seemed alarming. As old social customs and patterns of leisure began to give way to the pressure of new tastes and wider ambitions, football, too, was profoundly affected. Having emerged in the late nineteenth century as a function of the improvements in working-class living standards, from the early 1950s it began to respond to the changes brought about by prosperity and changing leisure interests.

It would have been difficult for football, like so many other leisure pursuits, to improve on the boom years of 1945–52. The game had begun to falter, though it was scarcely perceptible at the time, between 1949 and 1951, but the decline quickened and became a matter of alarm between 1952 and 1954 when attendances fell by a disturbing six million. By 1955–6 the annual attendance had fallen to 33.31 million (a fall of seven million from the post-war peak). In 1960–1 this slid down to 28.6 million and by 1964–5 to 27.6 million. By 1984–5 the figure stood at 17.8 million. Compared with the collapse of the cinema industry and considering the more comfortable attractions of TV for instance (to say nothing of the physical privations of attendance at a football match), it is remarkable that football retained such a considerable following. But it is significant that this fall in attendance up to the mid-1960s was not evenly distributed throughout all professional divisions. The best leagues and teams lost fans at a lower rate than others, an indication perhaps of increasing discrimination among spectators.

It was, above all else, the fact of alternative forms of leisure (some of them within the home) which undermined football's following at the turnstiles. There were many other, more comfortable – and even more attractive – ways of enjoying free time. Other social changes in British society were more subtle, less discernible initially but perhaps in the long term no less influential. Most notable perhaps were the changes in female expectations and demands. From the first, football had been a man's game; played and watched overwhelmingly by men. In the changing climate of a prospering Britain, more and more men were no longer able, as their forebears had been, simply to do as they wished. Many took heed of their womenfolk's interests; many wanted to spend their free time in the company of their spouses and companions. The sexually segregated world of masculine pleasures – of which the male team games had been (along with the pub) the best examples – were less attractive to women. And more and more of those women were able, unlike their female forebears, to have their say in the way their menfolk spent their free time – and money. The old icebergs of British social groupings were changing quite dramatically in the warmer climate of material prosperity.

More specific factors might help to explain the declining and changing attendance patterns, particularly of the 1960s. Television coverage of football which came to the fore in that decade understandably focused on top-class football, in domestic, European and World competitions. Football in lower divisions is, obviously, less attractive to viewers. But the consequences of exposing TV audiences to the very best football has had repercussions on football in lower leagues. The yardstick, the assessment of the game took on an entirely different character. Previously, spectators tended to see only the games they attended. Now, thanks to TV, they could see the best in the country – and even further afield. They began to compare the fare they watched locally with better football on display elsewhere. Of course allegiance to a team often transcended the team's obvious limitations, and local loyalties continued to survive despite these various changes in society at large.

To make matters more difficult for smaller clubs, many of them were progressively eclipsed by more attractive, bigger clubs in the region. The great majority of the bigger, professional clubs are concentrated in the major urban and industrial cities of Britain and have, in effect, acted as magnets, drawing fans from throughout their hinterland, often from towns which maintain their own local club. In this they have been helped by the improvements in roads and private transport. It is now almost as simple to travel to watch the nearest top-class team as it is to watch a closer local game. This pull of the bigger clubs in any region has become a key factor in the redistribution of fans. Leeds drew support from a wide area of Yorkshire, draining supporters from small clubs; Liverpool, Everton and Manchester United dominated the north-west of the country, while the currently successful, bigger clubs in the midlands and London can have much the same effect on their smaller neighbours. A similar story can be told of Glasgow. Why bother to watch a poorer local team when a first-class fixture is available close by? In all this, improvement in the road networks and the increase in car ownership have helped. The new network of motorways enables major teams regularly to draw thousands of spectators from a greatly expanded catchment area. It is the curse of managers of smaller clubs to watch coaches and carloads of local people setting off for the big cities while the local team plays before sparsely attended terraces. Many of the bigger clubs no longer have to rely solely on local support for their attendances, though it clearly still constitutes the bulk of their following. Fans' banners and signs paraded at the games, draped over railings, and waved from passing vehicles, proclaiming their local origins, testify to the remarkably diverse geography of support for the bigger clubs.

These new patterns of support, with a handful of clubs drawing the lion's share of the game's support – and income – created new contours to the professional game in Britain. But the overall geography remained recognisable to anyone familiar with the game's history. Bigger clubs have been able, on the whole, to maintain their pre-eminence, seeking to secure their success by buying new players. Of course, money does not always guarantee success, and there have been celebrated cases of major clubs sliding into footballing decline despite lavishing money on their teams. But it is certainly the case that smaller clubs have found it ever more difficult to live in the shadow of the bigger teams. Even when they develop their own talent, they generally find it impossible to resist the blandishments of hefty transfer fees; the players themselves, anxious to improve themselves in what is a short-lived career, are equally reluctant to remain with a smaller club when in demand by a major team.

The years of rising prosperity in the nation at large produced, then, a series of convulsions in the story of modern British football. It was inevitable that some of the old clubs would not survive the changed economic and social environment. Symbolically, it was Accrington Stanley, one of the oldest of English professional clubs, which was forced to withdraw from the League in 1961–2. Once a prosperous late-nineteenth-century industrial town, Accrington shared the fate of the declining fortunes of King Cotton and, in leisure and recreational terms, proved too close to bigger, more successful and attractive cities. Accrington Stanley was an extreme case of a wider problem facing all the minor professional clubs; namely how best to compete with illustrious neighbours for the support and money of increasingly discriminating spectators.

The story of British football in the generation from the mid-1950s cannot be told simply in terms of income and balance sheets – though at every turn the complex question of money intrudes into the debate. For a small band of idealists and leaders – in a game which was, year after year, characterised by a remarkable lack of vision – the game's future and well-being was ultimately tied to Europe. Any surviving instinct of insular sporting superiority was, as we have seen, dashed by the devastating visit of the Hungarians in 1953. As if the point needed reinforcement, in the following years the English were beaten 7–1 in Budapest. It was all grist to the mill of those who looked to Europe for the future of the game. Of course, it was no simple matter. Moreover, the fate of Europe's footballing future was clearly bound up with the development of the European Community. Here, once again, the British found themselves lagging behind the rest.

The movement towards political and economic integration, culminating in the establishment of the EEC by the Treaty of Rome in 1957, had gathered momentum in the late 1940s and early 1950s. Sustained by the post-war economic revival, European integration was borne along by a determination to eliminate the all-too-recent national antagonisms. At every level of society, from politics and high finance to education and sport, there were growing numbers of people who looked towards an integrated European future. The concept of a united European economy held enormous attractions for the captains of industry. Others, however, for a host of sectional, traditional reasons, found the idea much less attractive.

Few areas of European social life seemed more obviously amenable and geared towards international activity than sport – especially football. By the late 1950s the world football body, FIFA, was fifty years old and had, for all the political fluctuations of the past half-century, adequately supervised the evolution of football as a world game. At the global level, as in Britain, the strength of football was of course not institutional or bureaucratic but social. Football had become a world game for many of the reasons which had shaped its emergence as the British national game. Football had in fact become a sporting Esperanto – a form of human association which defied language and cultural divisions and which could be played between men who knew nothing of each other, who had little in common except their commitment and ability at football. By the mid-1950s, after some half-century of embryonic international football, it seemed feasible, in the new climate in Europe, to provide club football (where the professional game was at its strongest) with a European structure. Once again, however, the British remained on the fringes, watching events with interest but very little enthusiasm, excepting that small band of idealists.

In 1955 the French sporting newspaper *L'Équipe* convened a gathering of prominent European club officials. Their deliberations produced the European Cup, a knock-out tournament on a home-and-away basis for the continent's various champions. European club football was set in motion in the 1955–6 season. True to form, however, the English were prominent by their absence, for the Football League had persuaded the English champions, Chelsea, not to enter, for fear of interfering with their home commitments. (Few seemed to notice the Ruritanian quality of missives issuing from Lytham, the League's Lancastrian redoubt, designed to keep English football out of Europe.) Happily, the English game possessed managers of stature who, in contrast to the unduly influential sporting administrators, sought to reconcile football to the rapidly changing social circumstances (both in relation to TV coverage and European football). Moreover, the Scots, through Hibernian, had entered European football from the first and their example (and their profits) had pointed the way to a lucrative and enlightening experience. In 1956 yet another Scot, Matt Busby, whose youthful Manchester United team won the Championship, ignored the League's advice and committed his team to Europe. Busby had long been attracted to the idea of international club football and, with the ageing of his excellent team of the 1940s, had made elaborate preparations for the recruitment of young footballers. Indeed he was a pioneer both in youth football and in the European game, the one providing the necessary pool of talent for the heavy demands of the other. It was, yet again, no accident that English football was steered in the right direction by a Scot. It was an old story, as interesting as it remains perplexing.

1957-8 marked a turning-point in the story of English football and the story of those years belongs to Manchester United, for their success at home and in Europe, cut short by the Munich air crash of 6 February 1958, carved out for the club and the manager (and for one young survivor, Bobby Charlton) a special place in football history and in the memories of any sports fan old enough to remember those cold February days. There were, of course, other sporting disasters; other teams and games destroyed by accidents and killings. But it is impossible to discuss the recent story of British football without recognizing the ramifications of the Munich air crash, both on the game itself and on the creation of a mythology which seemed to grow more potent with the passage of time.

Thwarted of the Double in 1957 only by an eminently avoidable injury in the Cup final, defeated in the European Cup semi-final by the incomparable Real Madrid, Manchester United entered the 1957-8 season with a flair and a confidence which belied their youth. All seemed to be set for an even more successful season, only to be destroyed by the Munich air crash. England's most adventurous club, in their most exciting enterprise, was shattered. The city of Manchester, which had warmed to the team's unique talents, responded to their death with a grieving affection which carried the makeshift team of survivors and young players to an unsuccessful Cup final appearance that same year. No discussion about Manchester United and their subsequent successes and failures in the intervening years has any meaning unless set in the context of February 1958. It was the year of unrealised promise Any future achievements – and failures – would henceforth be set in the balance against what might have happened. Ten years later, Manchester United became the first English team to win the European Cup, in pursuit of which the earlier team had died, but the success of May 1968 was tempered by unavoidable thoughts of what might have been.

Ironically, despite the Munich disaster, the decision to enter European competitions was more than justified. Moreover, the accident raised a debate about the pros and cons of similar competitions. Nonetheless, European football rapidly became the prime ambition of Britain's leading clubs. It was only a matter of time before numbers of British teams jostled for places in the European competitions which soon proliferated; European Cup, European Cup Winners' Cup, Inter-City Fairs Cup, UEFA Cup and then a spate of minor and, in some cases, ill-fated competitions. But the very proliferation of such contexts is testimony to the continuing lure of European competition – and the financial rewards they are expected to bring. Once British clubs developed the taste for such competitions, or more important after they began to appreciate the profits involved, it was only a matter of time before the strength of British club football began to impress itself on Europe, though it is arguable that, with a few notable exceptions, they have failed to rise to the peaks of virtuosity displayed by the best European teams.

British football was transformed by the wider challenge of European competitions, which became an end in themselves. The financial rewards from Europe were/are enormous, and it soon appeared that the winning of prestigious trophies at home was valued merely as an entrée to Europe. Fittingly, the greatest prize, the European Cup, fell first to the Scots, and Celtic, and then to Manchester United (led by a Scot), though other teams won less prestigious trophies. In the process, the fans of the bigger clubs took to the air to follow their team. Tens of thousands of them, using the recently devised cheap travel and hotel organizations, were now able to fly throughout Europe simply to watch a football match. In what was a remarkable leap in the nature of support, tens of thousands of football fans took planes to distant cities. In the late 1960s and early 1970s, for instance, armies of Glaswegians descended from the skies onto the unsuspecting cities of Lisbon, Milan and Barcelona. Of course their travels were but another aspect of the burgeoning air-travel industry in those years. British holiday-makers had begun to desert their traditional seaside resorts at home for the guaranteed warmth of Southern Europe. And the more they travelled, the more commonplace the idea of air travel became. It also became cheaper. In an age of cheap charter air travel, a one-day visit to the far fringes of Europe seemed no more extravagant than an epic overnight journey on a steam train from Glasgow to London in the 1930s.

By the late 1950s the British could no longer ignore football in the wider world. They were actively involved in European competitions and, henceforth, keen to take part in the World Cup tournaments played every four years. Here was the world game played at its best; a stage on which countries and individuals displayed their sporting prowess and their individual flair. Though the British teams had ambitions of success in Sweden in 1958, the displays of the Brazilians – best remembered for the virtuosity of the teenage Pele (though he was only one of an array of dazzling stars) – removed any doubts about the nature and quality of football in other parts of the world. There were, it is true, some aspects of the South American game which the Europeans did not like (and which journalists tended to put down to vague factors such as 'national temperament' or the 'Latin spirit'). But there was no denying the levels of artistic achievement and athletic ability which underpinned such success.

The world's greatest teams and players were, by the late 1950s, more likely to be found in South America than in Europe. Indeed it was becoming clearer by the year that footballing talent had no obvious national boundaries; no natural source of local inspiration. Its historical point of origin mattered little, for it was a game driven forward, throughout the world, by a widening and infectious support among untold millions of people who knew nothing, and cared even less, about where and how the game originated. The pioneering British footballing traditions were of no more than passing or antiquarian interest. It was clear, by the end of the 1950s, that great footballers were just as likely to emerge from the shanty towns of Brazil as from the tough tenements of Glasgow. And as enthusiasm for the game spread world-wide, footballing talent began to appear in a host of societies – in Africa, Asia and in Arab states – places which would, not long before, have seemed hostile environments to football.

Many observers found it tempting to impute the success of new footballing nations – especially the South Americans – to flair, to local genius, but it was clear enough that training and preparation were no less important. Both in 1958 and 1962 much of the Brazilian World Cup success was the fruit of utterly unpredictable and intuitive athletic genius, the precise origins of which defy analysis. The Brazilians clearly had unrivalled talent, but they were also tuned physically and mentally to an intensity unknown in British football. The Austrian team of the 1930s and the Hungarians in the early 1950s displayed similar combinations of thorough preparation and natural talent. It seemed unusual, given the enormous popular bed-rock of British soccer, that no such combination had materialized in its national teams.

In fact a greater degree of professionalism had entered the management and preparation of British national teams by the late 1950s. Teams met as long in advance as possible and were provided with up-to-date facilities and expertise. But it was not until 1966, and then on their home ground at Wembley, that England was able to win the World Cup. The Scots fared even worse. Time and again, their efforts to make an impression in World Cup tournaments failed, despite a barrage of preceding promises and despite the obvious array of footballing talent. There was a curious conundrum here. Both in Scotland and England, the club traditions remained vital and attractive. Yet they failed to nurture success for the national teams. Of course it needs to be stressed that so many of the best English club teams hinged on their Scottish players. The English clubs were always going to be better than the national team because they relied so heavily on players – especially the Scots – from throughout the British Isles. As we have seen, this was a tradition which stretched back to the 1880s. But it also helps to explain the continuing discrepancy between the quality of club as opposed to national football.

The problem of British football – manifested in its international failing in the 1950s and 1960s – went much deeper than events on the field. While it is true that football was making determined efforts to close the gap which had widened, in the insular years, between British and foreign football, the professional players were employed on terms which would have scandalized footballers abroad and appeared inadequate even by comparison with other working men at home. Among international footballers, the British were the poor relations, for they were shackled to an industry which was characterized by appalling labour relations and by an attitude towards labour which had disappeared in all but football (and, worse still, cricket) and the domestic trades. Most clubs and the administration viewed footballers in an appallingly crude light; footballers were simply working men able to earn, for a few short years, moderate wages and the game was thought to offer a preferable alternative to the labouring and unskilled work into which they would otherwise have been forced. Even outsiders favourable to the game thought that footballers, basking in local popularity, were relatively well paid for their weekly work of one-and-a-half hours' football. From the players' viewpoint, however, the most important element which affected their working lives was the structure and personnel of league management.

The English Football League had changed little in its view towards footballers since the early twentieth century, as a report of 1966 noted: 'They were directed by people who in their professional lives (mainly in commerce and small industry) were accustomed, in common with industrial practice at that time, to govern in an autocratic manner.' The history of industrial relations in the game had been appalling. Throughout the twentieth century a string of players had fought back, sometimes alone, sometimes through their weak union, to secure the rights and treatment granted to other groups. But throughout, players seemed able to break out of the game's unjust restrictions on their earnings only by deals outside the game, by bending the rules, or by going abroad. The awareness of footballing rewards abroad, especially in the 1950s and 1960s, served to anger British players, and though the wage limits were progressively raised, the matter of principle remained; management and administrators insisted, as an article of faith, that players' earnings should be strictly capped. This had never been true in Scotland, however. But there, no less than in England, the game was held in the grip of paternalistic management which paid scant attention to the players' material well-being, preferring instead to pay wages which were only marginally above the level of local artisan earnings. The players, through their union the PFA, were struggling against a massive obstacle, but in 1958 had been able to force the maximum wage up to £20 a week (£17 in summer). The very concept of a maximum wage was a particular grievance but it was rooted in the voting power of the smaller clubs, who were generally afraid of the financial power of the bigger clubs in a free market. As if this were not bad enough for the players, the prevailing transfer system enabled a club to hang on to a player even against his wishes and, in extreme cases, made it virtually impossible for him to continue his career. Such restraints on trade guaranteed that footballers were perpetually and lowly paid indentured workers, and the system led, as unjust systems tend to do, to methods of circumventing the rules which were 'illegal' in the eyes of the law-makers. Skilled players were penalized and were able to earn little more than the honest artisans in lower divisions; there were few career prospects and players generally looked forward to humble positions on retirement.

For years until the late 1950s the players were represented by a doughty Scot, Jimmie Guthrie. But his pugnacious style often served to alienate rather than win over the clubs, and though he made notable gains for the players, he gained little personally, save for management hostility and even banishment from football grounds. Men who spoke the simple truths of trade-union rights were unwelcome to footballing authorities. In his successor, Jimmy Hill, however, the game's managers faced a more skilled and subtle opponent. An articulate man, a fine player and manager, and an accomplished speaker at ease before TV cameras, Hill proved more than a match for the industrial dinosaurs of football. Hill's success, however, was based on footballers' genuine complaints. Dissatisfaction among players was, justifiably, widespread and finally, though not for the first time, in 1960 after months of static negotiations, the PFA threatened to strike. Though the issue passed to the Ministry of

Labour, it took this strike threat, repeated in 1961, before the employers agreed to abolish the maximum wage. Even then, however, the arguments were not over and it was only in 1963, when George Eastham, in dispute with his club Newcastle United, challenged the club's legal right to retain a player against his wishes, that players were granted the freedom of movement which was long a basic right in other occupations. The High Court judgement in the Eastham case, that the rules under which football had operated for three quarters of a century were *ultra vires*, was eloquent testimony to the squalid nature of football's industrial relations for so long. 'The basic problem has been,' commented the PEP report of 1966, 'that the Football League have failed to understand and sympathise with the problems of the professional player, and have been slow to shed an autocratic attitude which the players could not be expected to accept in modern conditions.' The consequence of this freeing of trade is that today's best players can earn more in a week than their predecessors earned in a year. Some can earn more in a month than old stars earned in their lifetime.

Not surprisingly, top-class footballers sought to capitalize on their skills (often very briefly) in European countries where their commercial value was adequately rewarded. But in the unhappy industrial climate which prevailed in the ten years up to 1963, when foreign football seemed both superior in quality and offered a more rewarding profession, it was scarcely surprising that the British game was ill at ease with itself. One significant contribution of the victory of the Players' Union, admirably led by Jimmy Hill, was the creation of a more congenial working climate within professional football.

Looking back from a world which pays its modern football stars salaries, perks, lump sums, bonuses, percentages, sponsorships and more, amounting – for the very best – to a princely income, it seems hard to grasp the realities of players' lives a mere generation ago. Complaints about the current excesses of players' earnings need always to be weighed in the balance against the old system which subjected talented men to a regime of employment which was archaic, unjust, unrewarding and out of kilter with labour practices at large. Yet it is perfectly clear that the unshackling of players' earning power led, within a generation, to a dramatic change in the nature of the game at the senior level. The major clubs, with the bigger crowds and broader commercial appeal, were the only clubs able to pay the wages of the best players. Gradually there was to be a concentration of power – of money, commercial strength, sponsorship, and following – in the hands of a small handful of clubs. And the same pattern unfolded in both England and Scotland. From the first, from the days when maximum wages ended, it was feared that the major clubs would simply dominate and control the game as a whole. We shall see how far that worry was realised. There was, however, a certain recycling of money at work; a great deal of the money laid out by big teams for new stars found its way back into the smaller clubs whence many of those stars had emerged.

The senior British clubs became the game's pace-makers in a wide sense. Their excursions into Europe and, in the summer, around the world, were copied by smaller clubs. The wages they paid their players had the effect of inflating wages throughout the game. In fact the freeing of wages produced a dramatic increase in the costs of professional football. These added costs led inevitably to regular, increased admission prices. Clubs of all shapes and sizes resorted to ever more elaborate schemes for raising money – simply to pay the weekly bills – and all this was without spending any money on the much-needed improvements in the stadiums. In this they were greatly helped by their supporters clubs, by local sponsors and the like. In the lower reaches of the game, clubs were glad to receive free kit, free footballs; anything that might help defray the soaring costs of running the clubs.

The history of British football had been littered with the individual stories of famous stars. From the early days, the best players had traditionally been able to secure better commercial deals for themselves, both within the game and, more lucratively, in the broader commercial world which quickly came to realise the potential of attaching the stars to their products and services. Ghosted articles, sponsored products, names attached to sporting equipment; all these were familiar long before World War I. What changed from the late 1950s was not so much the involvement of commercial interests in and around the professional game of football, but the scale of that involvement, and the staggering amounts of money involved. In 1951 Stanley Matthews received £20 a week for sponsoring boots made by the CWS. A generation later, the figure earned for a similar sponsorship had increased a hundredfold.

Football's small elite quickly became marketable commodities (at least for the height of their fame) to a degree that their footballing forebears could scarcely have imagined. Obviously the rise of footballing superstars, whose names appeared on a multitude of goods and services, whose complex financial affairs require full-time managers, agents and advisers, is largely a function of a highly prosperous consumer society. Even had there been no maximum wage in the years before the mid-1950s it is inconceivable that footballers could ever have earned such money outside the game.

As British society became more prosperous from the 1950s onwards – or at least more consumer-minded – the best players were able to reap the transient benefits of that consumerism. In this process, they were greatly assisted by that other major change in the social life of the British people in these years; the rapid diffusion of TV throughout British life. Whatever else television achieved, it helped to transform the game of football in a number of fundamental ways. It helped, at its simplest, to make a small number of young footballers into very rich men (though many were unable to capitalize on that bonanza). Indeed it could be argued that television had a greater impact on football than any other single innovation since the late nineteenth century. Not since working men found themselves with spare cash and free time to follow their teams, almost a century before, had the game been subjected to such powerful changes as those wrought by the development of television from the late 1950s onwards. Even the BBC's radio coverage of football from the late 1920s paled into insignificance when compared to the impact of TV.

Certain sections of English football doggedly resisted the seductions of TV, fearing that its impact would be by no means necessarily beneficial for the whole game. But the bait dangled by the TV companies was very attractive: large fees negotiated for the recorded extracts of certain matches, live coverage for special games, headed by Cup finals and internationals, and a formula for spreading the proceeds among the clubs. While the resistance to televised football was greater in Scotland than England, the experiences of the late 1960s and early 1970s did not convince everyone that the income from TV compensated for the resulting loss of fans from the terraces. Throughout these years, with the occasional upward exception, attendances at football matches declined. It was easy to assume that television was responsible, even though that decline long predated the arrival of television. It was, of course, more complex than that. Television was itself part cause, part effect of massive social changes in British life. More and more people simply found the attractions of visiting a football ground less and less attractive. It was easier – and certainly more comfortable – to stay at home (and homes themselves were more comfortable) than enduring the out-dated facilities at a local football ground. Yet millions who would never visit a football match watched the game on television. Football rapidly became part of the Saturday evening entertainment at home.

Television did much more than drive away wavering supporters. It was crucial in confirming football as the most widely watched game in the world. Of course, by then, only a small percentage of people in western societies did not own a TV set. In 1966 in England and in 1970 in Mexico, the World Cup competitions attracted global TV audiences in excess of 400 million people, figures which greatly surpassed those watching man's first landing on the moon. By 1990 it was calculated that billions of people watched the final, played in Italy; even the Pope changed his weekly address so as not to clash with a game. On a more modest scale, the weekly TV coverage of football has attracted a regular audience of millions. On more ritualistic occasions, notably the Cup finals, the competing TV services vie with each other to capture the larger audience; their total viewing figures attract an absolute majority of people living in the British Isles. Indeed the TV world of football has become an industry in itself, involving hosts of highly trained commentators and technical staff, and masses of expensive equipment – which itself grows more sophisticated by the year, facilitating ever-more dramatic images, instant and for replay. And to make sense of the whole scene, there emerged a new breed of commentator, normally a player or former player, able to add the technical voice of experience to the analysis. In some respects, TV took over certain key roles previously filled by newspapers in moulding popular opinion about the national game. Since the origins of the modern game, it had been the printed word, later accompanied by photographs, which shaped the wider public image of the game. It was newspapers, magazines, boys' comics, which nurtured the interest in the game of football. From the late 1950s onwards, however, it was, increasingly, television which undertook a similar role. Moreover, TV began to encroach on the game itself; its detailed coverage, slow-motion replays (which often miss the speed and flash of spontaneity which is the essence of good football) and excessive analysis of teams and individual players provide the game with the empirical data for training and preparation. A vital part in the training for big games is a study of the opponents on the most recent video. Opponents' strengths and weaknesses, the home team's failings, all and more can be dissected as never before thanks to the impact of television coverage. As film equipment became cheaper and more manageable, clubs could even film their own games and avoid their earlier reliance on the television companies.

Apart from the obvious technical assistance television has brought to the game, it has transformed the very best footballers into major celebrities. For a fortunate few, television has brought fame and fortune often out of all proportion to their ambitions and even to their talents. Prominent players began to double their already considerable earnings simply by selling their names. This often led to absurd abuses; players recommending goods they never buy, tonics they never use and, perhaps worst of all, signing articles and books they do not write. Yet in essence this had been happening for the best part of a century. In the two decades from the late 1950s, however, it was a pattern which became more and more pronounced, with ever-higher stakes, and, inevitably, more and more money pouring into players' (and their agents') accounts.

It is easy to understand how this excessive commercialism emerged. Sponsors and players wanted to get the most out of their investment and their name. Players and their representatives felt the urge to capitalize on a short career, and to set aside money for when their playing days were ended. Yet there were great dangers. Many young men were simply unable to cope with the added fame and adulation healped on them in the prospering years of television coverage. Many came to believe the inflated claims about themselves. Drawn into a giddy world of showbiz, so many fell prey to people and circumstances they were ill-equipped to deal with. The fall from grace and fame was often as fast as the rise to prominence. For every football star who secured a decent long-term future during his years in the televised limelight, there were many more left with little save their bitter-sweet memories.

Televised football has also helped to break down the resilient barriers of insularity which for so long isolated British football. Widespread coverage of European competitions, the interest in which has been reinforced by the periodic success of British clubs, turned top British teams and players into European institutions. Similarly, British schoolboy footballers and fans became familiar with the teams and stars from Europe. As televised coverage spread, so too did awareness of the game in the most distant parts of the globe – helped by the technical improvements in television itself, notably satellite transmissions. Games could be beamed from the far corners of the world live, to the most distant communities. Games in Australia could be seen in Europe; African matches beamed to Europe. Players and teams from parts of the world which many British fans would have trouble finding on the map suddenly attracted attention (how many fans could point to the Cameroons?). Of course football was not alone in this. All the major sports were utterly transformed by televised coverage and the improvement in telecommunications. Indeed some games which were virtually moribund were given a remarkable lease of life by television; who could have predicted the rise of televised snooker?

The 1960s were the years when television made its seminal impact on football, and secured the game's following in armchairs throughout the country. Significant European Cup finals (in 1960, 1967 and 1968), the proliferation of other European competitions and British victories, and, of course, the perfection of television systems throughout Europe, all served to confirm televised football's huge popularity across Europe. The World Cup competitions proved even more popular, thanks again to TV coverage. The 1966 competition in England generated enormous enthusiasm, partly because it was played throughout the country, from Middlesbrough to London, but again, the focus on enthusiasm was TV coverage and not spectator viewing, with the obvious exceptions of the semi and final ties. The English victory in 1966 seemed to give the domestic game the kiss of life – for the short term at least. Crowds returned, the Labour government had invested money in the game, football's first knighthoods had been bestowed – on an Englishman and a Scot. Previously, sporting knighthoods had been restricted to cricket, yachting and horse-racing. Although there was an element of Harold Wilson's populist politics at work here, it was also true that football had become respectable by the mid-1960s, in part because of television and also because the game's universality seemed to cut across social divisions of all kinds. In a vague sense, the game – at least when the national teams were winning – seemed to unite people. (This was of course an article of faith with a string of South American dictators and generals.)

In creating this image of football as a classless, national game, television was clearly crucial. Yet it was, in many respects, quite deceptive. Football retained its strong working-class origins – even in societies where the cruder lines of social class were changing quite markedly. British football was rootedly working class; its players, managers and the rank-and-file of its spectators were from lower income groups. Moreover, even the material prosperity of the 1960s and 1970s which came to cling to the game could not totally mask the game's social origins. Anyone moving from a Rugby Union club to a football club would be forcefully struck by the marked contrast in their respective social tones (with obvious regional exceptions of course).

The sense that football had become classless was helped by the emergence of star footballers into celebrity status. Here were young men of overwhelmingly working-class origins able, by dint of their footballing skills, to move into the most select of neighbourhoods and to enjoy the most lavish of material life-styles. Such social mobility – for the few – was again not a true reflection of the game's basic core of players and supporters.

Television's impact on professional football was much more obvious, more immediate and widespread than its impact on the amateur game. Moreover, we need to remind ourselves that the amateur game was – and remains – the bed-rock of the game itself. What makes football the people's game is not so much the professional game, but that thick strata of popular activity on fields and playgrounds across the country. If television drove more and more people away from the professional game, it certainly did not have the same effect on the amateur game. Football remained as popular as ever. From school teams to works teams, from church teams to pub teams, all and more compete for the limited footballing space. Throughout the 1960s and 1970s there were more footballers in Britain than at any time in the game's history. Although the statistics are difficult to assemble and are often unreliable, it seems certain that more males played football each weekend than watched the professional game. In any one season, it is calculated that a similar number of schoolboys played football, and perhaps as many as one-and-a-half million men and boys played each weekend. The health of the grass-roots game had never been better and was in contrast to the regular complaints from within the professional game. But the two games were inextricably linked, for amateur football continued to be the nursery for the professional game, while the example of the professional game had an influential effect on the amateur.

Television was the most obvious change in the development of football by the mid-1960s. Other forces were also bringing about important changes. The changing economics of the game were bringing about change. In the teeth of rising costs – wages, transfer fees, daily running costs, etc. – clubs tried to increase their income. One method was simply playing more football. New competitions may bring in more cash, but they also serve to glut the fixture lists and to wear down the players. The cumulative result was an alarming increase in the total number of games played, and the stretching of the season throughout the whole year. The best players, in successful clubs, who also played for their national teams, found themselves playing football throughout the year, often twice a week, with scarcely a summer break. The most serious result of this was the emergence of physical and psychological problems for successful footballers, who might find themselves playing upwards of eighty games in a season. Players were forced on to the pitch even when unfit (with pain-killing injections) and made conscious of the economic importance, to the club, of their efforts. Whatever benefits they began to derive from their fame – and for a few they were very considerable indeed – the modern professional by the mid-1960s was working under severe pressure, the likes of which their footballing forebears had never experienced. Fans for their part tended to be unmoved by such arguments. Most remained ignorant of the physical demands and punishments of the professional game. In a game where success alone mattered, and where success involved increasingly high financial stakes, there was an ever-sharpening spiral of footballing activity in order to pay the players and to keep the club 'successful'. But excessive amounts of football can ultimately be counter-productive. A string of teams simply could not keep pace with these oppressive demands, often falling at the last hurdle of a very long season. And few observers doubt that the national teams have suffered from the weariness of the players they inherit from the successful clubs.

The high stakes on offer, and a new breed of hard-nosed management which sought to win by the narrowest of legal means, spawned a new commitment to 'gamesmanship' in the 1960s and 1970s. Though the statistics for on-field offences tend to reflect official policy, rather than a change in players' behaviour, there was no doubt that the will to win, at all costs, led to the intrusion of calculated football; a determination to play by the letter, if not the spirit of the law. To stop the opponent from winning became an end in itself. And the end result, in Britain and Europe, was the emergence of a style of football which was unattractive to watch and deeply frustrating to play. It was justified solely in terms of its results. Though euphemisms ('professionalism' the most common) were used to disguise the reality, it was hard not to see it as a cynical and ultimately short-sighted philosophy which served to kill the game's appeal and alienated spectators' support.

Yet it would be wrong to imagine that in these years of prosperity all was bad; that football lost its attractive and compelling qualities in the face of encroaching commercialism. Football, like all other forms of athleticism, showed marked improvements in performances. Players were healthier, fitter, faster and more acutely trained, and there seems no reason to doubt that football was more advanced than ever before. Some of the older qualities of football, of the slower, more leisurely game which allowed players to play at their own pace, may have disappeared, but there is no objective evidence to suggest that the game was worse than in past eras, and much to indicate that it was greatly superior. Yet the years of the late 1960s and early 1970s rang with complaints about the declining standards of the game. Certainly, spectators voted with their feet, leaving the stadiums in droves. But that pattern had been in train since the early 1950s and was to be explained by changes in society at large rather than within the game itself.

Football's decline as a spectator sport in the years 1953–73 derived from external factors over which the game had little

control. The game had become only one of a
leisure activities open to British people in t.
proportion of the spending power of working p
itself rose markedly), the amount spent on football dra.
decreased. With an expanding range of outlets for consu
spending (from more elaborate holidays to cars and house
improvements), traditional football fans found the attractions of
winter football, viewed from a wet, bone-numbing terrace,
eminently resistible, more so when the local team was no more
than ordinary and when it contrasted sharply with the edited
highlights of superior teams seen on TV in front-room comfort.

The development of hooliganism in and around football by
the late 1960s posed a distinct set of problems which the game
found troublesome in the extreme. Many fans saw hooliganism,
with its worrying levels of violence, of obscenity and – later –
racial abuse, as the final straw. Football was hard enough to
watch – costly, inconvenient, often uncomfortable and
sometimes unrewarding – without having to be alert to physical
dangers and verbal unpleasantness. Yet the evidence was
confusing. Attendances fell where crowd troubles never
happened, and remained stable where trouble seemed endemic.
Hooliganism in itself could not explain the continuing decline
in football attendances. But it certainly armed the game's critics
with more slings and arrows to hurl at the game at moments of
national and political debate. As we shall see later, those fans at
the heart of the troubles in and around the grounds were
helping to build a rod for football's back; a rod which would be
wielded with some vigour by a new breed of unflinching
politician from 1979 onwards. The damage caused by football
hooliganism was much broader than the immediate geography
of their actions, for they helped to sow the seeds of deep
disillusion about the national game. And that disillusion was to
bear fruit in the terrible aftermath of the disasters which
blighted the game in the 1980s.

By the early 1970s, football seemed at a crossroads. As ever,
it was sensitive to changes in society at large; its ups and downs
seemed to reflect more fundamental changes in British society at
large. By the late 1960s and early 1970s those changes were
quicker, more widespread and more fundamental. Quite simply,
the pace and nature of social change had quickened. Of course
this was true for all British institutions: there was nothing special

₁ distinctive about the game of football. Yet those aficionados of the game who sought explanations for what was happening solely within the game itself tended not to notice changes in society at large.

Football remained as sensitive as ever to fluctuations in social patterns; to population and urban change, changes within mass media, the influence of educational change and, above all else, the redirection of consumer spending. Some devoted fans, with money to spend on their passion, would think nothing of flying thousands of miles to watch a match. But many others chose to direct their extra earnings elsewhere.

Even before the enforced improvement in football grounds in the wake of recent major disasters, clubs were improving their facilities in order to woo wealthier patrons. Time and again, improvements were aimed at the upper end of the spectator market; the cheaper places remained untouched. It was surely a sign of the ambition and of the marketing aims of football's management that they saw their future more securely aligned with higher, rather than lower income groups. This was a pattern which was to be repeated across Britain in recent years, often to the outrage of 'traditional' fans, who (rightly) felt themselves being squeezed out to make way for lavish facilities for more prosperous clients.

The story of football up to the early 1970s poses a number of contradictions for observers. First of all, the television audiences were global and measured in their hundreds of millions; the World Cup in Mexico in 1970 was watched by unprecedented numbers – on television. Yet by 1973 attendances at home had fallen by eight million over the previous twenty years. At the same time, there were more players than ever before. In fact there simply were not enough pitches to satisfy demand. The story of the game was, again, a complex phenomenon; too subtle to be easily labelled by ready-made categories. If it was, as many claimed, in great decline, it had odd ways of manifesting that decline. No one could have stood at the edge of a Sunday-morning football pitch, surrounded on all sides by teams and supporters, and remotely felt that the game which had characterized British life for almost a century was anything other than booming. Such contrasts were at the heart of the game; they had been part of the game's continuing appeal for years. Whatever seemed to happen to the professionals, the game of football, of the common man, continued to thrive.

9 Disasters and Renewal

The physical face of British – but especially English – football changed more fundamentally and more quickly in the 1980s and 1990s than at any comparable period in its history. This was due initially to those tragedies at football grounds which killed so many people, which appalled millions who saw the tragedies unfold on television, at home and abroad, and forced the government and 'footballing' authorities to address the game's most pressing problems. The physical face of the British game – the stadiums which had remained virtually unchanged throughout their life and which stood as monuments to the crowded urban pleasures of the masses – were torn down and reconstructed. Like housing and the workplace, the architecture of pleasure had been found badly wanting. New styles, systems and comforts were needed to take the place of those outdated – and in many cases dangerous – buildings. With the exception of a few notable clubs, it is difficult to believe that these major changes would have been implemented (indeed would not even have been considered) without those terrible incidents. Football's disasters became a symbol of a nation in steep and apparently unstoppable decline.

Crowd troubles and major accidents had punctuated the history of British football. Large, unrestricted crowds cramming into facilities which were ill-designed to cope with such numbers, and physical pressures had been commonplace throughout the century. Looking back at the massive crowds, especially those following World War II, it seems remarkable that major accidents were not more common. But there were a number of disasters. In 1902 at Ibrox Park, part of the wooden stand collapsed, pitching 26 people to their deaths and injuring more than 500. Another 33 people died, and 400 were injured, when barriers collapsed in an 80,000 crowd at a Bolton Cup tie in 1946. The figures mounted; in 1971 66 died in a stairway crush at the end of a Glasgow derby. More shocking, perhaps, because it was shown live on television, was the fire which consumed the main stand at Bradford City's ground in May 1985, with the loss of 55 lives and dozens of serious injuries. Only weeks later, though further afield, 38 people (mainly Italians) died in a stampede of fans in the 55-year-old Heysel Stadium in Brussels. It was an incident prompted by attacks by British fans on their Italian opponents. Finally, the appalling crush in one section at Sheffield Wednesday's ground for a semi-final in April 1989 killed 95 people, most of them Liverpool fans. Here was an unacceptable litany of avoidable disasters; something clearly had to be done to prevent any more.

These last two cases involved Liverpool fans. The media instantly made the association between a decaying industrial, maritime city – the flagship of British urban decay – and the alleged violence and indiscipline of their football fans. The press portrait was of fans, from England's most blighted city, running out of control. Not for the first or last time, football was seen as a symptom of Britain's problems. Which other people were so beset by urban troubles; which other European fans visited such mayhem and destruction upon unsuspecting neighbours? Who else was too aggressive in their support, so loud (and crude) in their fanaticism, so threatening in their marauding bands? It was a portrait which was effective, eye-catching and politically persuasive. It was as if the British had become a nation of football louts (notwithstanding the fact that these incidents were entirely English). Commentators around the world 'focused' on football; teasing apart its every shortcoming to find answers to the British malaise. But almost every point they made could be countered or denied.

Of course it could be argued that this portrait merely inverted the British self-image proclaimed earlier in the century; that in their sports and games they flaunted their superiority. Now, in the troubled violence which flared around their football games, they revealed their collective shortcomings. It was, of course, much more complex than that. For a start the problems plaguing the game could be replicated in a host of European cities. But in the rush to judge it seemed important to find instant culprits. In the immediate aftermath of the Heysel, Bradford and Hillsborough disasters, there was an epidemic of finger-pointing; an almost national urge to single-out and denounce the guilty. Of course it *was* important to find out what had gone so horribly wrong in those (very different) disasters. The fierce arguments about Hillsborough continue to rumble on, more especially about the contribution to the disaster of local policing.

It was a dismal record of suffering, made all the more horrifying by the way those collective agonies were projected into the nation's living-room by the ever-present eye of the TV camera. We now know that the worst scenes – too grotesque, too horrifying for transmission – were left in the editing room. But what the nation and the rest of the world saw was bad enough. Old people incinerated as they stumbled for safety in Bradford; children with the life crushed out of them, wedged against the cages that penned them in; mounds of corpses – and of the dying – were horrifying, even to a TV audience numbed over the years by the parade of televised suffering from around the world. What on earth had all this to do with that wonderful game which brought such pleasure to millions? It is easy to see why so many people despaired, and why so many others demanded action to prevent any similar outrages. Football became a national issue in a way it had never been before.

First came the instantly dispensed punishment. The Brussels disaster was quickly followed by the banning of Liverpool Football Club, and then all the other English clubs, from playing in Europe. The country which prided itself in giving football to the world, now found itself a sporting pariah. At home there followed a long, drawn-out analysis; politicians, high-court judges, experts of various persuasions, all and more searched for explanations – and solutions. Under a Prime Minister who would brook no interference with her judgments, it seemed for a long time that the game would be subject to draconian restrictions (notably membership cards) which would have seriously damaged the game. It was saved from those prime-ministerial sanctions by yet another judicial inquiry, following another football disaster and by the level-headedness of the inquiring judge.

What became abundantly clear to the investigators (though it had been obvious to football fans for years) were the physical shortcomings of most stadiums in England (in Scotland, too, but they had not been plagued by recent disasters). Large numbers of people died because of the physical environment at Brussels, Bradford and Hillsborough. An old, tinder-dry wooden stand at Bradford, a crumbling section of stadium in Brussels, a corner of an overcrowded Hillsborough from which fans could not escape when pressured from behind. No one would argue that the problems were simply matters of design and safety. But it was abundantly clear that the stadiums involved (and many others) were utterly inadequate for the demands and pressures placed on them. They also represented a nightmare for the police, particularly since modern fans were not as easily marshalled and moved around as their fathers and grandfathers had been.

Whatever else was to be decided, the stadiums needed to be changed. In the wake of Bradford, scarcely a ground in England remained unaffected. The Popplewell Report into the disaster prompted major changes in stadiums around the country, though many of the bigger clubs had already set improvements in train as part of the commercial upgrading of their facilities. But those changes were mere tinkerings compared to the consequences of the Hillsborough disaster. The report by Lord Justice Taylor demanded – and got – massive changes to the physical environment of football grounds. All senior clubs were ordered to phase out their terraces – those bleak, stepped banks, interspersed with crude metal barriers – by 1994, the lower league clubs by a later date. Money was to be made available for those improvements through the Football Trust (itself financed by the ever-lucrative football pools).

The pace of change thereafter was staggering. One football ground after another became a building site. Tens of millions of pounds were invested, and the Edwardian facades of one club after another gave way to new, comfortable, seated stadiums. Many fans complained (especially about the added cost of sitting, rather than standing, at a football match). The capacity of many stadiums was reduced; Wembley, for instance, was lowered to 70,000 and Old Trafford packed, held 10,000 fewer people than it did 20 years earlier. But the income is proportionately greater. Moreover, the same trend was true of Scotland, though there the motive was different. Though Scottish fans had inflicted their fair share of mayhem on other clubs and countries, especially in the 1960s and 1970s, they did not enjoy the English reputation for crowd violence which culminated in the post-Taylor changes. Nonetheless, in Scotland as in England change was the order of the day; clubs moved to new sites, old grounds were reformed beyond recognition. And all this was supervised by the post-Taylor Football Licensing Authority. Everywhere the perimeter fences (initially introduced to stop crowd invasion, but the source of so many deaths at Hillsborough) were removed, clubs hired their own safety officers, their own armies of professionally trained and organised stewards. The number of police at the grounds has dropped, though thousands of them need to patrol the environs and routes to the bigger stadiums. By the mid-1990s, football looked remarkably different from the game of only three or four years earlier. Yet many of those changes would not have happened without the terrible disasters of the 1980s.

These changes did not meet with universal approval of course. Admission prices shot up. Some clubs, faced with consumers' resistance, were sometimes obliged to reduce prices. Many fans felt that seating would lead to an end of the vital 'atmosphere' – the cacophony of noise so basic to big games. Such objections aside, the truth remains that football quickly adapted to the new arrangements. Indeed it now seems bizarre that both clubs and fans should have clung so tenaciously to facilities which were outdated, uncomfortable and often dangerous. Here perhaps is the *real* British disease; that clinging to the wreckage of tradition, that refusal to contemplate alternatives to old habits, so characteristically British in so many areas. Remain faithful to the familiar. In the case of football, it was clear that such habits, overlaid by new and unnerving social problems, were both cause and occasion of serious disorders. It would be glib to claim that trouble could have been averted had football simply resolved to improve its physical environment. The simple truth remains that football did not change – perhaps could not change – until driven, reluctantly, to legally-enforced improvements. It was intrusive government edict which produced the biggest improvements in football in the twentieth century.

Football's problems could not be solved simply by improving the stadiums. What lay behind at least two of those disasters was the behaviour of the fans. Both at Hillsborough and Heysel (and in a number of other smaller, though sometimes fatal, incidents) crowd disturbances had bedevilled the game. Football had become synonymous with 'hooliganism'. Indeed in the 1970s and 1980s, football hooliganism became a preoccupation of the media. Often the game itself was relegated to a secondary item behind the lurid description of football's marauding fans, sometimes organised into gangs, hurling objects and abuse at their chosen targets. Here again, the game became the symbol of a nation's broader troubles. The violent, foul-mouthed football fan seemed a perfect personification of much that was wrong with the nation.

Many people abroad had an image (nurtured by the local media) of the English as a loutish, beer-drinking mob of football hooligans. And there was evidence enough in those years that organised, and less formal, hooligans were indeed making their own distinctive impact on the game. There was, of course, a rich and diverse youth culture associated with turbulence and disorder for decades past. And it is salutary to remind ourselves that the concept of a hooligan originated in the 1890s. There had been plenty of crowd disturbances in the past, though it is generally recognised that football was largely peaceful and untroubled between the wars. There had been nothing quite like the hooliganism which blighted the game in recent years. Nor is it possible to discuss its emergence simply – or even largely – in terms of football itself. Here was a phenomenon whose roots and inspirations lay deep within the sub-strata of British life.

Crowd troubles began to manifest themselves in the years when football attendances had begun to thin out; when more and more older men quit football for the new domesticated pleasures provided by improved homes and car-ownership. They left behind increasingly sparse terraces in the hands and control of younger fans. At the same time, the clubs themselves changed – appearing to grow more distant from their fans in style and substance. The bigger stars were whisked away, thanks to the pleasures of material bounty, from the often meagre world of their rank-and-file supporters. Where once the players and fans had travelled home together on the bus and tram, they were now unapproachably divided, in life-style as well as transport. In more ways than one, the clubs began to uproot themselves from their local communities. In many cases those communities – in the heart of the inner cities – were themselves transformed by urban decay, by migration, by industrial change and by the arrival of new immigrant groups with no local or traditional loyalties.

Trouble began on the trains. Football excursion trains were wrecked. Disturbances then spread into the stadiums, into those sections of the crowds reserved for youths. Those centres of youthful support began to attract youths who enjoyed the new climate and who added their own violent and foul-mouthed contribution to the game. Their styles – of clothing, haircut, songs, etc. – changed periodically and from place to place. But the cumulative impact was similar; a rise in turbulence in and around football grounds – and *en route* to games throughout the country. City and regional rivalries were no longer a matter of vocal support for a particular team. Now they often spilled over into public acts of violence, sometimes on a frightening scale. Gang fights over territory became a feature of the game and time and again innocent bystanders found themselves caught in the mêlée. It demanded – and got – a new form of police control which involved careful intelligence work, a rough management of all suspected people and inevitable infringements of the rights of everyone involved. Attending certain football grounds became an intimidating exercise in running the gauntlet of violent youths on the one hand and a visored, mounted and heavily protected police presence on the other. It was a daunting prospect which hardly seemed worth the effort. By the mid-1990s, football hooliganism had developed an international dimension, with links (fostered by computers) between neo-fascist groups across Europe.

Here were sensational, almost weekly stories which provided rich pickings for the media. Every incident, however trivial, received full (sometimes distorted) publicity. The antics of the footballing fringe were projected around the world, on television, to convey an impression of deep-seated urban unrest (compounded by other, unrelated urban troubles). The impression took hold of football as a deeply troubled game – a reflection of a society ill-at-ease with itself. Cameras from TV companies around the world followed those small bands of rowdies (who were of course eager to oblige), capturing their every action and feeding the image (and those young men's sense of importance) with an attention and importance it often did not warrant. Myth and realities converged and fused. At times it was hard to see the real football hooligan for the televised image. But as control and scrutiny tightened at home, those fans keen to find trouble could find it more easily in Europe – where restrictions were much lighter – and where drink was more freely available. The arrival of mobile phones gave such groups an extra ability to organise more easily. Mass computer ownership similarly allowed them to forge links, via the internet, with like-minded groups in other countries. There was even a forging of links between European neo-fascist groups. British governments and police forces resolved to tackle the problem.

To add to the whole ghastly business, a new overt racism, directed against a new generation of black players, began to surface and to pollute the game more deeply than any other disagreeable element. Racists found a fertile soil in football; a perfect arena in which to vent their bizarre views, subjecting black players – and anyone at hand – to a barrage of abuse and gestures which shamed the game and its followers. Organised racist and fascist groups – and their publications – wallowed in the attention they received. And for years football's authorities chose to ignore the problem. A handful of clubs struck out against it, but most did not. In part, this was perhaps because such sentiments struck a rich vein of populist racism which surfaced throughout society in those years. Time and again, the clubs, managers and owners made utterances, and controlled their own players, in a style which was itself deeply racist. The game began to reflect the confusions of feelings – that complicated animus about race – which has so bedevilled British life since the 1960s. But it was, once again, more English than British. There were racial incidents in Scotland, but Scottish teams rarely attracted the virulent racism which so characterised the English game in the 1970s and 1980s.

There was growing evidence that football's racists had developed links with like-minded friends in Europe. It was of course but one aspect of the emergence of the far right which began to plague Western Europe, especially afer the collapse of the communist regimes in the east. However international the phenomenon, critics were in no doubt that the centre of footballing racism, its influential heartland, was England. It was in England that the disaffected, often unemployed youths, turned to the game for that vicarious mix of physical challenge, racial edge and attention-seeking. It had become a problem – or a set of inter-related problems – which no British government could afford to ignore. This association between racist groups and football violence convinced government that steps had to be taken to purge the national game of its obnoxious elements.

Few doubted, in the late 1980s, that football was in a crisis. Not surprisingly, the game attracted more than its usual share of study and criticism. An army of critics stepped forward to offer their own view of football's problems. Much of the resulting debate developed from the serious research by scholars (most notably from de Montfort and Leicester Universities). Thanks to those efforts – and to the rapid emergence of other scholarly investigations – it was possible, for the first time, to engage in serious debate about the problems which underpinned the game. There had, of course, been arguments before. Now, however, there was an expanding body of data available. The Home Office and police similarly created their own research facilities. There was, for many, too much theory and literary opaqueness. And much of the ensuing debate smacked too much of those internal academic debates which outsiders find so obscure and unenlightening. Yet, for all those quibbles, it was indisputably clear that the study of football had come of age as a serious intellectual issue. The quality of research, the seriousness of the issues addressed, the importance of the debate – all and more confirmed the game's right to be taken seriously. Any waverer had only to read the current research to be persuaded that here, at last, was an important issue finally receiving appropriate intellectual attention.

It was perhaps easy to convince outsiders because so many of football's problems were of such deep-seated social concern to people with no brief for the game itself. It was hard to have a sense of social concern without feeling alarm, for example, about the rise of hooliganism. Here, and elsewhere, football seemed to hold up a mirror to the puzzling, changing face of British life. To study the game in its broader setting was to effect an entrée to the sociology of modern Britain. Such an approach was not without its problems. It was easy to ridicule, more especially for the British with their infamous track-record of anti-intellectualism. Here was a perfect whipping-boy; scholars devouring large research grants, creating academic empires and securing professional preferment on the back of football and its modern social problems. Yet why should that game *not* attract serious intellectual and research interest?

The end result, however, by the end of the 1980s was a quite remarkable outpouring about football and its recent problems. A generation earlier it had been a common remark among serious critics of the game that little serious research had been done; there was not very much data available and the game's importance seemed to go unrecognized by serious critics and commentators. That, clearly, is no longer the case.

At the heart of much of that scholarly interest lay the serious social problems thrown up by football, problems brought into focus by football's disasters. The disasters at Heysel and at Hillsborough, whatever their real, deep-seated origins, seemed closely associated with fans' misbehaviour. In the anguished aftermath, few doubted that the game cried out for reform. Before the Popplewell and Taylor Reports, a great deal of the debate about football had been about 'law and order' issues. And it was surely significant that both inquiries were headed by judges. But the consequences – especially of Taylor – were to be more profound, more far-reaching than anyone imagined at the time. Yet it is surely a depressing irony that it took grievous loss of life before the game changed. And only then because it was forced to change.

One of the most chilling realisations in the wake of the Hillsborough disaster was that it had been brought about in part by the very measures designed to re-assert control over the game. People were crushed to death in the pens designed to stop football fans spilling out, invading the pitch and possibly hurting others. At Sheffield, this solution to one problem turned out to be a death trap. Whatever other conclusions were drawn from Hillsborough, most people were agreed that football grounds were hopelessly out of date. Football's physical environment was inadequate. Yet this had manifestly been the case for many years past – as any football fan could confirm. Of course improvements had been introduced (not least at Hillsborough). By and large, however, football grounds were crumbling and dangerous museums to the physical world of leisure in the first half of the century, though adapted to deal with modern problems of crowd control. What so many critics overlooked was the shocking philosophy which underpinned the corralling of fans into such dangerous pens; the belief that problems were best dealt with by physical structures and human containment.

Initially, that accident merely confirmed old prejudices; here was yet further, ghastly evidence of the barbarism that lay at the heart of English football. It was of course no such thing (notwithstanding the evidence of bravado and foolishness which were unquestionably mixed into the disastrous social chemistry of that day). Most unnerving of all perhaps was the fact that the Sheffield disaster was just the latest of a long list of public catastrophes in the late 1980s, mainly in transport, which suggested a persistent and ubiquitous disregard for public safety. The physical structures of British life seemed to be corroding at a remarkable rate – taking hundreds of people to their death.

It was a very British response to appoint a judge to examine a disaster. For a change, however, it produced an enlightened and refreshing assessment. Most striking of all was Taylor's independent line, paying little heed to Thatcher's proposals to deal with footballs problems. The fences came down and the proposed membership cards were rejected. But, most crucial of all, it was decreed that the wholly inadequate and dangerous physical environment of most grounds should be brought to a speedy end. Terraces were to be converted to seating. Not everyone liked these changes. We need to remember that many football fans are as wedded to bad habits as the management. But in essence the Taylor Report was demanding a humanising of football's ugly habitat. It hinged on the belief that the game treated its fans badly and that they deserved better from the clubs they supported.

Taylor's report also made an important assumption that took the debate to the heart of crowd control. Treat people like animals in pens and they are likely to behave that way; treat them decently and they might behave better. Yet many fans, many clubs and their organisations remained resistant to the removal of traditional terraces, claiming that removing them was to tear the heart out of the people's game. But many others saw such arguments as dangerous nostalgia; a redundant harking-back to the days of the outside lavatory and steam trains. Almost immediately, many clubs – notably the smaller, poorer clubs – began to drag their feet, hoping to avoid necessary change by the simple passage of time. As memories of disasters dimmed, the urgency might be dissipated.

Whatever the cause, in the immediate aftermath of the Taylor Report and the modernisation of football grounds, there was a marked decline in hooliganism. True, there were periodic outbursts among fans travelling abroad. But even there, local police (now in cahoots with their British colleagues) were generally ready and prepared for the arrival of the English fans. Once again, their heavy-handed tactics often hurt innocent fans, caused huge resentment and marched rough-shod over civil liberties. At home, the crowds began to come back to the game; almost 20 million in 1989–90 (compared with 16.4 million in 1985–6). And to crown the resurgence of the game's respectability, it spawned an unprecedented literary outburst – including in 1992–3 a best-selling book on football (Nick Hornby's *Fever Pitch*) which clearly transcended the traditional market for books on football. There was, too, a remarkable flow of thousands of fanzines, excellent periodicals (*When Saturday Comes*) and a regular issue of books covering every conceivable aspect of the game. The game entered the 1990s in an up-beat, optimistic mood.

For those who cared to brood about how the game might move forward, they had only to cast envious looks at Italy. The dramatic upsurge of interest in Italian football in the 1990s was related to the 1990 World Cup, to televised coverage of the Italian game, and to the transfer of British players to Italy. British fans could only stare in some amazement at the spectacular Italian stadiums. (Closer, subsequent scrutiny revealed corruption involved in their construction.)

The contrast could not have been greater. The management of the local game continued to bicker over how much was needed to comply with the Taylor requirements, and where the money was to come from; funds drawn from football pools provided only part of the total sum required. Once again – and presumably not for the last time – the people's game faced the future in that curmudgeonly mood which so characterised its proceedings, at so many levels, throughout its modern history. In truth the game and its fans deserved better.

The physical changes in football's outward appearance were only the most visible of a host of changes which were transforming the game more rapidly than in any comparable period. There were complaints about some of those changes. There was, quite simply, too much football. Players were obliged to play too many games, with scarcely a break in summer; far more than their European rivals (hence the explanation for continuing British failures to compete successfully abroad). Tired players, poor coaching, too great a reliance on strength and running; all these and more were offered as reasons for the apparent inferiority of British teams and players.

The structure of the game was also changing. Bigger clubs became more powerful, retaining more of their income from gates, and they acquired an even greater control over the conduct of the game. They also generate income for the smaller clubs – in television fees, for example – which percolates down throughout the game, and in effect provides senior clubs with a powerful weapon. Furthermore, the threat that a small handful of 'super-clubs' might withdraw completely from the current arrangements to create a super-league of their own has periodically been used to intimidate the minnows. Even the creation of the Premier League (and the consequent rejigging of lower leagues) did not satisfy the bigger clubs. The major clubs, keen to win trophies at home as an entrée to the more lucrative tournaments against European rivals, have willy-nilly drifted towards competing in European leagues. Time and again, those men who speak about the future of the game (in the major clubs at least) continue to aspire towards a European league as the main basis for regular competition. While there is a certain logic to that development, it also threatens to wrench the game loose from its social moorings at home.

The arrival of satellite TV, and its saturation coverage of football, and the amazing salaries consequently paid to better players has transformed the game still further. British football could now compete with European neighbours, in wages and facilities. Televison income has enabled teams to buy players from Europe and South America. Foreign players became so commonplace in the 1990s that fears were expressed for the future of British-born players. Clubs were floated on the stock exchange, the best players became millionaires enjoying a celebrity unknown even a decade earlier.

The story of British football since the Hillsborough disaster is the story of a major British institution scrambling to catch up with the dramatic changes in society at large, changes which it had in the main chosen to ignore for decades. Like Lloyds of London and the monarchy, football initially found itself isolated and increasingly disliked because of its backwardness. Ever more people had simply lost patience; had lost sympathy with the elevation of bad habits to the status of tradition. Like other major forms of British popular culture – the cinema, and seaside holidays, for example – football had been by-passed by developments which, at once, threatened to undermine the game and yet which, paradoxically, could be harnessed to the game's benefit.

It was, as one scholar has pointed out, no accident that the Football League faced serious challenges to its very existence at the same time as London Zoo; another hallowed nineteenth-century institution which found itself out of favour as the world turned slowly upside-down. Football, for much of its administrative history, was in the hands of men who, publicly, like Joe Richards of Barnsley, claimed they were happier to see Barnsley win the Third Division championship than England win the World Cup. Here was a sense of footballing loyalty which was local almost down to the parochial level. It was, of course, this fierce pride which, for almost a century, had given the game its strength and its vitality. But it was a local pride which, by the 1980s, stood four-square against many of the changes which the game needed.

True to the traditional spirit of the English League, the outcome – the establishment of the Premier League – was bitterly resisted by most of the smaller clubs, and by the Football League itself. The problems of modernisation prompted an insistence on traditional structures. Yet in a sense they were right to resist. The restructuring of the game was driven by commercial interests; by a small band of elite clubs anxious to confirm their position and to enhance their wealth. And they intended to do this in conjunction with those powerful commercial interests who, through sponsorship and television, appreciated the commercial value of a modernised game. There were undoubted grounds for concern as football headed into the arms of the mega-rich; as the big clubs slide into bed with corporations and wealthy businessmen. The role of major magnates threatened not only the specific clubs they targeted, but the whole structure of the game. At times football seemed ready to go the way of so many other businesses; picked off, stripped down and recycled by millionaires and investors who viewed them as just another speculative venture.

Set against this danger, however, were the benefactors; the millionaires who – like the backers of major clubs in Europe – seemed happy to pour good money after bad in supporting their favourite team. At Watford, Glasgow Rangers, Wolves and Blackburn Rovers, wealthy patrons disgorged millions. Sometimes it yielded dividends on the field, sometimes not. But for many fans it seemed a dangerous game; it could just as easily go badly wrong – and did in some cases and narrowly avoided doing so in many others. In essence the millionaire backers provided some charismatic reminders of a central problem facing the game; that clubs (large and small) could barely survive on the income they generated at the gates. They needed other sources of income – sponsorship, television deals, philanthropic support – merely to survive.

The particularly acrimonious disputes which swirled around the formation of the English Premier League reinforced the traditional rift between the London-based Football Association and the Lytham-based Football League. They were separated by more than simple geography, though geography was important; the one metropolitan and committed to an aggressively commercial future for football, the other provincial – even parochial – anxious to safeguard what it took to be the game's traditional values and support. In a way, both were right. The major clubs – the core of the Premier League – could not continue to be wagged by the Lancastrian tail of the Football League. Yet, in its turn, the League was also right to persist in the defence of that broader community of footballing interests which were rootedly local and yet which formed the rich mosaic of English football.

In what could stand as a *leitmotif* for British industry and commerce as a whole, the one element in this story (and throughout its previous history) which has been consistently ignored was the fans. It was a familiar story; society's foot soldiers, the very people who gave the game its rationale and strength, were the last item on the agenda. Indeed the persistent refusal to improve football's physical environment was eloquent testimony to the game's refusal to consider their interests. At times, the fans seemed an inconvenience; at best a necessary evil, at worst the source of a host of problems which deflected football's management from the pursuit of its own interest. For years, few people wrote about the fans. Suddenly, in the 1990s, there was a blizzard of literature about them. It was even possible to launch specialist sports bookshops – where the largest single section was devoted to football, and its fans.

The fans were the backbone of the professional game; without them it was nothing. Indeed it is surely revealing that one of the most severe penalties inflicted on erring teams is to oblige them to play behind locked doors; to keep out the paying spectators. Too often acting as the mere poodles of the clubs they supported, the supporters' clubs formed a network of enthusiasm and energy which brought great strength to the game itself. But not until very recently were they given a voice in the running of their clubs. Few in the game even considered that fans had any rights. They were, above all, spectators; punters whose weekly loyalty was vital yet unheeded. Their only reward was admission to crumbling facilities to watch their favourite team. Here was one more example of British management choosing to ignore the shop floor. Had the clubs listened to the recurring complaints which flitted through the proceedings of the supporters' clubs, decade after decade, they could have detected – and possibly deflected – many of the problems which lay at the heart of the game, none more fundamental than the grounds themselves. Only the absence of fans, and loss of income, seemed to impress football directors. Until, that is, the disasters of the 1980s.

Fans were consulted and heeded only when problems arose. When hooliganism broke out, when attendances declined, when the game needed direct access to fans whose behaviour at home and abroad seemed incomprehensible, football authorities began to turn to spectators for information and advice. With some striking exceptions, however, there was little effort to form a constructive relationship between the clubs and their supporters. In this, it merely continued as it had begun; a game of the common man, managed and controlled by his betters. Here, yet again, was a glaring illustration of problems which transcended the game itself; of management and rank-and-file operating in different spheres. It was, again, a very British problem.

Yet it would be wrong to suggest that nothing had changed. For a start, British teams were very different from their forebears. A generation before, they were built around the most talented players from throughout the British Isles. Few English teams were without their Scots. Now, teams had become remarkably cosmopolitan. Russians and Scandinavians, Americans and Africans, South Americans and South Africans – all and more rubbed shoulders with players from every nation in Europe; and all play together in British teams.

Even more startling, one Scottish team (Rangers) began to fill with Englishmen. Some of the best English teams in the 1990s contained scarcely an Englishman. Finding a *lingua franca* at times proved a coaching nightmare. Many players do not understand the language – to say nothing of the accents – of the fans who adore them. Yet here is a remarkable testimony to the strength of the global game. While it might seem to reflect on the paucity of local, British talent, in fact it speaks to the broadening of the game's horizons. British teams are now catching up with competitors in Europe. For decades past, a similar pattern had been noticeable in Europe. The great Real Madrid team of the 1950s and early 1960s, for instance, was led by an Argentinian, a Hungarian and a Frenchman.

Players began to criss-cross Europe in search of a more lucrative career. The end result is that European top-class club football has become remarkably cosmopolitan. In 1990, for example, a majority of the squads playing for Argentina and Brazil played their club football in Europe. Footballing authorities have sought to staunch this international flow, and have resisted the free movement of labour within Europe (in contrast to the legal freedoms). There is a widespread fear that if the bigger teams simply buy the world's best players, this will stunt local talent and adversely affect the emergence of local players. There have been periodic bans on imported footballers (in Italy, for instance). The Bosman ruling greatly eased the movement of footballing talent (and may have helped the rise in players' salaries). But it is now inconceivable that Europe's major clubs can function in their current format, in their leagues and competitions, without large squads drawn from around the footballing world.

In a Europe drawn ever more closely together it seemed natural that football, like other institutions, should seek a European arena. Yet that can only make sense for a small number of elite clubs. At a time when most smaller professional clubs have difficulty paying transport costs across their own country – and when the obvious move would be towards more regional leagues – games in Europe seem unimaginably costly and ambitious. What drives the urge towards European football is that vague sense that it is part of the emergence of the new Europe. But lurking behind the whole movement are powerful commercial interests. It is no accident that much of the impetus within the game itself comes from men with enormous financial – and television – investments and who see in a European league an ever more lucrative cornucopia. Multinational companies, transnational tycoons, all and more have been striving to overcome national loyalties – and institutional inertia – to create European leagues and competitions. Television and global marketing has even created audiences and markets for European football in far corners of the globe.

There are of course a host of practical complications, but few that seem insurmountable. It is hard to envisage European football without its local, national game. After all, European politics and administration is an addition, not an alternative, to local, national government. But the favourite example offered by football's Europeans is that of major sports in the USA. There, and in Europe, sport hinges on massive commercial sponsorship – and the ease of jet travel. A century ago, it seemed a wonder of modern life that a Glaswegian team could be whisked off to London by the steam train. Today no one blinks when British teams play midweek games throughout Europe – or even take off for a friendly in the Gulf, in Asia or the Americas. Players compete in Australia one week, and are back before their fans in Britain the next week. By the time the European ban on English teams was lifted in 1990 the face of their own domestic game was undergoing a remarkable change.

One of the most obvious changes on the field has been the rapid emergence of black footballers. A generation ago they were unusual – and hence more easily targeted by racists on the terraces. Now, they form a highly visible and significant element in most teams. Most major clubs have a core of black players. Indeed, when teams do not have a black player in their ranks, the assumption arises that the club/manager have chosen to ignore them. Those who are the sons of West Indian immigrants come from poor homes in the inner cities, following the route which had been traditional for professional players over the past century. Now joined by African players, they have become role models for other black youths, and they have also been the object of extraordinary and sometimes virulent racism, on and off the field. But as they have grown in numbers, in confidence, collective strength and as powerful and impressive spokesmen have emerged from their ranks, they have led the attack on racism in football. They have embarrassed the game into confronting the issue; into trying to secure football as a racist-free environment. Of course, pockets of virulent racism persist, and latent animosity periodically erupts against black players. But it seems clear enough that a new generation of black players refuse to allow themselves to be subjected to such abuse, from fans, other players – and from management. But what they need – and so rarely got (initially at least) – is active support from football's authorities. Clubs can make great strides against this problem. Current signs are that they will be propelled towards action by a new generation of professional black players weary of the game providing a forum for the nation's more unpleasant forms of behaviour.

The discussion about the problems of football in recent years naturally focused on the English game. It was, after all, English grounds, English fans and English teams which were blighted by disasters and troubles. When Europeans prepared for trouble from visiting fans, above all others they feared the English. In the long term this seems curious because for a long time the English had thought of the Scots as the most troublesome of supporters. Indeed there had been a string of infamous Scottish footballing visits – to London, Barcelona and to various English grounds. For years the English had been awed by those banks of Scots streaming south for major games, fuelled by lashings of booze, buoyed up by their own brand of nationalist bravado, bedecked in distinctive regalia and dress, and heralded by a cacophony of noise. It was (is) a footballing fanaticism which can hold its own with the best from South America. It is also a source of an amazing and durable mythology – part of that identity of urban Scotland (especially Glaswegian) which Scots carry with them around the world. Of course it is a fanaticism which flares most colourfully and aggressively in the face of the English. And if the Scots cannot beat the English, they will support anyone else who can. The old enemy remains *the* enemy.

But old patterns began to change. Even in Glasgow, where footballing allegiances bore many of the traits of sectarian markings, where the game reflected old (but now changing) social and geographic divides, the game registered the seismic changes at work throughout society at large. Millionaire backers, new stadiums, players from throughout Europe – even English players (sometimes black Englishmen) now appeared for Scottish teams.

Those changes were heralded and driven forward initially by Rangers, with a multimillionaire backer and a manager who had played part of his career in Europe and for whom European football (with Liverpool) had become a way of life. Though much of his work was deeply disliked by many, he was successful and remarkably influential. After Souness, the Scottish game would never again revert to its old habits. He was a Busby – but shorn of Busby's humane instincts. In the long term, his work was of enormous significance for it propelled the local game away from its traditional grooves. Glasgow and Scotland *had* changed in a host of important ways. The vernacular and images used to describe its football took little notice of those changes, preferring instead to linger on old stereotypes which (however real their core) were becoming less persuasive by the year.

These were years of a new and assertive Scottish identity. In part it was forged by the impact of Scottish oil, but mainly because, under successive Tory governments, Scotland was a nation with scarcely any political representation. The political system left many Scots feeling they were governed by an occupying power. At the same time, the drift to Europe threatened Scotland with further loss of independence. The tide turned with the return of a Labour government in 1997 and the launch of devolution. Again, the broader patterns were reflected in the story of football. Viewed from Europe, there were many within football who saw no reason to allow the British four separate footballing authorities (and four automatic entries to various competitions). Even at the world level, African and Asian countries began to gib at the rights of access of all the British countries.

Throughout the past century, football has been more than a mere game to armies of Scots. It has, in common with other politically marginalised places in Europe, provided a platform and a voice for expressions of local identity. However we look at the story, Scotland is rich in football. It has 38 league clubs (for a population of only five million), many of them pioneers in the earliest days of the modern game. Yet it has been a game which has depended for much of its money on the English; on transfers south, and money flowing north. It has also needed the safety valve of players drifting south. Too good, too numerous for their own regional well-being, Scottish players needed to escape the more restrictive economy of Scotland to find their true value in more prosperous regions.

Through all this, the Scottish flagship has been Rangers – to the continuing chagrin of Celtic. Rangers' successful team, their wonderful new stadium, their state-of-the-art finances and backing can stand comparison with any other British club and with many of the major European clubs. But all this success, mass following, millionaire life-style sits uncomfortably within the old structure of traditional Scottish football. More than that, if the biggest clubs were diverted towards games in Europe or even to a British league – the local Scottish base would suffer. Home teams need the visits of Rangers (or Celtic).

In Scotland, as in England, the footballing convulsions of the 1980s and 1990s saw threats to many entrenched and established ideas and systems. The amalgamation of old rivals, uprooting from old venues, looking to new competitions and new regions – all and more threatened to turn footballing loyalties upside-down; to deracinate them from the soil in which they had thrived, in some cases for a century. In Edinburgh and Glasgow, in London and the North East, brash entrepreneurs threatened to take local clubs and shake them into a new shape; shapes which seemed to owe little to their past. Reactions were similar throughout; a populist, gut dislike – often led by the local media and by fans from the professional classes – with arguments couched in the powerfully mythical phrases of traditional loyalties. Though historians of football frequently claim that the British do not know much about the game's history, its traditions – real and mythical – clearly mean a great deal to many fans.

In a curious and ironical twist for a game so often acting with little sense of its powerful history, club history became a potent weapon in the hands of opponents of threatened upheavals. One side looked to the entrepreneurial, sponsored, TV-based European super-leagues; a footballing vision of the future which was of a piece with the greater urge towards European integration. But the other, more traditional camp sought to maintain the game as it was; rooted in powerful local loyalties and communities, a source of traditional local pride, and an expression of a particular set of identities which might be parochial, urban, regional, national – or sectarian. It was, in a particular form, an argument about the changing face of Britain. And it was difficult to reconcile the two (though in fact to divide opinion into two distinct camps is to ride rough-shod over a host of confusions and subtleties).

In truth the game north – and south – of the border needed much more money than government proposed to invest or is available from levies via the football pools. Thus it was that local politicians, entrepreneurs and more old-fashioned football directors became bogged down in a mire of discussion; about new sites, improvements, sources of funds – and of course variations on all those themes (including joint use and amalgamation of clubs). Once again, prospects of dramatic change clashed with historical loyalties.

This debate was mainly about the major clubs. But it had gloomy implications for smaller clubs; those, in the words of one Scottish scholar, which 'face a bleak future in bleak places'. Plans to modernise – even if money were available – are likely to destroy more than they enliven in Scotland. For a country which attached great store by its footballing history – quite properly – these are troubling questions. Indeed, the dazzling improvements in one major club served not merely to enhance the fame and prospects of Rangers but to throw into sharp relief the inadequacies of the others. Nor is this unique to Scotland. The transformation of the major English grounds contrasts with the continuing poverty of some of their neighbours. The list is long and is, in effect, merely a way of illustrating the qualitative gulf which exists between the rich and the poor; between a small elite and the great majority.

Yet the rich need the poor. Not unlike society at large, the well-to-do depend on humbler folk in ways they often do not recognize to maintain their own position. But in the people's game of football, people guard their loyalties and their clubs with enormous passion and pride. No one can assume that the ideal world of multinational corporations, their backers and television supporters will of necessity get their own way. Here, as elsewhere, history has a way of playing tricks on people who ignore its potent symbols and power.

In the councils of football, power seems to be wielded more and more by media magnates; the men who rule the airwaves and command extra-terrestrial equipment, beaming down their products to the remotest corners of the globe. At first, it was a more earth-bound issue, as the two major TV channels (BBC and ITV) fought for a commanding share of the expanding armchair market. TV companies then began that guerrilla war against each other in order to capture the best football schedules (and other sports of course). But it was the rise of satellite coverage which confounded the older TV agencies, promising ever-greater riches in return for global coverage. And of course global coverage of the game created an unimaginably large audience for commercial sponsors; access to markets measured in their thousands of millions. It was hard to think of a more revolutionary impact on football than the unleashing of global, free-market pressures on the development of the game. It was a pressure which served to accumulate the existing forces of concentrated power and wealth within the game. Indeed it seemed merely an upping of the tempo and pace. It divided still further the haves from have-nots. (Football fans in Shanghai or Jakarta are unlikely to clamour for a live game from Stockport, Airdrie or Carlisle.) At the end of the century, the people's game had become a global game of extraordinary commercial power. Its major teams and tournaments were watched by unrivalled numbers, from Barcelona to Bhutan.

The major British clubs simply do not need the small clubs in their TV deals; yet the small clubs need the money from those deals (and from any other they can manage). But it was this indisputable power – and the simple economic clout of the major clubs – which enabled them to recast voting power within the game, giving the big clubs an in-built advantage. It was a circular process; to the lions went the lions' share. TV survives on audience competition and the marketing of its programmes via advertisement. It was, then, perhaps inevitable that the more illustrious names – of the bigger clubs – would be able to dictate terms which favoured themselves and disadvantaged their weaker colleagues. It was an altogether more aggressive commercial approach to the game, in tune with the economic climate of the 1980s and 1990s, but out of line with the game's tradition of a crude (though paternalistic) egalitarianism.

Successful clubs could even strike their own TV deals. Here was a cornucopia unknown in the history of European sports (although it was already well-established in the USA and in Olympic deals). To compete at the highest level brought riches greater than the GNP of many nations; to be eliminated was a financial disaster. It involved a major element of risk, however; the massive fees paid for players (transfers and salaries) could only be justified – and paid for – from international competitions and television income. The financial imperatives were starker than ever. The curious decision to award the 1994 World Cup to the USA was built in large measure around the commercial, TV-based potential of US marketing. That decision made little sense unless we remember the importance of TV in the shaping of the modern global game.

All this seemed utterly unreal when viewed from the sparse, windswept terraces of the lower leagues. Yet all were part of the same game. In Scarborough, as in Milan, in Stranraer and in Munich, it was the same game; same rules, conventions and passions, recognisable from one place to another. It was, in essence, that simple game of collective strength, speed and athleticism, flavoured by those dashes of individual genius which defy analysis. And fans responded similarly from one part of the world to another. But more and more of them – measured in their tens of millions – know the game from a distance; watching it not in their nearest stadium but on the screen of the nearest TV set. Yet, for all that, it remains what it has always been; the people's game. Those who forget the strength of its roots – who seek to remove it from the social warp and weft which have fashioned football for more than a century – may find that it is a game which has a life of its own.

Whatever else has happened to football – a very British institution – over the past century, its rise to global prominence has served to underline its claim that it, more than any other sport, is the people's game.

Bibliography

Chapter 1 Pre-Industrial Football

Anscomb, J.W., 'An 18th century Inclosure and Football Play at West Haddon', *Northants Past and Present*, 1968–9.

Brailsford, D., *Sport and Society; Elizabeth to Anne*, London, 1969.

Cambridge Review, 'Football in the 16th and 17th centuries', 1909.

Cambridge Review, 'Football in the 17th century', 1911.

Coulton, G.G., *Social Life in Britain from the Conquest to the Reformation*, Cambridge, 1919.

Emmison, F.G., *Archives and Local History*, London, 1966.

Emmison, F.G., *Elizabethan Life: Disorder*, Chelmsford, Essex Record Office, 1970.

Lennard, R. (ed.), *Englishmen at Rest and Play*, Oxford, 1931.

Malcolmson, R.W., *Popular Recreations in English Society, 1700–1850*, Cambridge, 1973.

Manning, P., 'Sports and Pastimes in Stuart Oxford', in H.E. Salter, *Surveys and Tokens*, Oxford, 1923.

Magoun, Jnr., F.P., 'Football in Medieval England and in Middle English Literature', *American Historical Review*, XXV, 1929–30.

Magoun, Jnr., F.P., 'Scottish Popular Football, 1424–1815', *American Historical Review*, XXXVII, 1931.

Magoun, Jnr., F.P., *History of Football from the beginning to 1871*, Cologne, 1938.

Parker, Enid, *Cambridgeshire Customs and Folklore*, London, 1967.

Poole, A.C., 'Recreations', in *Medieval England*, A.C. Poole (ed.), Oxford, 1958, II.

Strutt, Joseph, *The Sports and Pastimes of the People of England*, 1801.

Victoria History of the Counties of England; Derbyshire, 1901, II.

Chapter 2 The Public Schools and Football

Armytage, W.H.G., *400 Years of English Education*, Cambridge, 1964.

Bamford, T.W., *Thomas Arnold*, London, 1960.

Briggs, Asa, *Victorian People*, Pelican Books, 1971 edition.

Carleton, J.D., *Westminster School*, London, 1965.

Checkland, S.G., *The rise of industrial society in England, 1815–1885*, London, 1964.

Dunning, Eric, 'Football in its early stages', *History Today*, 1963.

Dunning, Eric, *Early Stages in the Development of Football as an*

Organised Game, MA thesis, University of Leicester, 1961.

Fry, C.B., *Life Worth Living*, London, 1939.

Halévy, E., *History of the English People in the Nineteenth Century*, 6 vols, I, London, 1961 edition.

Hughes, Thomas, *Tom Brown's School Days*, London, 1858.

Kitson Clark, G., *The Making of Victorian England*, London, 1966.

Mack, E.D., *Public Schools and British Opinion, 1780–1860*, London, 1938.

McIntosh, P.C. (ed.), *Landmarks in the History of Physical Recreation*, London, 1957.

Newsome, David, *Godlinesse and Good Learning*, London, 1961.

Oldham, J.B., *A History of Shrewsbury School*, London, 1952.

Shearman, M., *The Badminton Library, Athletics and Football*, London, 1888.

Shearman, M. and Vincent, J., *Football: Its History for Five Centuries*, London, 1885.

Thring, J.C., *The Winter Game*, Uppingham, 1863.

The Victoria History of the Counties of England, Essex, 1907, II; Middlesex, 1911, II; Staffs, 1967, II.

Wymer, N., *Sports in England. A History of Two Thousand Years of Games and Pastimes*, London, 1949.

Chapter 3 The Rise of Working-class Football

Arnold, Matthew, *Reports on Elementary Schools, 1852–1882*, London, 1910.

Best, G., *Mid-Victorian Britain, 1851–1875*, London, 1971.

Betts, J.R., 'The Technological Revolution and the Rise of Sports 1855–1900', *Mississippi Valley Historical Review*, XL, 1953.

Briggs, Asa, *Victorian Cities*, London, 1968.

Briggs, Asa, *The Age of Improvement*, London, 1962.

Briggs, Asa, *Mass Entertainment: The Origins of a Modern Industry*, Joseph Fisher Lecture, University of Adelaide, 1960.

Chesney, Kellow, *The Victorian Underworld*, London, 1972.

Clapham, Sir John H., *An Economic History of Modern Britain*, Cambridge, 1957, III.

Dent, H.C., *1870–1970. Century of Growth in English Education*, London, 1970.

Fry, C.B., 'Football', *Badminton Library of Sports and Pastimes*, London, 1895, I.

Golesworthy, M. and Macdonald, R., *The ABC of World Football*, London, 1966.

Hammonds, The, *Age of the Chartists, 1832–1851*, London, 1933.

Hobsbawn, E.J., *Industry and Empire*, London, 1968.

Inglis, K.S., *Churches and the Working Class in Victorian England*, London, 1963.

Keating, J.W., 'The Rise of Sport', *Mississippi Valley Historical Review*, IV, 1917.

Kellett, J.R., *The Impact of Railways on Victorian Cities*, London, 1969.

Mandle, W.F., 'Games People Played: Cricket and Football in England and Victoria in the late 19th century', *Historical Studies*, 15, 1973.

Masterman, G.F.G., *The Condition of England*, London, 1909 edition.

Molyneux, D.D., *The Development of Physical Education in the Birmingham District from 1871–1892*, MA thesis, University of Birmingham, 1957.

Pickford, R.W., 'The Psychology of the History and Organisation of Football', *British Journal of Psychology*, 30–31, 1939–41.
Pimlott, J.A.R., *The Englishman's Holiday*, London, 1947.
Sherrington, C.E.R., *100 Years of Inland Transport*, London, 1934 (1969).
Slugg, J.T., *Reminiscences of Manchester Fifty Years ago*, Manchester, 1881.
(Wright, Thomas) A Journeyman engineer, *Some Habits and Customs of the Working Classes*, London, 1867.
Yearsley, Ian, *The Manchester Tram*, Huddersfield, 1962.

Chapter 4 Football to 1914

Alcock, C.W., *Football, the Association Game*, London, 1890.
Alcock, C.W., *Football, Our Winter Game*, London, 1874.
Alcock, C.W., *The National Football Calendar*, 1881.
Alcock, C.W., *The Book of Football*, 1906.
Budd, A. and Fry, C.B., *Football*, 1897.
Bulletin of the Society for the Study of Labour History, 23, Autumn 1972.
Churchill, R.C., *60 Seasons of League Football*, London, 1958.
Corbett, B.O., *Football*, London, 1901.
Creek, F.N.S., *A History of the Corinthian Football Club*, London, 1933.
Delany, C., *A Century of Soccer*, London, 1963.
Dunning, Eric (ed.), *The Sociology of Sport*, London, 1971.
Edwards, Charles, 'The New Football Mania', *Nineteenth Century*, XXXII, 1892.
Encyclopaedia Britannica, 11th edition, 1910–11.
Gibson, A. and Pickford, W., *Association Football*, London, 1906.
Grayson, N., *Corinthians and Cricketers*, London, 1957.
Pelling, Henry, *Popular Politics and Society in Late Victorian Britain*, London, 1968.
Pickford, W., *A Few Recollections of Sport*, Bournemouth, 1939.
Pickford, W., *The Hampshire FA*, 1937.
Rees, R., *The development of Physical Recreation in Liverpool during the 19th Century*, MA thesis, Liverpool University, 1968.
Sutcliffe, C.E. and Hargreaves, F., *History of the Lancashire FA 1878–1928*, Blackburn, 1928.
Wall, Sir F., *Fifty Years of Football*, London, 1935.

Chapter 5 Britain's Most Durable Export

Bonser, Keith, 'Soviet Sport', *Bulletin of the GB–USSR Association*, No 38, Winter, 1972–3.
Catton, J.A.H., *The Real Football*, London, 1900.
Ducommun, F.M., *Le Football, son histoire, ses systèmes et ses lois*, Neuchatel, 1957.
Enciclopedia Universal Ilustrada, Madrid, 1924.
Ghirelli, Antonio, *Storia de Calcio in Italia*, Torino, 1967.
Jeffrey, G., *European International Football*, London, 1963.
Koppehel, C., *Geschichte des Deutchen Fussballsports*, Frankfurt, 1954.
Le Livre d'Or du Football Suisse, Basle, 1953.
Meisl, W., *Soccer Revolution*, London, 1955.
Mercier, J., *Le Football*, Paris, 1966.
Nello, Paulo Coetho, *Historia do Fluminense*, Rio de Janeiro, 1952.
Perel, A., *Football in the USSR*, Moscow, 1959.
Robinson, J.F., *The History of Soccer in the City of St Louis*, PhD thesis, St

Louis University, 1966; *Dissertation Abstracts*, 27A, pp 2655–4379, 1967.
Scanio on Tennis (1555), English edition, 1951.
Schidrowitz, Leo, *Geschichte des Fussballsports in Österreich*, Vienna, 1951.
The Times, 18 April 1925.

Chapter 6 The Insular Game 1915–39

Allison, G., *Allison Calling*, London, 1948.
Blythe, R., *The Age of Illusion; England in the 1920s and 30s*, London, 1963.
Briggs, Asa, *The Birth of Broadcasting*, London, 1961.
Briggs, Asa, *The Golden Age of Wireless*, London, 1965.
Brunson, N. and Heinemann, M., *Britain in the 1930s*, London, 1971.
Economist, 17 April 1937.
Golesworthy, M., *We are the Champions*, London, 1972.
Johnston, Frank (ed.), *The Football Encyclopedia*, London, 1934.
Johnston, Frank (ed.), *The Football Who's Who*, London, 1935.
Joy, B., *Forward Arsenal*, London, 1952.
Listener, 29 Sept 1937; 4 March, 18 March, 1938; 4 May 1938; 13 Oct 1938.
Mowatt, Charles Loch, *Britain Between the Wars*, London, 1952.
The Professional Footballer, London, 1952.
Spectator, 14 February 1936.
Taylor, A.J.P., *English History, 1914–1945*, Oxford, 1965.
The Times, 1919, 1937.
Yates, Ivan, *Forty Years in Football*, London, 1952.

Chapter 7 Leisure in Austerity, 1939–52

Calder, Angus, *The People's War*, London, 1969.
Cox, Jack, *Don Davies, An Old International*, London, 1962.
Easterbrook, Basil, 'The Golden Years', *Football Monthly*, 1971.
Football Annual, Sunday Chronicle, 1946–7.
Hopkin, Harry, *The New Look*, London, 1967.
Harrison, Tom and Modge, Charles (eds.), *War Begins at Home*, Mass Observation, London, 1940.
Longmate, Norman, *How We Lived Then*, London, 1971.
Marwick, Arthur, *Britain in the Century of Total War*, London, 1970.
Scleppi, J.R., *A History of Professional Football in England During the Second World War*, PhD thesis, Ohio State University, 1972.
Sunday Spectator, 30 June, 6 February, 16 April, 30 April 1948.

Chapter 8 More Prosperous Times

Davies, Hunter, *The Glory Game*, London, 1972.
Evening Standard, 3 May 1973.
Glanville, B., *Soccer Nemesis*, London, 1955.
McIlvanney, Hugh, *World Cup '66*, London, 1966.
McIlvanney, Hugh, *World Cup '70*, London, 1970.
Marwick, Arthur, *Britain in a Century of Total War*, London 1970.
Observer, 31 December 1972; 4 March 1973.
PEP, *English Professional Football*, London, 1966.

Taylor, Ian, 'Soccer Consciousness and Soccer Hooliganism', in *Images of Deviance*, S. Cohen (ed.), London, 1971.
Vinnai, G., *Football Mania*, London, 1973.

General

Delany, T., *A Century of Soccer*, London, 1963.
Douglas, Peter, *The Football Industry*, London, 1973.
Dulles, Foster, R., *A History of Recreation*, New York, 1965.
Farror, M. and Lamming, D., *A Century of English International Football*, London, 1972.
Frewin, L.R. (ed.), *The Saturday Men*, London, 1967.
Golesworthy, M., *The Encyclopedia of Association Football*, London, 1963.
Glanville, B., *The Footballer's Companion*, London, 1962.
Glanville, B., *History of the World Cup* London, 1973.
Green, G., *History of the Football Association*, London, 1953.
Green, G., *Soccer, The World Game*, London, 1953.
Green, G., *The Official History of the FA Cup*, London, 1959.
Green, G. and Fabian, A.H., *Association Football*, London, 1960, 4 vols.
Hill, Jimmy, *Striking for Soccer*, London, 1961.
Hole, Christine, *English Sports and Pastimes*, London, 1949.
Marples, M., *A History of Football*, London, 1954.
McIntosh, P., *Physical Education in England since 1800*, London, 1952.
McIntosh, P. (ed.), *Landmarks in the History of Physical Education*, London, 1957.
McIntosh, P., *Sport in Society*, London, 1963.
Pawson, Tony, *100 Years of the FA Cup*, London, 1972.
Pawson, Tony, *The Football Managers*, London, 1973.
Rafferty, John, *100 Years of Scottish Football*, London, 1973.
Rothman's Book of Football.
Sharpe, Ivan, *The Football League's Jubilee Book*, London, 1963.
Somers, Dale A., *The Rise of Sports in New Orleans*, Baton Rouge, 1972.
Sutcliffe, C.E. (ed.), *The Story of the Football League, 1888–1938*, Preston, 1938.
Young, Percy, *Football, Facts and Figures*, London, 1950.
Young, Percy, *The Appreciation of Football*, London, 1951.
Young, Percy, *The Football Year*, London, 1956.
Young, Percy, *The Wolves*, London, 1959.
Young, Percy, *Manchester United*, 1960.
Young, Percy, *Football in Sheffield*, London, 1962.
Young, Percy, *Football on Merseyside*, London, 1963.
Young, Percy, *A History of British Football*, London, 1966.

Bibliography for revised (1994) edition

Specialists in the field need no guidance to further reading. What follows is designed to help interested readers who might want to consult literature published (mainly in book form) since the mid-1970s. This list supplements the sources cited above. Much important work is to be found in scholarly articles. Many of the best can be found in the 'Annual Bibliography of Publications on the History of Sport', published in the December issues of *The International Journal of the History of Sport*, Cass, London.

Chapter 1

Brailsford, D., *Sport, Time and Society*, London, 1991.
Burke, P., *Popular Culture in Early Modern Europe*, London, 1979.
Clark, P., *The English Alehouse*, London, 1983.
Dunning, E. (ed.), *The Sociology of Sport*, 1970.
Golby, J. and Purdue, W., *The Civilization of the Crowd*, London, 1984.
Guttman, A., *From Ritual to Record*, New York, 1978.
Hargreaves, J. (ed.), *Sport, Culture and Ideology*, London, 1982.
Pimlott, J.A.R., *The Englishman's Holiday*, Brighton, 1976 edition.
Storch, D. (ed.), *Popular Culture and Custom in Nineteenth Century England*, London, 1982.
Thompson, E.P., 'Time, Work Discipline and Industrial Capitalism', *Past and Present*, December 1967.
Yeo, E. and S. (eds.), *Popular Culture and Class Conflict, 1590–1914*, Brighton, 1981.

Chapter 2

Cunningham, H., *Leisure in the Industrial Revolution*, London, 1980.
Dunning, E. and Sheard, K., *Barbarians, Gentlemen and Players*, Oxford, 1979.
Haley Bruce, *The Healthy Body and Victorian Culture*, Cambridge Mass., 1978.
Holt, R., *Sport and the British*, Oxford, 1989.
Mangan, J.A., *Athleticism in the Victorian and Edwardian Public School*, Cambridge, 1981.
Mangan, J.A. (ed.), *Pleasure, Profit and Proselytism*, London, 1988.
Mangan, J.A. and Walvin, J. (eds.), *Manliness and Morality*, Manchester, 1987.
Mason, T., *Association Football and English Society*, Brighton, 1980.
Richards, J., *Happiest Days*, Manchester, 1988.
Wiener, M.J., *English Culture and the Decline of the Industrial Spirit*, Cambridge, 1981.

Chapters 3 and 4

Hole, R., *Sport and the British*, Oxford, 1989.
Hutchinson, J., *The Football Industry*, Edinburgh, 1982.
Inglis, Simon, *League Football and the Men who Made it*, London, 1988.
Mason, T., *Association Football and English Society*, Brighton, 1980.
Mason, T. (ed.), *Sport in Britain*, Cambridge, 1989.
McCrone, K.E., *Sport and the Physical Emancipation of English Women*, London, 1988.
Mangan, J.A. and Parks, R. (eds.), *From Fair Sex to Feminism*, London, 1987.
Murray, B., *The Old Firm*, Edinburgh, 1984.
Vamplew, W., *Pay up and Play the Game*, Cambridge, 1988.
Wagg, S., *The Football World*, London, 1984.
Walton, J.K. and Walvin, J. (eds.), *Leisure in Britain*, Manchester, 1983.

Chapter 5

Arbena, J.L. (ed.), *Sport and Society in Latin America*, Westport, Conn., 1988.

Arbena, J.L. (ed.), *An Annotated Bibliography of Latin American Sport*, Greenwood, Conn., 1989.

Cashman, R. and McKernan, M. (eds.), *Sport in History*, Queensland, 1979.

Crampsey, Bob, *The Scottish Footballer*, Edinburgh, 1978.

Hobsbawm, E.J. and Ranger, T. (eds.), *The Invention of Tradition*, Cambridge, 1983.

Lever, Janet, *Soccer Madness*, Chicago, 1983.

James, C.L.R., *Beyond a Boundary*, London, 1963.

Mackenzie, J.A. (ed.), *Imperialism and Popular Culture*, Manchester, 1986.

Mangan, J.A., *The Games Ethic and Imperialism*, London, 1986.

Mangan, J.A. (ed.), *The Cultural Bond*, London, 1992.

Mangan, J.A. (ed.), *Pleasure, Profit and Proselytism*, London, 1988.

Riordan, J., *Sport in Soviet Society*, Cambridge, 1977.

Redmond, G., *The Sporting Scots of Nineteenth Century Canada*, Toronto, 1982.

Sissons, R. and Stoddart, B., *Cricket and Empire*, London, 1984.

Tischler, S., *Footballers and Businessmen*, New York, 1981.

Chapter 6

Fussell, P., *The Great War and Modern Memory*, Oxford, 1979.

Jones, S.G., *Sport, Politics and the Working Class*, Manchester, 1988.

Korr, C., *West Ham United*, London, 1986.

Veitch, Colin, 'Play Up! Play Up! and Win the War!', *Journal of Contemporary History*, 20, 1985.

Wagg, S., *The Football World*, Brighton, 1984.

Chapters 7, 8 and 9

Addison, P., *Now the War is Over*, London, 1985.

Critcher, C. and Clarke, J., *The Devil Makes Work: Leisure in Capitalist Britain*, London, 1985.

Dunning, E., Murphy, P. and Williams, J., *Hooligans Abroad*, London, 1984.

Dunning, E., Murphy, P. and Williams, J., *The Roots of Football Hooliganism*, London, 1988.

Dunphy, E., *A Strange Kind of Glory: Sir Matt Busby and Manchester United*, London, 1991.

Glanville, B., *The Story of the World Cup*, London, 1993 edition.

Hargreaves, J., *Sport, Power and Culture*, London, 1986.

Hennessy, P., *Never Again*, London, 1993 edition.

Humphries, S., *Hooligans or Rebels?* Oxford, 1981.

Inglis, S., *The Football Grounds of Great Britain*, London, 1993 edition.

Marsh, P. and Campbell, A. (eds.), *Aggression and Violence*, Oxford, 1982.

Mason, T., *Sport in Britain*, London, 1988.

Pearson, G., *Hooligan: A History of a Respectable Fear*, London, 1983.

Rollen, J., *Soccer at War*, London, 1985.

Taylor, R., *Football and its Fans*, Leicester, 1992.

Walvin, J., *Football and the Decline of Britain*, London, 1986.

Williams, J. and Wagg, S. (eds.), *British Football and Social Change*, Leicester, 1991.

Index